PAUL

THE APOSTLE

PAUL

THE APOSTLE

MISSIONARY
MARTYR
THEOLOGIAN

ROBERT E. PICIRILLI

MOODY PUBLISHERS

CHICAGO

All Scripture quotations, unless otherwise indicated, are taken from the *New American Standard Bible®*, Copyright © 1960, 1962, 1963, 1968, 1971, 1972, 1973, 1973, 1977, 1995 by The Lockman Foundation. Used by permission. (www.Lockman.org)

The use of selected references from various versions of the Bible in this publication does not necessarily imply publisher endorsement of the versions in their entirety.

Selected references and quotations from F. F. Bruce, *Commentary on the Book of Acts,* NICOT (Grand Rapids: Eerdmans, 1934), used by permission of Wm. B. Eerdmans Publishing Company.

Selected references and quotations from the *Randall House Bible Commentary: 1, 2 Corinthians* by Robert E. Picirilli used by permission of Randall House Publications, Nashville, Tennessee.

Edited by Kevin Emmert
Interior design: Ragont Design
Cover design: Erik M. Peterson
Cover painting: "The Apostle Paul" (© 1657) by Rembrandt van Rijn

Library of Congress Cataloging in Publication Date

Picirilli, Robert, 1932- Paul the Apostle.
Includes bibliographies.
1. Paul, the Apostle, Saint. 2. Christian Saints—Turkey—Tarsus—Biography.
3. Tarsus (Turkey)—Biography. I. Title.

ISBN-13: 978-0-8024-6325-8

BS2506.P48 1986 225.9/24 [B]   86-18246

We hope you enjoy this book from Moody Publishers. Our goal is to provide high-quality, thought-provoking books and products that connect truth to your real needs and challenges. For more information on other books and products written and produced from a biblical perspective, go to www.moodypublishers.com or write to:

Moody Publishers
820 N. LaSalle Boulevard
Chicago, IL 60610

23 25 27 29 30 28 26 24

Printed in the United States of America

CONTENTS

Foreword   7

Preface   11

1. Paul's Dispersion Background   13

2. Paul the Jew   31

3. The Conversion and Commission of Paul   51

4. From New Convert to Missionary Traveler   63

5. The Gentile Mission Expands   103

6. The Third Missionary Journey   141

7. Paul the Prisoner   187

8. The Last Years of Paul   241

Recommended Resources   265

Notes   271

FOREWORD

It is difficult to overstate the apostle Paul's contribution to the early
Christian mission. While he cannot, and would not want to, take ul-
timate credit for his work (for he was drafted into service by the risen
Christ), he devoted his entire life to advancing Christ's kingdom and
to propagating the gospel—and with remarkable impact. Few, if any,
rival Paul's influence on Christian theology. In fact, the Reformers'
teaching on justification by grace through faith alone derived directly from Paul's letters to the Romans and Galatians. While for a
time scholars viewed Paul as the writer of systematic treatises such
as Romans or church manuals such as the so-called Pastoral Epistles,
in recent years a phalanx of scholars has recognized that Paul wrote
primarily as a missionary and only secondarily as a theologian.[1] That
is, Paul's primary interest did not lie in formulating abstract theology. Rather, he sought to make converts to the Christian faith and
for that reason established local communities of believers, raising up
leaders who could nurture and grow these outposts of Christianity
in the Greco-Roman world of his day.

There are several helpful treatments of the apostle Paul as a man
and as the founder of Christianity.[2] Any such treatment must include
an assessment of Paul's relationship to Jesus, without whom there
would be no Christianity at all.[3] If recent, it should also include an
assessment of the so-called "New Perspective on Paul," which seeks
to recover the "real, historical Paul" beneath two millennia of church
history (including the Reformation), remaking Paul at times, at least
in part, in its own image.[4] One should expect to find a section on
Pauline chronology—that is, a discussion of Paul's ministry and writings in proper temporal sequence, starting with his early life and then
his conversion, his missionary work, and his final years, including his
martyrdom. In fact, it is a tribute to Paul's stature as a missionary

and early Christian leader that any such chronology spans the period of expansion of Christianity from Jerusalem to the ends of the then-known earth, regardless of whether the apostle reached Spain as we know he intended to do.[5] Finally, there might be a survey of Paul's letters included in the New Testament canon—thirteen out of the twenty seven documents—or at least a summary treatment of Paul's theology as it developed over the course of his three decades of ministry.[6]

Enter Robert Picirilli, seasoned Bible teacher and Christian scholar, and the book you are holding in your hands. Picirilli believes that most books about Paul are either too shallow or too detailed to be used profitably for informed personal study or as a college-level textbook. To remedy this deficiency, he has written a treatment that seeks to understand Paul in his first-century Jewish and Greco-Roman contexts and to equip students who possess general background knowledge of the New Testament with a more thorough appreciation of Paul's contribution to Christian thought and practice. Chapter 1 provides a description of Paul's birthplace, the city of Tarsus, and a discussion of his Roman citizenship, a matter of considerable significance. Chapter 2 introduces "Paul the Jew," including his background in Pharisaic Judaism, his education, and a discussion of "Paul the rabbi." This leads seamlessly to a discussion of the conversion and commission of Paul—essentially his encounter with the risen Christ on the road to Damascus—in chapter 3. The following chapters (4–8) are devoted to following Paul's steps on his missionary travels, and include discussions of Paul's letters (their form, language, general character, and chronological arrangement), until his final years. The letters are presented in four groups: (1) the letters to the Thessalonians; (2) the letters to the Corinthians, Romans, and Galatians (which Picirilli dates later than is sometimes done); (3) the "prison epistles"—Colossians, Ephesians, Philemon, and Philippians; and (4) the "Pastoral Epistles"—Timothy and Titus. Appealingly and sensibly, Picirilli examines and surveys each of Paul's letters in the context of his mission against the backdrop of the book of Acts. This gives the book an organic and intuitive feel, making it ideal as an introductory survey for college students or for personal study. This is exactly what I seek to convey to my students as I teach them about Paul, his mission, and his letters.[7]

The virtues of this book, then, are many. First, it is written with the serious student of Scripture in mind rather than for fellow academics or scholars. Second, it is written in an accessible style that avoids unnecessary jargon and cuts to the heart of the matter on any given issue. Third, it organizes the material chronologically, as mentioned, which enables the reader to gain a valuable historical perspective on how Paul's ministry and thought unfolded over time. This understanding, in turn, is essential for an appreciation of Paul's seminal contribution to the early Christian mission and to Christian theology. While much Pauline scholarship has been conducted since this book was first written, the author and publisher rightly believe that it retains its usefulness as an introduction to Paul the apostle. For this reason, the bibliographic references throughout the book have been left in their original state. That said, readers will appreciate the references to standard evangelical treatments such as those by F. F. Bruce, Donald Guthrie, and many others.

In my own teaching ministry, I typically start with the book of Acts as a backdrop to Paul's life and mission, moving to his conversion, missionary travels, and letters to the churches he planted as well as to his apostolic delegates. Additionally, Paul's letters to Timothy and Titus are firmly grounded in his apostolic mission and ought not to be relegated to a pseudonymous author following Paul's death.[8] Like the author of the present volume, I believe an appreciation of Paul's life and work within the context of his first-century Jewish and Greco-Roman environments is vital. For example, understanding Paul's metaphor of the church as "God's household" within first-century Jewish and Greco-Roman culture is highly illumining as it is predicated and builds upon the household as an orderly, God-ordained structure in which every member has a clearly defined place, space, and contribution to make.

In these and other ways, I appreciate and concur with Picirilli's methodology. Not only does *Paul the Apostle* therefore contribute to

a better appreciation of Paul's life and work, it also makes a meth-
odological contribution, modeling how to study Paul in his original
life-setting in a way that integrates Pauline chronology with his letter-writing activity. For these reasons, I am very grateful that Moody
Publishers has chosen to publish this new edition of Robert Picirilli's
Paul the Apostle. May this volume continue to serve students and
teachers well, to the greater glory of God in Christ.

> Dr. Andreas J. Köstenberger
> Founder, Biblical Foundations™
> Senior Research Professor,
> Southeastern Baptist Theological Seminary
> Wake Forest, North Carolina, Fall 2016

PREFACE

I am gratified, and grateful to God, that *Paul the Apostle* has been in print and useful to the church for over thirty years.

I remain convinced that, except for Jesus Himself, Paul is the most central figure of the New Testament. Knowing him and his inspired writings well is absolutely essential for understanding the Christian faith. By him we learn how the teachings of our Lord are fleshed out for everyday living. More than any other New Testament writer, he instructs us on how the church functions. He is the Christian theologian *par excellence*. He embodied the ideal missionary, evangelist, pastor, and gospel preacher. Every new generation of believers must become familiar with this man and his message.

Before writing this book, I found that most books about Paul were either too shallow or that they assumed too much for the serious student at the college level. Some were general and devotional; some were written for the seminary student who already has a good background in biblical studies.

What I wanted was a volume that would put Paul, his ministry, and the occasion of his letters in his world as it really was: one written for a student who has only a general background in the New Testament, not assuming things he or she would not know; at the same time, one written for a serious student who desires depth and detail, which takes advantage of recent research in the field; a book, finally, that would serve either for the individual who does not have the benefit of classroom teaching or as a textbook for a course on Paul at the college level.

I am satisfied that the contents of this volume are still pertinent and relevant, a medium between the academic and the overly simple treatments of the man and his mission. The basic overview of Paul and his writings given here continues to be reliable and current. Even the works listed in the "Recommended Resources" section in the back of the book are still useful, and it will be relatively easy for the user to update the list with helpful publications that have appeared since the first edition of this book.

Since I wrote and taught in the early 1980s, perhaps the most influential movement in Pauline studies has been what we call the "New Perspective on Paul," tracing back to E. P. Sanders's 1977 work *Paul and Palestinian Judaism*. This approach to interpreting Paul has a number of varieties that are too diverse and complex to discuss here. Primarily, New Perspective proponents interpret Paul's interaction with Judaism in the light of contemporary scholarship on Second Temple Judaism. That scholarship, they say, shows us today that Judaism was not a works-based religion after all. Instead, the Jews observed special Jewish traditions like circumcision, dietary laws, and Sabbath keeping as "boundary markers" that distinguished them from Gentiles and maintained their covenant relationship with God. In that case, when Paul argued against salvation by works, he was focusing on these special observances rather than good works of obedience to the law of God.

I am confident that the traditional understanding of Paul is at least fundamentally correct: namely, that he contrasted salvation by grace through faith with salvation by *any* works. In other words, salvation is a gift and cannot be earned. At the same time, Paul's message accorded with James's: faith is not sterile or mere intellectual belief. Genuine faith expresses itself in obeying God, in works of love and trust, under the lordship of Jesus Christ.

As I did in the first edition, I thank my wife, who was gladly patient about my preoccupation; members of the board of trustees of my college, who provided the sabbatical that made the work possible; my daughter, who did the typing; and Ron Pitkin, without whose encouragement I probably would not have followed through. I also appreciate Moody Publishers for the decision to release the book again in this new edition.

May a new generation of students of Paul find that this book contributes to their understanding of how God has revealed Himself in the life and writings of that eminent apostle!

1

PAUL'S DISPERSION BACKGROUND

We call him the apostle Paul. His mission takes up at least half of Acts, and his epistles dominate our New Testament. If we are to understand him, we must look into his background in order to form as complete a picture as we can of the kind of person he was and of the various influences that shaped him.

We first meet Paul in Acts 7:58 as the "young man" at whose feet those who stoned Stephen laid their coats. One way to characterize him is as a Dispersion Jew. In the time of Jesus and Paul there were millions of Jews who lived in various places throughout the Roman Empire. Of a world Jewish population estimated at from 3 to 8 million, "The consensus seems to be that about two thirds of the Jews lived outside of Palestine."[1] These were significantly affected by cultural influences that were not as strong in Palestine. Paul was born into such a family and had been partly reared in the Dispersion ("the Diaspora").

This characterization of Paul as a Dispersion Jew serves as a convenient means of organizing our study of his background. In this chapter we will explore those influences on Paul that arose especially out of the fact that he was born in and affected by the non-Jewish culture of his world. In the next chapter we will consider those aspects of Paul's background that reflect his Jewish heritage.

We have no authentic biography of Paul. The New Testament gives no account of his life before he appears as a fully mature man at the scene of Stephen's martyrdom. But there is a surprising number of references, in Acts especially, to Paul's background. These provide considerable insight into Paul's experiences between his birth and his conversion.

Two passages in particular, Acts 21:37–22:3 and 22:25–29, provide helpful information regarding the time and place of Paul's birth and rearing, his language, and his standing in the non-Jewish world.

PAUL'S BIRTHPLACE:
THE INFLUENCE OF TARSUS

Paul said, "I am a Jew of Tarsus in Cilicia, a citizen of no insignificant city" (Acts 21:39). "No insignificant city" designates Tarsus as no average, or ordinary, city, a city not to be looked down on. He also said that he was born there (Acts 22:3). Paul apparently had a sense of pride about the city of his birth. He regarded it as a city to be taken note of, an important city; he knew that those to whom he spoke would not disagree.

There are at least four reasons Tarsus would have been reckoned important. First was its size. In Paul's time Tarsus probably boasted a population of half a million, packed a little tightly into an area of some eight to ten square miles. Not many cities in the Mediterranean world would have been any larger.

Second was its trade. Tarsus was one of the busy and competitive centers of the Mediterranean's bustling commerce. A little time spent with a map (see the beginning of chap. 4) will show that its location was ideal. Tarsus was positioned on the southern side of that peninsula we call Asia Minor (now the land of Turkey), along the coastal plain of the province of Cilicia. It was a port city, a natural and well-protected harbor, a dozen miles upriver from where the Cydnus emptied into the Mediterranean. About twenty-five miles to the north of Tarsus were the Taurus Mountains, rich in the minerals and timber that made trade with Tarsus so desirable. By way of illustrating their zeal for trade, the Tarsians could proudly point to the Cilician gates. They had built that road across one of the passes in the Taurus Mountains earlier in their history; it was reckoned a mighty feat indeed.[2]

In addition to the mountains' resources, the Tarsians also traded in leather goods and *cilicium* (from the name of the province), a cloth woven from the hair of the black goats that populated the slopes of the Taurus range. "The black tents of Tarsus were used by caravans, nomads, and armies all over Asia Minor and Syria."[3]

A third reason for the importance of Tarsus was its political standing. A city so well situated could hardly fail to be a center of power, and Tarsus had been such a center for nearly a thousand years when Paul was born. In the earlier times of the empires of Assyria, Babylonia, and Medo-Persia, Tarsus was a leading city in Asia Minor. When Alexander's Greek empire was divided after his death, Tarsus was part of the territory controlled by the Seleucids. The famous Antiochus Epiphanes took special interest in Tarsus. He gave it his own name, Antiocheia, and made it self-governing (in 171/170 BC). It thus had the standing of a Greek city-state and was one of the most important in all of Antiochus's empire.

When Paul was born, Tarsus had passed into Roman control, and still its standing was recognized. The Romans designated many districts as *provinces* (see further, below), and Tarsus was the capital city of the province of Cilicia.[4] It was also awarded, by the Roman senate, the privileged standing of *libera civitas*.[5] These Latin words (Latin was the language of the Romans) mean "free city." Such a standing gave the city the right to govern itself apart from the provincial government as well as freedom from major Roman taxes, including duty on trade. It would also have been garrisoned by its own soldiers.[6]

One more reason for the importance of Tarsus should be mentioned briefly. Tarsus was a university city, surpassing even Athens and Alexandria in the general learning of its natives.[7] John Pollock mentions two of the more famous students of Tarsus, Athenodorus (a tutor of Augustus) and Nestor. In old age both of those men returned to the city from illustrious careers in Rome. They would have been alive during Paul's boyhood.[8] However, Paul himself, being the son of a strict Jewish Pharisee, would not have been exposed to the pagan education of those schools.

So Tarsus was a city of recognized significance. One does not have to be very imaginative to sense the kind of awareness Paul would have had if he spent the first years of his life there. He would have become familiar with the sea and with the ships that unloaded cargo at the docks of Tarsus from all over the Mediterranean. He would have heard the strange native tongues of the ships' crews and conversed with them in Greek, the most common language of the empire. He would have observed many travelers from Rome; Tarsus was a favorite vacation spot for highborn Romans. Many people mixed in Tarsus, and Paul could not have avoided being exposed to them and their ways. He would have obtained considerable understanding of the shape and culture of the Roman world and of the heterogeneous peoples that populated it.

In recent years some scholars have cast doubt on these possibilities, arguing that Paul, though born in Tarsus, did not spend any of his formative years there. W. C. van Unnik's little book *Tarsus or Jerusalem* may be considered the bellwether of this viewpoint. Van Unnik contends that Paul's family moved to Jerusalem when he was but an infant. His argument rests entirely on the meaning of one word (and the punctuation) in Acts 22:3: "brought up." It is beyond the scope of this text to respond to that view except to say that I remain unconvinced. What we know of Paul fits better with the view that he spent a considerable part of his boyhood in Tarsus. In the final analysis van Unnik is forced to account for Paul's "Hellenistic" (*Hellen* is the Greek word for Greece) awareness as a result of later years in Tarsus (following his conversion), and so the end result is not very different after all. Furthermore, if Paul's parents lived in Tarsus for some period before his birth (as will be seen below), then the subtle influences of Tarsus would have been felt in the home even if the family did move to Jerusalem during his infancy. Regardless, the next chapter will show that Paul's *primary* background was certainly Jewish; in that respect, at least, van Unnik is right.

When we evaluate the influence of Tarsus on Paul, we have to deal with more than his birth and boyhood there. Paul was a "citizen" of Tarsus (Acts 21:39). Just living there would not automatically make him a citizen. Only the privileged were named citizens of a city; the general population, including most of the working and poorer classes, did not have that standing.

The citizens of a city were responsible for its government, and that was especially important in a city that was *libera civitas* like Tarsus. Those named citizens were the ones who would assemble to conduct the affairs of the city and make the decisions that affected its corporate life.[9]

Being a citizen of the city, by the way, was *not* the same as being a Roman citizen. Paul was that, too, as will be discussed below. Certainly the two often went together, but they were two distinct privileges. In the eastern provinces of the empire, being a citizen of a city was often of more practical advantage than Roman citizenship. Paul "thinks of himself first and foremost as a citizen of Tarsus, and only refers to his latent Roman status when it is expedient to do so."[10]

A person who was a citizen of a city was therefore automatically a person of influence. Conversely, the standing of citizenship was usually awarded to those who were more influential. Inasmuch as Paul spent no more than his boyhood in Tarsus, we can be confident that he became a citizen of that city in the same way he got his citizenship from Rome, namely, because his father was already a citizen (Acts 22:25-29). This has some fairly strong implications for our understanding of Paul's background. For one thing, it suggests that Paul was from a family of some influence and probably wealth. One thing required for inclusion in the roll of citizens was that one had to own property of certain worth.[11]

For another thing, we can safely assume that Paul's family had lived in Tarsus for a significant length of time before his birth; otherwise it is difficult to explain how this orthodox, Pharisaic, Jewish man (Paul's father, Acts 23:6) had gained Tarsian (and Roman) citizenship.

Long ago Sir William Ramsay offered a theory that would account for this family's privileged standing. Antiochus Epiphanes, a Seleucid ruler, took special interest in Tarsus, renaming it Antiocheia and settling a large colony of Jews there in 171/170 BC. Under such circumstances, that colony of Jews would have been given the large measure of responsibility for the affairs of the city.[12] Such families would have established themselves as being of influence and power in the city, a standing that would continue to be recognized even under later administrations, including the Roman structure. Ramsay suggested that Paul was born into one of these "original" families of Tarsus. If so, then Paul's family had been there for four generations or so when he was born.

Whether or not that is the case, there were probably, as Ramsay suggested, many Jewish citizens in the city. The reason for drawing this inference is that membership in the citizenship assembly carried with it social as well as political implications. The citizens were generally organized into one or more "tribes"[13] that made provision for social and even religious activities together. We cannot imagine an orthodox Jewish family participating in such activities unless there were enough Jewish citizens to have a tribe of their own.

While we are considering Paul's birth*place*, a word is in order about the *date* of his birth. As already noted, we meet him first in Acts 7:58 as a young man. The trouble is that this Greek word (*neanias*) could refer to a person anywhere in the twenty to forty age bracket. All this tells us, then, is that Paul was somewhere between twenty and forty at the time of Stephen's martyrdom in about the year AD 33, and even that date may be off two or three years, depending on one's view of the date of Jesus' crucifixion.

There is also the fact that, when writing to Philemon in approximately AD 60 (see chap. 7), Paul called himself "the aged" (Greek, *presbytes*), a word not usually used until a person had reached sixty or so.

One other consideration is that Paul was certainly old enough to be given a leadership role among the Jews by the time of Stephen's death. And leadership was not generally accorded truly young men in our modern sense of that word. Some think that at the time of or immediately after Stephen's stoning Paul was a member of the Jewish Sanhedrin, a question we will examine in the next chapter. If so, according to rules expressed later but probably in force then, he was at least thirty-five.

We can be no more specific. Paul's age at Stephen's stoning was about the same as the date we attach to that year. He was born then about the time we change the dating to the Christian era (AD), probably a few years after the birth of Christ.[14] There is a traditional supposition (based on an inference in a sermon attributed to Chrysostom) that he died in the year 66 at the age of sixty-eight; thus he was born in 2 BC. F. F. Bruce suggests that he was born "probably in the first decade of the Christian era."[15]

PAUL'S ROMAN CITIZENSHIP

As already noted, Paul was partly reared as a Jew in the Dispersion. The world he was part of is now known as the Greco-Roman world: Greek in language and culture, Roman in government.

When Alexander the Great conquered that world for the Greeks, in the period leading up to 323 BC, he deliberately tried to establish Greek culture in the lands conquered. The Greeks believed that their language and culture were superior to all others, and it was part of their mission to "civilize" the world. Even after the Greek Empire was divided, following Alexander's death, the process of enforced Hellenization went on in many places.

Then along came the Romans and conquered that world again. But the Romans did not desire to challenge the established Greek culture. What they wanted was to rule by their legions and collect the taxes. Indeed, the Romans themselves were strongly influenced by the culture of the Greeks in art, philosophy, dress, athletics, and religion. They made Latin the official language of the empire and expected Roman citizens everywhere to have an adequate knowledge of it, but in fact many did not, and Greek was by far the more common language, especially in the eastern provinces. Indeed, "Greek was an official language of the public administration in Syria and Palestine, Latin being normally confined to the internal organization of the army, and to documents affecting Roman citizens."[16] That accounts for the significant differences in the western and eastern parts of the empire in the time of Paul. In the western provinces, Roman culture was stronger; whole communities were granted the status of Roman citizenship. In the eastern provinces, the dominant Hellenistic culture made the process of Romanization much slower.[17]

ROMAN EMPERORS DURING PAUL'S LIFETIME

Paul lived under five Roman emperors. All are sometimes indiscriminately referred to as Caesar.

Octavian, better known as *Augustus* (31 BC–AD 14), became the unchallenged ruler after defeating Mark Antony's forces at the battle of Actium, which produced the suicides of both Antony and Cleopatra. He reorganized the Roman government, renouncing dictatorial powers and restoring many of the functions of the senate with himself as *princeps* (first citizen). The emperor directly supervised imperial provinces, where the largest military contingents were stationed, like Egypt, Gaul, Syria, and Spain. The senate controlled the other provinces, ruled by civil rather than military governments. In practical effect, the emperor was sovereign.

During Augustus's reign, many thought the "golden age" had come. He put down insurrections in various areas, conquered new territories, and consolidated governments: additions included Egypt, Illyricum, Galatia, and others.

Tiberius (AD 14–37) was Augustus's stepson. Early in his reign he faced unrest in eastern provinces, including Cappadocia and Cilicia, and more serious problems in Armenia involving the never vanquished Parthians. Most problems he settled with firm diplomacy, but some disturbances (as in Africa, in AD 20) required the use of the army. At death, he left perhaps three billion *sesterce* (150 million dollars) in the treasury.

Gaius, nicknamed *Caligula* (AD 37–41), was the son of Germanicus (an adopted son, and nephew, of Tiberius). A weak and unstable ruler, he wasted the financial reserves left by Tiberius, raised taxes, acted the monarch, and took seriously his "divinity" as an emperor.

Claudius (AD 41–54), the brother of Germanicus, thus another nephew of Tiberius and uncle of Gaius, attempted to undo Gaius's errors and restore the principles of Augustus, often replacing incompetent aristocrats as senators with more capable persons of lower social/political rank. He was poisoned by his (fourth) wife (who was his niece), the mother of Nero.

Nero (AD 54–68), son of Claudius, began ruling at age seventeen, though he was more interested in pleasures than politics. His military tacticians succeeded in crushing rebellion in Britain and regaining Armenia from the Parthians. His second wife, Poppaea, may have been a Jewish proselyte. Nero alienated the populace. He blamed Christians for the famous fire of 64 and persecuted them as a result, which action may have included the execution of both Paul and Peter. This ruler committed suicide in 68, which brought rejoicing in Rome.

There has probably never been a greater empire than the Roman Empire, and Paul lived when it was in its glory. The extent of the empire varied from one time to another, but its basic dimensions were settled by about 27 BC under Augustus. In Paul's day the Roman dominion extended across Europe westward into Spain and Great Britain and eastward through Asia Minor, Syria, and Palestine. All of North Africa was included, from Egypt across to the Atlantic. There was no land bordering the Mediterranean not under Roman control. "Except for the Parthian Empire on the eastern frontier and the turbulent tribes of northern Europe east of the Rhine, there was no serious threat to Roman domination."[18]

The "peace of Rome" (*pax Romana* was the official Latin expression) was therefore a peace that had to be enforced by military power. Roman legions, a professional army, were stationed at strategic points. The basic unit of the army was the *contubernium* ("sharing one tent") of eight men; ten *contubernia* formed a *century* (originally, a hundred), under a *centurion*; six centuries made a *cohort*; and ten cohorts (the first being double size) were in a *legion*, with an additional one hundred-twenty cavalry. At full strength, then, a legion included nearly six thousand troops. When Augustus died (AD 14), there were twenty-five legions, four of them stationed in Syria (which in the broadest sense included Palestine under its jurisdiction). Legionaries were Roman citizens. They served for twenty years and often became wealthy. Officially they were not permitted to marry. (There was also a standing "auxiliary" army made up of noncitizens who would become citizens on retirement. Lesser paid, they were used for secondary missions. The size of this army probably matched that of the legions.) Retired soldiers and their families were often settled in colonies at strategic places.[19] "The army was . . . the force that established and maintained the peace which made the spread of Christianity possible."[20] Paul often used the Roman soldier as a metaphor or illustration in his writing (as in Eph. 6:13–17; 2 Tim. 2:3–4).

Much of the empire was subdivided into provinces of two kinds. Senatorial provinces were governed by *proconsuls* appointed by the Roman senate. Most of these had only small military forces, not legions, at their disposal. Imperial provinces had governors appointed by the emperor. The more important of these were *legates*, with legions at their disposal. Syria (with Cilicia) was an imperial province governed by a legate. Lesser governors were *prefects* or *procurators*; Judea, when dealt with as a province (see insert in chap. 2), was governed thus.[21] In addition to provinces, there were *client kingdoms*, ethnic districts that were permitted to remain semi-independent under their own native "kings." Even these had to have Roman approval and could exist and exercise self-government only as Rome chose to allow. Some of the time, Judea was dealt with in this fashion (again, see insert in chap. 2).[22]

The empire was therefore generally stable, even though force was often required to quell uprisings in various areas, and a sense of unity was fostered. Contributing to that was a remarkable network of roads built to promote travel, especially the movement of troops, over important routes. The Roman roads still win admiration as an outstanding achievement of administrative and engineering skill. They were hard roads (something like our macadam roads), well maintained, with mile markers. (See the insert on page 79 for a description.) The Mediterranean was also kept busy with sailing vessels following well-established sea lanes and carrying cargo from one port to another.

Both the roads and the ships, therefore, greatly promoted trade and travel, and there was freedom of movement throughout the empire. It was a busy, bustling world, unified under one military power and one political administration. The coinage of Rome, Roman troops, and the Roman-approved officials who judged civil matters all testified to this identity. Add to that the freedom of travel and communication between all parts of the empire and one can understand the influences that were at work to "develop wider horizons, a more cosmopolitan spirit, and a continuous interchange of intellectual and spiritual treasures."[23]

But Paul was not just born and reared in such a world; he was a Roman citizen. Once again, that must not be taken for granted. Most people who lived in the Roman Empire in Paul's time were not Roman citizens.

Paul was one of the privileged ones, as seen in Acts 22:25–29. He had been seized by a mob in Jerusalem, then rescued by the Roman troops stationed there. The commander of the troops gave orders that Paul be beaten so the truth could be learned, but when Paul made known that he was a Roman, the beating was immediately canceled. The discussion between the two of them is revealing. Captain Lysias was a Roman citizen, too, and had purchased his citizenship "with a large sum of money." Paul, on the other hand, was "actually born a citizen," meaning that his father was a citizen before him, and he inherited the status. This Roman citizenship is in view whenever the word *Roman* appears in Acts (see 16:21, 37, 38; 23:27; 25:16).

Roman citizenship, originally limited to freeborn natives of Rome, came to be granted under various circumstances to large numbers at once or to individuals. Sometimes colonies of citizens were settled in various places in the empire both to reduce the population in Rome and to contribute to the maintaining of order. (Such colonies usually included heavy contingents of military veterans.) Philippi in Macedonia was such a colony (Acts 16:12, 21), as were Corinth, Antioch, Iconium, Lystra, and Troas, other cities of importance in Paul's ministry.

In a few instances other cities were granted the standing that made all free residents citizens. In some cases, people in an area loyal to the emperor during a time of civil rebellion might be granted citizenship. Such practices brought about the rise in number of citizens from 400,000 to 4,000,000 during the civil wars of the first century BC.[24] There were also freedmen, former slaves granted freedom by the emperor or other residents, who were made citizens. Soldiers of the auxiliary army received the citizenship at retirement.

Obviously such privileges are often given as personal favors. Money may even change hands, as seen in the case of Claudius Lysias above. Although we know that Paul inherited the status from his father (Acts 22:28), we do not know how Paul's father or earlier ancestor obtained the citizenship. But we have already seen that Paul was most likely born in a prominent Jewish family, part of a Jewish community influential in Tarsus. We have also seen that his family were citizens of Tarsus. And we have seen that Tarsus was frequented as a popular vacation spot by highborn Romans. With all this, it is not hard to imagine any number of circumstances that might have led to some father or grandfather of Paul's having the kind of relationship with some Roman nobleman that resulted in citizenship being granted on an individual basis.[25] As A. N. Sherwin-White puts it, speculation is "a fruitless task, though lack of evidence has not deterred the ingenious."[26]

Being a Roman citizen did not mean participation in government like United States citizenship means for us. The empire was governed primarily by the emperor and the Roman senate. But the citizenship status was a coveted privilege, carrying with it certain legal rights and confirmed by local registers of Roman citizens in each community. "Each legitimately born child of a Roman citizen had to be registered within (it appears) thirty days of his birth."[27] Written proof could be obtained, if needed; if challenged, the testimony of seven witnesses was required.[28] Under Claudius those who falsely claimed the citizenship were executed.[29]

A Roman citizen, for example, could not be condemned or punished without a fair hearing, a right ordinary people did not possess. That is why the Philippian authorities were frightened about the beating that had been administered to Paul and Silas in Acts 16:35–39. He could not be scourged, which is the reason Paul escaped the beating in Acts 22:25–29. A Roman citizen could also appeal his case to the emperor if he felt he was not being treated fairly. That is what is involved in Acts 25:10–12, with Paul's appeal to Caesar and the transfer of his case from procurator Festus in Caesarea to emperor Nero at the imperial court in Rome. The citizen was also exempt from the poll tax but not the land tax.[30]

We understand Paul much better, then, if we remember that he was a citizen, born to a citizen, of the Roman Empire. His outlook and attitudes toward the world could not possibly have been unaffected by that relationship. He had a sense of identity with a heterogeneous world community, of being part of a united arid far-flung empire, and of enjoying a certain standing in the established political structure.

PAUL AND THE HELLENISTIC CULTURE

Paul's world, as already noted, was a Greco-Roman world, with the Greek influence culturally dominant. Being "civilized," in that time, meant being Hellenistic. Emil Schürer summarizes:

> It was the grandiose plan of Alexander the Great to found a world empire that would be held together, not only by unity of government, but also by a unity of language, customs, and culture.[31]

In Acts 21:37 we learn both that Paul spoke Greek and that the
Roman military tribune Lysias (referred to above) was surprised that
he did. That reflects the fact that Jews reared in Palestine tended to
be more provincial than those reared in the Dispersion, and were
less likely to speak Greek. Ever since the intertestamental days of the
Maccabees, there had been considerable resistance to Hellenization
among the stricter Jews in their homeland.[32]

Had Lysias known of Paul's rearing in Tarsus, he would not have
been surprised at his fluency in Greek. Even today we call that period
in the history of the Greek language the *Koine* period (a Greek word
that means "common"). The Greeks called other languages barbarian,
an onomatopoeic word they coined because speech in another language sounded to them like so much "bar-bar-bar," and the word came
to have the underlying connotation of uncivilized (e.g., Acts 28:2).

Given his use of the Greek language and even more his boyhood
background as a member of an influential Jewish family in Tarsus, we
cannot doubt that Paul was a Hellenistic Jew. Still there were degrees
of Hellenization. When people of one nationality live in another
country, the culture of that country may affect them to a greater or
lesser degree, depending on various factors.

One of those factors is the length of time a family has lived in a
different country. In light of what has already been said about the citizenship status of Paul's father, both of Tarsus and of Rome, it seems
probable that Paul's family had lived in Tarsus for more than one
generation. If Ramsay's theory discussed above is true, then the family had been there for several generations.

Another factor that affects the extent of cultural conditioning is
religion, and that has always been a key consideration for Jews living
among other peoples. Even in twenty-first-century America, many
Jews whose families have been here for generations maintain distinctive Jewishness, whereas others do not, and their religious concerns
play a large role in making the difference. The same was true then,
and so we may say that *Paul's family was Hellenistic, but they were
not Hellenizers.*

This distinction, sometimes drawn,[33] is more or less artificial, but it is a convenient one for making an important point. The evidence is that they were Hellenistic in the sense that they were culturally influenced; they were not Hellenizing, in that they maintained the purity of their orthodox Jewish faith, free from modifications under the influence of Greek philosophy.

There were Dispersion Jews who did make serious adjustments in their theology for the sake of lessening tensions with Greek thought. Philo of Alexandria can be cited as a good example. There was a large Jewish population in Alexandria in Egypt. Having been there for hundreds of years, they were well established and influential. Alexandrian thinking was looked to by many Dispersion Jews, especially those interested in doing as much as possible to adapt to the ways of their neighbors whose thinking was Greek. It was characteristic of the Jewish community in Alexandria to set the pace in this; the translation of the Hebrew Scriptures into Greek[34] had been made there in about 280 BC.

Philo was one of the influential Jewish thinkers in Alexandria. His life (c. 20 BC–AD 42) overlapped that of Paul. He was deeply influenced by Greek philosophers, especially Plato and the Stoics. Though he remained strictly monotheistic, he conceived of God as less knowable and personal, more like the pure Being of Greek philosophy than the God of the Old Testament. He accepted the Greek dualistic distinction between spirit and matter, with the material world being less real than the ideal world, partly created by angelic intermediaries, with the *Logos* (Greek for pure "reason") at their head. And in typical Alexandrian style, he interpreted the Jewish Scriptures in a strictly allegorical manner so that the stories could represent any philosophical notions he wanted to read into them.

The result was a synthesis between Old Testament theology and Greek philosophy, a serious departure from traditional Jewish orthodoxy. And many Jews out in the Greco-Roman world welcomed that kind of compromise. But many others, truer to the faith of their fathers, rejected such Hellenization of their thinking, even though they were clearly influenced by Hellenistic culture in less serious ways.

Paul's strictness as "a Pharisee, a son of Pharisees" (Acts 23:6) and "a Hebrew of Hebrews" (Phil. 3:5) testifies that his family was among these latter. The Pharisees were the strictest sect of Judaism, and "Hebrew" here refers to the language spoken at home and probably in their synagogue. Both expressions refer to Paul's father as well as himself, and therefore Paul was raised in a thoroughly orthodox atmosphere. (The next chapter will deal with these matters.) In religious matters Paul's family apparently looked more to Antioch in Syria (next door to Cilicia) than to Alexandria. The Jewish community in Antioch represented much more conservative thinking.

Still, the main point should not be forgotten. Although not Hellenizing in religion, even as a Jew, Paul's background was in a Hellenistic world. As a Greek-speaking native citizen of busy Tarsus and mighty Rome, his outlook could not help being affected.

There is clear evidence of that effect in the picture of Paul we get in Acts and in his writings. He knew and quoted Greek poets (Acts 17:28; Titus 1:12). He obviously enjoyed the Greco-Roman athletic games and used them often as illustrations in his letters,[35] even though many less tolerant Jews regarded these games as reprehensible.[36] Throughout his writings he displayed understanding of the customs of his world.

All one has to do to appreciate this is to contrast Paul's general outlook with that of an equally famous apostle, Simon Peter. Peter was not a Dispersion Jew; he was reared in provincial Palestine, in "the isolated district of Galilee."[37] He fished on Galilee, where no ships from lands afar ever docked. His acquaintance with the peoples and customs of the great Roman Empire would not have been as wide as Paul's. Greek was not nearly so common a language in his hometown. Roman citizens were not numerous even in Judea. Even as a Spirit-filled Christian, he found it difficult to reach out to the Gentiles, as the incidents in Acts 10 and Galatians 2:11–14 show.

Paul had no such problems. He could already identify with the world. He was truly cosmopolitan, a citizen of the world. No wonder then he was God's chosen vessel to the Gentiles (Acts 9:15), whereas Peter's responsibility was primarily to the Jews (Gal. 2:7–8).

Someone may object that Paul's love for the Gentiles was the result of his conversion and not of his background. Surely God could have miraculously changed a narrow, provincial outlook to a broad, cosmopolitan one. But we must not forget that God works His will in the circumstances of a person's background, too. He prepares the vessels of His service to be usable even before they know Him. Thus it was with Paul. God's hand had been at work from his birth (Gal. 1:15) to make him the man He could use. And one of the main ingredients of that preparation is found in his Dispersion background as Tarsian, Roman, and Greek.

2

PAUL THE JEW

The previous chapter explored one side of the fact that Paul was a Dispersion Jew. The fact that he was partly reared in Tarsus, a consciously Greco-Roman city, contributed much to the making of the man. But there is no doubt that his Hebrew heritage as son of an orthodox Jew contributed even more.

The fact that Paul was bilingual, fluently speaking both Greek and Hebrew (Acts 21:37, 40), represents the two cultures that blended in him. But even though Hellenistic culture had affected his outlook, he prided himself on being "a Hebrew of Hebrews" (Phil. 3:5).

This phrase refers especially to the language spoken in his home, his native tongue. He was a Hebrew-speaking Jew born to Hebrew speaking Jews. Actually, the language was not the original Hebrew but Aramaic, a Chaldean tongue that had supplanted the older Hebrew from the captivity. We have already noted that Paul's family was not among those Hellenizing Jews who sacrificed the purity of Old Testament theology for adjustment to Greek philosophy. They were also not of those who adopted Greek as their native language. This difference between Greek-speaking Jews and Aramaic-speaking Jews is precisely what is involved in Acts 6:1 and 9:29, where the word *Hellenistic* (kjv, *Grecians*) appears.[1]

Above all else, then, and in the fullest sense, Paul was a Jew. That fact accounts for the greater part of his background. And because we know much about the Jew in New Testament times, we can tell much about Paul.

Before we explore any other facet of this, a word is in order about his name. "Paul" is a Greek spelling (*Paulos*) of the Latin *Paullus*. To

Aramaic-speaking Jews, his name was Saul (from *Saoul*). The strong probability is that he had both names from birth.[2] As to the origin of the name *Saul* we can be confident: Paul was of the tribe of Benjamin (Phil. 3:5), and Saul was a famous name in that tribe, going back to Israel's first king. Of the origin of the name Paul, we can only speculate; it may reflect some Roman benefactor in the family history, perhaps even the one responsible for the Roman citizenship.[3]

PAUL'S RELIGION: JUDAISM

To be a Jew has always meant more than nationality. Thus, when Paul laid claim to being a Jew (Acts 21:39; 22:3), he spoke as much of religion as of race. In Galatians 1:13–14 he identified himself as one who practiced and profited in the Jews' religion (Greek, *Ioudaismos*, "Judaism").

What sort of religion was the Judaism of Paul's day? Obviously the Jews of the first century shared much in common with their forefathers so well known in the Old Testament. Even so, in its essence as a way of relating to God, Judaism was not the faith of the Hebrew heroes.

Judaism, as a distinctive religion, and to this day one of the world's most influential ones, was a development of the captivity and post-captivity experiences of Judah. The earlier history of Israel is a mixed record. Many had a vital relationship with God, observing the system of worship He gave them in the Mosaic law, but many more practiced insincere ritual or, worse still, became heavily involved in idolatry and other heathen wickedness. For such things God brought judgment and captivity, at the hands of the Assyrians on the northern kingdom (Israel) and of the Babylonians on the southern kingdom (Judah).

When the Jews[4] returned from captivity under men like Zerubbabel (537 BC) and Ezra (458 BC), they were different. Idolatry would never again be a major problem. In that respect God's chastisement had been effective. They had learned that their distinctiveness consisted both in their racial identity and in the Mosaic law that was so uniquely theirs.[5]

It may be that they learned the lesson too well, for Judaism became a religion of the law. Four things can be cited as illustrative of this emphasis. First, the rabbis had arisen as a lay order to be teachers of the law, displacing the priests in that function. There were no rabbis in pre-captivity Judah, and the Mosaic system made no provision for that office. But by Jesus' time the rabbis were the dominant interpreters of the law among the Jews.[6]

Second, scribes had arisen to be copiers and professional scholars ("lawyers," as in Luke 10:25) of the Mosaic law. These, too, did not exist before the captivity. Most of the scribes and the rabbis shared common origins and interests.

Third, synagogues had developed as places devoted primarily to the study of the law. Again, there were no synagogues prior to the exile in Babylon; by New Testament times the synagogue was the center of Jewish education and everyday life. Synagogue life revolved around the law that was taught there, especially by the rabbis. The synagogue "pulpit" was not "clerical," for any qualified layman could bring the message. Still, the well taught are naturally preferred over those with lesser knowledge, so that "the natural superiority of the Scripture expert asserted itself in the synagogue."[7]

Fourth, the office of the priesthood was redirected. The priests were originally meant to be the teachers of Israel. But the rise of the scribes and rabbis and the hold they had on synagogue life (along with other developments during the intertestamental period) shifted the emphasis for the priesthood in two other directions: to political activity and to being perpetrators of the sacrificial ritual of the law associated especially with the Temple.

We do not know precisely how all this took place. In captivity the Jews had to survive without Jerusalem and the Temple. No doubt they began to arrange to assemble (*synagoge* is a Greek word meaning "assembly") to worship and study the law. Teachers were needed. Copies of the law were needed. "Expert" interpretations were needed. One thing led to another, and the new system carried back to Judah after the captivity became more and more formalized. Ezra, for example, was already being called a scribe (Ezra 7:6).

As each of these has been mentioned, emphasis has been placed on their relationship to the law, for that is where the emphasis belongs. Judaism, involving both the priestly-sacrificial ritual and the rabbinic educational-ethical teaching, revolved around the law, or Torah. Religion came to be a way of living according to the law.

It is certain that when Jesus and Paul were born, there were devout Jews who had a warm and vital relationship with God. Zechariah, Mary, Anna, and Simeon surely represent many more. Even so, in its formal expression Judaism, especially in the Pharisaic form that dominated rabbinic-synagogue teaching, was already a religion of law when Jesus came into the world. The personal knowledge of God communicated by the Old Testament revelation tended to be supplanted by a moral-ceremonial code. Justification before God was likely to be understood as earned by the keeping of Moses's law, and that had never been God's intention.

PHARISAISM: PAUL'S BRAND OF JUDAISM

There were different sects within Judaism. Like his father before him (Acts 23:6), Paul was with the Pharisees (Phil. 3:5), which he calls "the strictest sect of our religion" (Acts 26:5).

The precise origins of the Pharisees are also difficult to trace, involving historical developments during the intertestamental period. In some way they probably had roots in the *hasidim*,[8] who opposed liberalizing Hellenistic trends under the Seleucid rulers. The word *Pharisees* apparently means "separated ones."

Regardless of origins, the character of Pharisaism in Paul's time is generally clear. A fundamental feature was legalism, the effort to reduce life to a system of rules that cover every conceivable circumstance. In this respect the Pharisees were wedded to the kind of teaching that issued from the scribes and rabbis.[9] No doubt there were scribes, or legal scholars, among the Sadducees, too, but their influence was much more limited, and their teachings disappeared from tradition under the dominance of the Pharisees.[10]

By Jesus' time there had grown up a body of oral tradition passed on from one generation of rabbis to another, later to be recorded in the Talmud. As Schürer explains,

Biblical law gradually became a complex and intricate branch of knowledge. And as this law was not fixed in writing but was mainly handed down by word of mouth, continuous study was necessary even to become familiar with it.[11]

This rabbinic tradition dealt with duty and ceremonial purity in incredible detail, attempting to tell how to apply the Mosaic law in any situation, right down to whether it was lawful to carry a needle in one's pocket on the Sabbath, for example, or precisely how to wash one's hands before eating in order to be ceremonially clean. Of special concern were the laws that related to Sabbath observance, food restrictions, tithing, and ceremonial purity. At the same time it would be misleading to say there was no concern for inner purity and spiritual quality among Pharisees. At least some of them, at times, expressed such concerns.[12]

These rabbinic rules went far beyond those contained in Moses's law but were considered essential to keep and protect that law. This tradition was called a "hedge about the law." As the legalistic sect of Judaism, the Pharisees upheld this body of tradition. They regarded it as equally inspired as the Old Testament,[13] tracing it to Moses. Rabbis, therefore, who were the teachers of the law in the synagogues, tended to be Pharisees.

The Pharisees were also known for their belief in the spiritual realm: angels, resurrection from the dead, and an afterlife. The Jewish historian Josephus further relates that whereas the Essene sect believed in strict predestination, and the Sadducees that all things happen by man's free will, the Pharisees afforded room for both divine predestination and human choice.[14]

Beyond these key characteristics, several others can be briefly noted. The Pharisees generally frowned on luxurious indulgence, preferring a simpler life. They took little interest in political pursuits so long as the existing government left them alone. They were closely knit and tended to withdraw from others, with spiritual pride often marking their separatism. They regarded the common folk (the *am ha'aretz,* "people of the land") as incapable of true piety. Even so, the

Pharisees were a large sect (according to Josephus, six thousand were in Palestine shortly before Jesus' birth) and very influential, identified as they were with the rabbis who were the respected teachers of Judaism's synagogue-centered education in the law. Schürer demonstrates clearly that the course of Pharisaism finally became the course of Judaism: "No peculiarity emerges from this characterization of Pharisaism which might distinguish it from Judaism in general during the period of the Second Temple."[15]

The chief opposition to the Pharisees was furnished by a much smaller sect, the Sadducees. The origins of this group, too, are somewhat obscurely traced to developments during the intertestamental period, no doubt to a more wealthy, politically minded, liberalizing, priestly tradition. Even the name is uncertain, perhaps derived from "Zadok" (often pronounced "Saddouk"), the patriarch of the priestly line since Solomon's time.[16]

The Sadducees rejected the rabbinic extrabiblical tradition; indeed, they regarded only the written Torah as inspired and binding. They did not take literally the references to angels,[17] resurrection, or an afterlife. (This is what is involved in such incidents as that recorded in Mark 12:18–27; see also, as particularly instructive, Acts 23:6–10.) "Their real interests were concerned more with this life and the present than with the life to come and the future."[18]

The Sadducees therefore tended to identify with the Temple sacrificial ritual rather than with the rabbinic-dominated, synagogue-centered legalism that the Pharisees loved. The priests tended to be Sadducees.[19] But in the last decades preceding the destruction of the Temple, "a number of priests themselves belonged to the Pharisees."[20]

Dating back to trends that developed during the intertestamental period, the priestly Sadducean party was very politically active, concerned with power and influence. Schürer summarizes:

> From the priestly circles emerged the Sadducean party, and from those of the Torah scholars came the party of the Pharisees, the lay experts in religious matters. . . . The Pharisees were essentially concerned with strict legality. The Sadducees were at first simply

aristocrats persuaded by historical development into opposing Pharisaic legalism. . . . The Pharisees' characteristics proceeded from their legal orientation, whereas those of the Sadducees derived from their inherited social standing.[21]

There were other sects of lesser importance. The Essenes were even more extremely separatistic than the Pharisees, usually living in such ascetic communities as the one we have come to associate with the famous Dead Sea Scrolls. The Herodians (somewhat like a lobby in our day) were interested in keeping the Herodian dynasty in power (see the insert on pp. 44–47), and that involved influence at Rome. Zealots were a small group of patriots devoted to the overthrow of Rome by armed revolution.[22]

So Paul was a Jew, and a Pharisaic Jew at that. As such, he was a member of the sect that played the largest role in Jewish life. He was zealously devoted to upholding the law of God and strongly identified with rabbinic-dominated synagogue life.

One further word about this. Paul was not necessarily like the picture of a Pharisee we tend to see in the gospels. Whether the gospel writers actually intended this, we generally characterize all Pharisees as narrow, mean, and hypocritical, insincerely pushing off their external conformity on others, secretly delighting in wickedness. Doubtless, some of the Pharisees were like that; doubtless, also, most of them confused outward behavior with true righteousness and tended to avoid evidences of their own depravity, covering up with devotion to rules and rituals. Even so, many were earnestly devoted to their religion and genuinely, if misguidedly, hoped to stand before God blameless in the keeping of the law. From all we know of Paul, his zealous activity recorded in Acts (7:58–9:2) and his own references to his background (Phil. 3:3–6; Gal. 1:13–14), he was certainly such a Pharisee.

PAUL'S EDUCATIONAL UPBRINGING

We cannot fully appreciate the impact of Judaism on Paul without considering the role of education in Jewish life in the time of

Paul. For the Jew, religion and Jewishness and education were insepa-
rably interwoven.[23]

When we explore the subject of Paul's education in particular,
we have to look at two things: at the typical education that would
have been any Jewish boy's and at the specific education that was
given to those who were to become rabbis.

The Jewish writers Philo and Josephus have given us a general
outline of the informal but thorough education of the young men
in New Testament times. Teaching the law of God was expected to
begin in the home. According to the rabbis, a father had three duties
(after circumcision and redemption) in the rearing of a son, and the
first was to teach him the law. Philo said this began while the child
was still in "swaddling clothes"; no doubt the impetus was supplied
by such passages as Deuteronomy 6:6–7.

We do not have a good picture of the shape of formal education in Paul's day. Later on, the Talmud indicated that boys began
to attend weekday classes at the synagogue at age five, beginning
studies with the Pentateuch. At age ten the student advanced to the
Mishnah, a part of the Talmudic tradition that dealt with the detailed laws of ritual observance. At age thirteen the boy reached his
majority as a "son of the law," and at fifteen he was deemed ready for
the meat of the Talmud. At eighteen the young man was expected to
marry and at twenty to be pursuing his trade.

How much of this was practiced in the time of Jesus and Paul we
cannot tell. Schools probably operated in the time of Jesus, though
perhaps not yet as a general and well-established institution.[24] "By
New Testament times, the Jews had adopted a more formal approach
to education. They set aside classrooms and qualified teachers to instruct all the children in the village."[25]

John Townsend thinks that primary schools (up to age ten?)
were "probably not widespread outside Jerusalem until after the first
Jewish revolt" (AD 66–73), partly because of the great emphasis that
was placed on learning at home the Scripture knowledge expected in
the secondary school.[26] But he goes on to point out that the scribes in
New Testament times taught young boys to read.

The students began by learning to recite and read the Hebrew Bible, starting with Genesis. (After the revolt, they began with Leviticus.) They would also have had to memorize the Targums, standard translations of the ancient Hebrew into either the spoken Aramaic or Greek. Writing may or may not have been given much instruction.

The secondary schooling was concerned more with the oral Torah, the rabbinic traditions, including *midrash* (traditions arranged under topical headings.) If education was to be continued, the student progressed from "Mishnah" to Talmud, which "involved advanced juridical learning and discussion."[27] Education somewhat similar to this was the experience of Paul.

The question arises whether Paul followed normal practice and was married. The discussion yet to come about his training as rabbi will not answer the question. Like everyone else, rabbis were expected to be married. Later, the Talmud would specifically decree that an unmarried man must not teach children.[28]

Some may think we have a biblical answer in 1 Corinthians 7:8, proving that Paul never married. But all that verse shows is that Paul had no wife when he wrote 1 Corinthians in about AD 55 (he would be about fifty-five at the time). Many a married man has been widowed by the age of fifty-five, and that could have been Paul's experience. In fact, the association between "unmarried" (masculine) and "widows" (feminine) in the verse may suggest that "unmarried" is being used in the sense of widower (for which there was no Greek word); some think Paul was classifying himself with widowers and widows.

We cannot be absolutely sure. What we can be sure of is the attitude of Jews toward marriage, an attitude grounded in the Old Testament itself, where both marriage and children are emphatically blessed (as in Prov. 18:22; Ps. 127:4–5). If the first of a father's three duties toward his son according to the rabbis was to teach him the law, the second was to find him a wife.

Below we will examine the question of whether Paul was a member of the Sanhedrin. Perhaps he was not. But their rule that one must be married to be a member[29] at least serves to show their high regard for marriage and family responsibility as a requisite for a leadership role in Jewish life. And by the time of Acts 8–9, Paul was certainly occupying a role that would have required the confidence of responsible men.

What we can say then without hesitation is that if Paul did not marry, he was an exception, especially considering the prominence he achieved. If he did marry, we know nothing at all about his wife or her fate, but the absence of any reference to her is no more significant than the absence of almost any other references to Paul's personal experiences before his conversion or for quite a few years thereafter.

PAUL THE RABBI

Above we have explored the normal course of a Jewish boy's education. Such was the course of almost any youth's rearing in any conscientious Jewish family anywhere in the world of Paul's day. But there is more that can be said about Paul's education: He trained to be a rabbi. In Acts 22:3 Paul indicated the very rabbinic school he attended in Jerusalem.

According to the usual procedures of that period, as an aspiring rabbi, Paul would have transferred to a school for rabbis in Jerusalem. The age for that is somewhat uncertain. Some think it may have occurred when Paul was as young as eight or ten. More likely is the age of thirteen, when the lad received the *bar mitzvah* and so became responsible as an adult "son of the law." The studies outlined above, as typical for all, would not have been foregone; instead, they would have been intensified and supplemented.

During Paul's life there were two main schools for rabbis in Jerusalem.[30] One had been begun by Rabban Hillel; the other, by Rabban Shammai—contemporaries of the first-century BC. When Paul says he was brought up in Jerusalem at the feet of Gamaliel, he reveals which school he attended; Rabban Gamaliel[31] was the grandson of Hillel.

The two rabbinic schools were somewhat different in character, and the difference has bearing for our understanding of Paul. The school of Shammai was known as very strict and orthodox—

puritanical, dogmatic, emphasizing maximum requirements. The Shammaites, for example, regarded the breaking of one law as a breaking of the whole; the Hillelite attitude was that God's judgment would take into account the preponderance of good or bad in one's life.[32]

The more influential Hillel school was more flexible and open, in some measure concerned about the spirit as well as the letter of the law, more inclined to be satisfied with minimum requirements. Hillel is reported to have summarized the whole law as saying, "What is hateful to yourself, do not to another."[33] The distinction between the two schools should not be absolutely pressed, for both represented the scribal-rabbinic-Pharisaic approach we have already examined. Still, there was strong tension between the two, so much that it was said, "Elijah the Tishbite would never be able to reconcile the disciples of Hillel and Schammai."[34]

Gamaliel, Paul's own teacher and grandson of Hillel,[35] was an outstanding rabbi and headmaster. His name is famous in Jewish circles even to this day. He was apparently more tolerant and large-hearted than we would normally expect of a Pharisee. The reference to him in Acts 5:34–39 as a member of the Sanhedrin illustrates his attitude. He was honest, sincere, frank—known for his love of nature. He appreciated and used Greek authors and was an acknowledged expert in the Mosaic law and the rabbinic-Talmudic tradition. He has often been called by Jewish writers the "Beauty of the Law." The Talmud says, "Since Rabban Gamaliel died, the glory of the Law has ceased."[36] The openness of Paul's family to some aspects of Hellenistic culture, though not to Hellenized theology (as discussed in chap. 1), may account for the decision to send him to Gamaliel. And Gamaliel, in turn, contributed to the attitude of Paul.

Rabbinic methodology called for each generation of rabbis to pass along to the next that body of oral tradition already described, to be memorized and preserved. These traditions included all the rules and ceremonies that governed life and served as the hedge about the law. Also included were standardized interpretations of various Old Testament portions and a methodology for teaching the law to a synagogue community.

All these things were included in Paul's rabbinic studies, called by various formal names: the Midrashim, expositions of the Hebrew Scriptures; the Halacha, legal customs and practices added by the rabbis to the Old Testament practices; the Haggadah, nonlegal narratives exegeting the Scriptures. Nothing was more important in interpreting a scripture or defining a duty than to quote some famous rabbi of antiquity as a final word.[37] Methodology included the representation of truths by allegories and symbols, as well as allegorical exegesis of Scripture. Such approaches frequently show up in Paul's epistles.[38]

One more thing we know about Paul can be related to his role as a Jewish rabbi. The rabbi was expected to have a trade. He would probably not be supported by his synagogue ministry but by the labor of his own hands.[39] Paul would be no exception. We know his trade from Acts 16:3. He was a tentmaker, and he pursued that craft as diligently during his Christian ministry as he would have as a rabbi, as various references in Acts and his letters confirm.

That is not meant to imply that Paul learned his trade in rabbinic school. The Jews felt strongly about the value of labor, and any young man would be expected to master a trade to support himself and his family. Reference has already been made to the three duties of a father toward his son. The third was to teach him a trade. Rabbi Judah is quoted as saying: "He that teacheth not his son a trade, doth the same as if he taught him to be a thief."[40]

Paul no doubt learned tent-making in Tarsus. As noted in chapter 1, the Tarsians traded in leather goods and *cilicium*, a cloth made from the hair of the black goats of the region. This cloth was the basic stuff of the well-known black tents of Tarsus that were popular across the empire. Because a son usually followed his father's trade, we can safely assume that Paul's father was a tentmaker, too, no doubt prospering in that business.

PAUL'S PLACE IN JUDAISM

So far we have seen that Paul was a practicing Jew with that religion of the law at the center of his rearing and education. He was devoted to the Pharisaic interpretation of that religion and so was a separatist and legalist following "the strictest sect," as he expressed it, of his faith. More, he was a trained rabbi; for him, religion would not be a peripheral thing but at the center of his life.

Nor should we conceive of Paul as just one more of the nameless hundreds for whom everything just said would be true. The picture we get in the New Testament is that Paul's zeal for these things was outstanding, that he was destined for a leadership role.

In Galatians 1:14 Paul's own inspired evaluation is, "I was advancing in Judaism beyond many of my contemporaries among my countrymen, being more extremely zealous for my ancestral traditions." We have every reason to believe that is a sober assessment. When we first meet Paul in Acts 7:58, those stoning Stephen had laid their coats at his feet. That probably suggests that Paul was there in a responsible role rather than as an accidental bystander (compare Acts 22:19–20). Stephen's slaying was a Sanhedrin matter, and Paul may well have been an official observer, appointed by the Sanhedrin.

Immediately following that, we read (8:1) that a great persecution of the Christians followed, and the clear indications are that Paul played the leading role; in 8:3, for example, the responsibility is put directly on him. This could not have transpired without active Sanhedrin involvement and encouragement, as confirmed in 9:1–2: Paul intended to extend his inquisition into Syria, and he easily obtained the necessary authorizing papers from the high priest, the presiding officer of the Sanhedrin. (See also Acts 26:9–12.)

Add to this that Paul's conversion brought the persecution to a halt (9:31), and there is no doubt that he was acting in an official capacity, as agent of the Sanhedrin, to put down this new heresy.

That does not necessarily mean that he was officially a member of the Sanhedrin, which was the highest Jewish court. Whether he was is another question that may never be finally proved. Many think he was. In Paul's own testimony in Acts 26:10, referring back to his role as chief persecutor of Christians, he says, "When they were being put to death I cast my vote against them." The Greek speaks of casting down one's "stone," referring to the use of black or white pebbles for voting whether to condemn or acquit the accused.

That would seem to settle the matter, but a measure of uncertainty remains because we may not be able to say absolutely that only the official members would have cast stones for or against those on trial. The Sanhedrin employed various attendants to assist them, and they or others involved in some way in specific cases might have taken part in formally expressing their wish to set free or condemn. We can confidently say, however, that if Paul was not a member of the Sanhedrin before his conversion to Christ, he was at least a trusted servant of that body.

As the highest Jewish court, the Sanhedrin in Jerusalem (often translated "council" in English Bibles) had to operate within limits prescribed by the Roman government. But most matters involving Jewish affairs were left by the Romans to be settled by that court. (This will be discussed in chap. 7.)

JUDEAN GOVERNMENT
UNDER ROMAN DOMINION

Judea had enjoyed a measure of independence during the intertestamental period under the leadership of the Maccabees and their successors. That came to an end in 63 BC when the Roman general Pompey occupied Jerusalem. From then on, any government in Judea was Roman appointed and subservient to Roman interests.

During Paul's lifetime, Judea was sometimes dealt with as a province, sometimes as a client-kingdom. Here is a brief survey of Judean governors during Paul's lifetime.

Herod (the Great) (37–4 BC). First named king under Antony's sponsorship and later confirmed by Augustus, Herod ruled until his death. The Herods were Idumaeans (the Old Testament Edomites) who had been conquered by the Jews (under John Hyrcanus, one of the Maccabees' successors), forced to submit to circumcision, and thus made to be Jews, even though the Jewish aristocracy regarded them only as half Jews and thus inferior.[41]

Herod's rule was both cruel and adroit. He executed competitors, including members of his own family. He built prolifically and magnificently, including the city of Caesarea and the Jewish Temple in Jerusalem. At the height of his power, his domain extended almost as far as had Solomon's, encompassing Judea, Samaria, Idumaea, Galilee, and most of the surrounding districts. King when Jesus was born, he ordered "the slaughter of the infants" in Bethlehem (Matt. 2:1–18). "It should also be mentioned that Herod applied his influence with his Roman masters to securing Jews in the diaspora against oppression."[42]

Judea was thus a client-kingdom under Herod. Such kings could not hold title without the emperor's approval. "The title was, as a rule, only conferred on princes reigning over larger territories; lesser princes had to be satisfied with the title of tetrarch or something similar [like ethnarch]."[43] Such titles were not hereditary.

Archelaus (4 BC–AD 6). One of Herod's sons, *Archelaus*, was made ethnarch (not king) of Judea, Samaria, and Idumaea by Augustus; his brother *Philip* was made tetrarch of Batanaea, Trachonitis, and other northeastern districts (4 BC–AD 33/4). Another brother (*Herod*) *Antipas* was made tetrarch of Galilee and Peraea (4 BC–AD 39). (Of these, only the last plays any role in the New Testament, being the Herod who had John the Baptist executed, feared Jesus as John risen again, and refused to take Jesus' case off Pilate's hands.)

Archelaus was the worst of Herod's sons, and the leaders of the Judeans and Samaritans laid grievous complaints of his tyranny before Augustus in Rome. As a result, he was deposed and his territory placed under direct Roman rule, largely at the insistence of Jews who wished to be done with the Herods. Thus Judea's client-kingdom status ended, and provincial rule followed.

Roman prefects (AD 6–41). Technically, Judea (with Samaria and Idumaea) was annexed to the province of Syria, but it continued to have its own emperor-appointed prefect (or *procurator*, as later used; the terms are largely interchangeable), who would come from the equestrian class (i.e., knights) rather than the higher senatorial rank. Only in serious circumstances would the legate of Syria intervene in the affairs of the Judean prefect.

From AD 6–41 there were seven prefects in Judea: Coponius (6–9); Marcus Ambibulus (9–12); Annius Rufus (12–15); Valerius Gratus (15–26); Pontius Pilate (26–36); Marcellus (36–37); and Marullus (37–41).[44] Of these, only Pilate is mentioned in the New Testament, being the judge of Jesus. The prefects resided in Caesarea, in a palace built by Herod (the Great), but would reside temporarily in Jerusalem on special occasions, "especially during the main Jewish festivals."[45]

(Herod) Agrippa I (AD 41–44). Grandson of Herod the Great, Agrippa I ("Herod" in the New Testament) had insinuated himself with Caligula and was named by him king, first over Philip's territory in AD 37, and then over Antipas's territory in AD 39 or 40. When Claudius succeeded Caligula in AD 41 (partly with Agrippa's aid), he was also named king over Judea and Samaria and thus "united under his rule the whole of his grandfather's kingdom."[46] Thus Judea once again became a client-kingdom rather than a province.

This Herod is the one who had James executed and planned the same for Peter (Acts 12). His death in AD 44 at Caesarea is viewed in Acts 12 as divine judgment for his pride. At his death, his son, young Agrippa, was not named king; all of Palestine was once again placed under provincial rule, technically under the general supervision of the Syrian legate.

Roman procurators (AD 44–66). From the death of Agrippa I until the Jewish revolt against Rome in AD 66, there were seven procurators: Cuspius Fadus (44–46), Tiberius Iulius Alexander (46–48), Ventidius Cumanus (48–52), Antonius Felix (52–60), Porcius Festus (60–62), Albinus (62–64), and Gessius Florus (64–66).[47]

Only two of these are mentioned in the New Testament, and both are of importance for Paul—Felix and Festus (to be discussed in chap. 7). The entire period was one of growing dissatisfaction among the Jews, leading up to the ill-fated revolt that culminated in the destruction of Jerusalem in AD 70 by the Roman general Titus. Afterward, Judea became a province permanently, completely independent of Syria.

One other point should be mentioned. Up until 44, the power to name the Jewish high priest lay with whoever governed Judea: with the king while Judea was a client-kingdom, otherwise with the Roman prefect/procurator. But when Agrippa I died in 44, his brother Herod of Chalcis (a small territory in the former Ituraea) requested and received from emperor Claudius the right to supervise the Temple and appoint the high priest. That power stayed with him and his successor (and nephew) Agrippa II (son of Agrippa I, above) until the time of the Jewish rebellion. Agrippa II, in AD 53, was given, in exchange for Chalcis, a larger territory that included the former tetrarchy of Philip (above) and, later, important parts of Galilee and Peraea. This Agrippa and his sister/consort Bernice also played a role in Paul's affairs. (See chap. 7.)

Each local synagogue community had its own Sanhedrin to deal with issues arising at that level, but the Great Sanhedrin at Jerusalem was looked to as the highest voice of Judaism by Jews everywhere. Normally, there were seventy-one members, and the number included representatives from the scribal-rabbinic-Pharisaic tradition, the priestly-Sadducean tradition, and elders, who were more or less hereditary heads of influential families, a sort of lay nobility who would also tend to be Sadducees.[48] As already mentioned, the high priest was the presiding officer, and the priests tended to be politically dominant, even though the learned opinions of the scribes could not be ignored.[49]

We are warranted in concluding, then, that Paul had risen to a place of respected leadership as a rabbi who was destined for greatness, perhaps even for a seat on the Sanhedrin. He was a learned man, zealous, capable. One thing remains to be mentioned in passing. We know Paul spent the time of his rabbinic training in Jerusalem, probably from age thirteen to eighteen. When he appears in the record at Stephen's stoning, he is probably thirty or thirty-five years old, having drawn the attention of prominent Jewish men as one who can be given important responsibility. What of the ten to fifteen years in between?

All we can do is speculate. In all probability he became a rabbi and lived and taught in some local synagogue community, perhaps in his own hometown. No doubt he continued to study and learn. It is likely that he distinguished himself and began to draw attention, although we know not how. At some point (if he ministered elsewhere most of that time) he moved to Jerusalem to advance even further in his chosen devotion to Judaism, perhaps shortly before Stephen's martyrdom,[50] perhaps at the invitation of powerful people there. Whatever the various possibilities are, the results we have outlined are reasonably clear.

Did Paul have contact with Jesus during those years? He does not refer to such contacts if he did,[51] and that may be one reason for thinking that most of his ministry during those years was away from Jerusalem. But that is an uncertain assumption at best. It is highly likely that wherever Paul ministered as rabbi, he would have been occasionally if not frequently at Jerusalem, at least during the Passover-

Pentecost season each year. And it would have been impossible, given his zeal and keen interest, that he could have been in Jerusalem during such occasions without at least hearing of the controversy stirred by Jesus' presence and teaching in Jerusalem on the same occasions. It would be strange if their paths did not cross, but we cannot say much beyond this.

It has often been said that Paul was a product of three civilizations, the Greek, the Roman, and the Jewish. As we saw in chapter 1, to the Greeks Paul owed some of the cultural influences that contributed to his cosmopolitan attitude, his sense of identity even with the Gentile world, and the language he could use freely almost any place in the empire. To the Romans he owed a sense of the unity of the world he lived in and the privileges of citizenship he enjoyed in that structure.

This chapter has shown us that he owed far more to his Hebrew heritage: his religion, his rearing, his education, his life's pursuit. Out of this came his concept of God and the theological doctrines (all Old Testament based and thoroughly mastered by him) that went with that: his values, moral and otherwise, not the least being his regard for the dignity of labor and the blessedness of the family before God; his zeal for religion, for Judaism in particular as the only true religion, a religion of careful obedience to the Mosaic law and the rabbinic traditions that served as a hedge about it; and the work that gave his life meaning also, providing the structure for realization of the great capabilities he had as a gifted scholar. Such a man was Paul when we meet him, when our interest is first aroused in him as the persecutor of the church who later met Jesus Christ.

W. J. Conybeare and J. S. Howson speak of a Christian's view of the world when Jesus appeared:

> He sees the Greek and Roman elements brought into remarkable union with the older and more sacred elements of Judaism. He sees in the Hebrew people a divinely-laid foundation for the superstructure of the church, and in the dispersion of the Jews a soil made ready in fitting places for the seed of the Gospel. He

sees in the spread of the language and commerce of the Greeks, and in the high perfection of their poetry and philosophy, appropriate means for the rapid communication of Christian ideas and for bringing them into close connection with the best thoughts of unassisted humanity. And he sees in the union of so many incoherent provinces under the law and government of Rome a strong framework which might keep together for a sufficient period those masses of social life which the Gospel was intended to pervade. The City of God is built at the confluence of three civilizations. We recognize with gratitude the hand of God in the history of His world.[52]

Yes, and we also recognize with gratitude the hand of God in the unique preparation of Paul to preach Christ in that very world.

The Conversion and Commission of Paul

In the first two chapters we have examined Paul's background prior to his conversion in Acts. From passing references in Luke's record and his own writings, we have pieced together a reasonably clear picture of the Dispersion Jew he was and of the outstanding rabbi he became.

This is as good a place as any to observe that we have no certain picture of what Paul was like physically. A late second-century apocryphal work called the Acts of Paul contains this description: "And he saw Paul coming, a man small of stature, with a bald head and crooked legs, in a good state of body, with eyebrows meeting and nose somewhat hooked, full of friendliness."[1] We have no way of knowing whether this is in any way dependable, even if W. M. Ramsay did suggest that "this plain and unflattering account of the Apostle's personal appearance seems to embody a very early tradition."[2]

For the Christian world, however, the most significant thing is that this first-century Greco-Roman citizen and Jewish rabbi became the most outstanding Christian preacher and theologian of all time. Luke's Acts introduces us to Paul for the very purpose of describing his conversion and ministry. That history, in turn, was no doubt intended by the Holy Spirit to provide grounds for the inclusion of his epistles as the interpretation of the gospel that dominates our New Testament.

From here on, then, we have basic material to guide us. Of Paul's conversion we have three accounts. Acts 9:1–31 is Luke's own historical description of the event. Acts 22:1–16 and 26:9–20 are two different Pauline testimonies of what happened as recorded by Luke. As would be expected even apart from inspiration, the accounts are essentially the same. The so-called discrepancies are minor and will be mentioned later in this chapter.

THE SETTING OF THE INCIDENT

All three accounts of Paul's conversion put it in the context of the persecution of the church. The point has already been made in the previous chapter that Paul was clearly the leader of the persecution and that the stoning of Stephen was the match that ignited the fire. Acts 11:19 calls it "the persecution that occurred in connection with Stephen." Acts 8:1–3 confirms both that the persecution arose "at that time" (KJV) and that Saul specifically was responsible for the havoc: *He* entered the houses of the disciples and dragged believers off to be beaten and jailed. The specific point of Acts 9:31 is that Paul's conversion brought this persecution to an end; his were the energies that had kept the effort alive.

Paul's own testimony in Acts 22:4, "I persecuted this Way," and 22:19, "I used to imprison and beat those who believed in You," confirms his role, and Acts 26:9–11 is even clearer (cf. Phil. 3:6; 1 Tim. 1:13). We do not have much detail and no record other than Acts, but the summaries show the intensity involved. Punishments were administered by the synagogues (22:19; 26:11), which often took the form of lashings,[3] imprisonments (8:3; 22:4; 26:10), and even death (9:1; 22:4; 26:10). Paul was "furiously enraged," determined to compel the followers of Jesus to "blaspheme" (26:11), that is, "to call Jesus accursed, and thus repudiate His claims."[4] Later on, he often remembered with deep sorrow the seriousness of his crimes (Gal. 1:13; Phil. 3:6; 1 Cor. 15:9; 1 Tim. 1:13).

That does not mean that Paul could have done all this independently or that he was alone in his zeal to stamp out the spreading flames of the faith of Jesus' followers. Before Stephen's execution the Sanhedrin had wrestled with the problem, stymied by a measure of uncertainty about how to proceed (Acts 4:1–21; 5:17–42). Even Paul's old mentor, Gamaliel, experienced cautious frustration

(5:33–40). But Stephen so angered them that they hesitated no longer (7:51–60), and the die was cast. When Paul, especially enraged by the situation, volunteered to take the lead, the Sanhedrin was quick to approve.

Thus the first great persecution of the church flourished under the leadership of this rabbi, exceedingly zealous that the ways of his beloved Judaism should not be undermined. The new Way threatened to do just that, and Paul was determined to cut down the flower before it could bloom. He recognized that the old ways and the new way were incompatible. One fact alone, regardless of others, made that clear: "Jesus had been crucified. A crucified Messiah was a contradiction in terms. . . . [According to] Deuteronomy 21:23, a hanged man is accursed by God."[5] Furthermore, Stephen's impassioned speech no doubt convinced Paul that Jesus' followers would forsake both the law and the Temple. No zealous Jew could tolerate that.

THE ROAD TO DAMASCUS

In the context just outlined, Paul made plans to go to Damascus. We can assume from Acts 26:11 that he had already taken the inquisition into other places ("foreign cities") outside Judea. Even so, Damascus was probably the farthest city he had aimed at yet.

As in other places, Paul needed official documents from the Great Sanhedrin addressed to the synagogues in Damascus, certifying that he was authorized to act as an official representative of the Sanhedrin, to arrest those regarded as heretics and bring them to Jerusalem for trial. He had no trouble obtaining such letters from the high priest as chairman (9:1–2; 22:5; 26:12). Probably he was primarily concerned to seize those who had fled to Damascus from Judea to escape him, but he might also have been interested in any believers who lived there already. The Sanhedrin's religious (not civil) authority was considered binding even on Jewish synagogues outside Palestine. Such authority was recognized within limits by the Roman overlords,[6] even if it was "a *de facto* authority that took no account of formal administrative or even provincial divisions."[7]

Damascus was an ancient and large Syrian city some 130–40

miles from Jerusalem (see the map at the beginning of chap. 4). There was a large Jewish population as evidenced by Josephus's report that ten thousand Jews were massacred there in AD 66.[8]

The trip would take several days, perhaps nearly a week: "A person could average thirty to fifty miles per day traveling at a normal rate of speed on horseback or in a carriage."[9] But Paul and his companions might have walked, and then the pace would have been slower. They probably stopped over in Jewish homes along the way.[10] Although it was not customary to travel during the hottest part of the day, Jesus appeared to Paul near Damascus at noon (9:33; 22:6; 26:13). Some have therefore speculated that they were pressing on, on Friday, to make the city before sundown when the Sabbath began and the faithful Jew was forbidden to travel any significant distance.

ENCOUNTER WITH JESUS

A careful reading of the three accounts shows that the main elements in the appearance of Jesus to Paul on the Damascus road were these:

1. A light brighter than the sun (9:3; 22:6; 26:13)
2. Paul's falling to the ground (9:4; 22:7; the companions also: 26:14)
3. The voice of Jesus, asking (in Aramaic): "Saul, Saul, why are you persecuting Me?" (9:4; 22:7; 26:14)
4. Paul's response, asking who this was (9:5; 22:8; 26:15)
5. Jesus' identification of Himself as the one speaking and whom Paul was persecuting (9:5; 22:8; 26:15)
6. Paul's submissive question, "What shall I do?" (22:10)[11]
7. Jesus' response, telling Paul to arise and go on into Damascus where he would receive directions (9:6b; 22:10; 26:16a)

First, we may profitably discuss Paul's mental state at the time Jesus appeared to him. An important clue is contained in Jesus' words: "It is hard for you to kick against the goads," which probably appear in their proper place in 26:14. The "goads," used metaphorically here, were ox goads, sharp sticks that prodded them on when they were inclined to balk. The saying was probably a common proverb.[12] Thus Jesus represented Paul's angry persecution as manifestation of an inner prodding.

The best way to understand this is that Paul was already in the grip of conviction. The intensity of his struggle against the church represented that inner turmoil. One often fights all the harder against the truth when he is half-consciously resisting it. No doubt Stephen's brave martyrdom had made a deep impression on the zealous Paul,[13] and the demeanor of others had added to that. The argument of Stephen and the claims of the other believers may well have made more sense than Paul was willing to admit.

It was probably in large measure to stifle this conviction and impression that Paul threw himself into the campaign of repression. But the goad kept on pricking his conscience until at last the truth that Jesus was risen burst forth into full realization and acknowledgment when He appeared to Paul in person and spoke to him by name outside the walls of Damascus.[14]

In other words, Jesus' appearance to Paul did not come as something totally against Paul's thinking. He was already fighting the conviction that Jesus was the risen Messiah. The relative inactivity of the several days en route had provided much time for reflection and reconsideration of all he had seen and heard. When Jesus appeared, he was probably on the verge of decision. Neither Calvinists nor Arminians believe a man is converted against his will or discount the influences within and without that prepare the way. Paul's conversion, as unique as it is, need be no exception:[15] "It involved the intelligent and deliberate surrender of his will to the risen Christ."[16]

Second, it is clear that Jesus appeared bodily to Paul, even though the three primary conversion accounts do not stress this point. Ananias and Barnabas said so in 9:17 and 27 (see also 22:14; 26:16). Most important, Paul himself always ranked this experience right alongside those of others who had actually seen the risen Lord (1 Cor. 9:1; 15:5–8).

Third, in light of the points just made, we do not have to accept the view that Paul's first vocal response meant no more than "Who are you, sir?" It is true that the words could have meant that; the Greek noun (*kyrios*) could be addressed respectfully to humans as well as to God (much like the English word *lord*). And so the RSV used "you" rather than "thou" in this verse. But the conviction of Paul and the bodily appearance of Jesus, which Paul may well have been familiar with in one way or another, may just as well indicate that Paul's recognition, albeit resisted by the question, was instantaneous, and thus the "Who art Thou, Lord?" of the NASB may be justified.

Fourth, the three accounts are not really discrepant. (One would credit even an uninspired writer with the intelligence to avoid real contradiction in his own volume.) The thing most often mentioned is that 9:7 says Paul's companions were "hearing the voice," whereas 22:9 says they "heard not the voice of him that spake to me" (KJV). There are two possible explanations. For one thing, the contradiction is not as direct in the Greek. In 9:7 "voice," the object of "hearing," is in the Greek case (genitive) that indicates the kind of thing heard, whereas in 22:9 "voice," although still the object of the verb "hear," is in the case (accusative) that indicates the extent of hearing. Thus they heard a voice but did not understand the words (cf. John 12:9). We all know that sometimes we hear but do not hear. It is also possible that 9:7 means they heard *Paul's* voice, "although they could neither see nor hear the person whom he appeared to be addressing."[17]

An even less significant difference is the "stood" in 9:7 versus "fallen" in 26:14. Most likely both are precise, with all falling down at first and then all but Paul getting up immediately and standing by in amazement. Paul of course remained prostrate, and his fall was the significant one (9:4; 22:7). (It is also possible that the "stood" in 9:7 means "stopped" and does not refer to posture at all.)

One other internal objection to the integrity and harmony of the three accounts is that Paul's testimony in 26:16–18 appears to represent Jesus as giving the commission to Paul on the road, whereas chapters 9 and 22 save all this for the session with Ananias in Damascus. It is possible that both Jesus and Ananias said these things to Paul; more likely the testimony in chapter 26 is simply Paul's own condensation of his conversation and commission, with the unessential role of Ananias omitted for brevity's sake.

COMMISSIONED IN DAMASCUS

We can imagine the mixed emotions of this rabbi as he arose, blinded, to be led by the others into Damascus. There would be anticipation, aroused by the Lord's promise that he would receive instructions in Damascus. There would also be a measure of bewilderment, at least a sense of having been torn loose from his moorings. Uncertainty about what lay ahead, fear, a need to sort things out, a consciousness that everything must be reassessed—such feelings must have washed over him again and again like the ocean's waves, all intermingled with excitement and wonder.

Certainly fasting and prayer were called for, and that is precisely how Paul spent those three strange, sightless days (9:9, 11). We know very little about that time. He was at the house of one Judas on a street named "Straight" (v. 11). Judas is otherwise unidentified, although the street is still shown to visitors in our day.[18] Paul did receive one vision, of the coming of Ananias and the restoring of his sight, but he probably learned nothing else. No doubt he meditated on everything he had seen and heard, including the teaching of the Scriptures and the rabbis. No doubt he had heard enough from the believers he had encountered, and his own mind was sharp enough that the Scriptures were already beginning to fall into place in the new light that Jesus was the crucified and risen Messiah. He was well prepared when Ananias came.

Ananias is also completely unknown to us apart from this incident. He was a disciple of Jesus (9:10), though he carefully observed the law of Moses and therefore was respected in the Jewish community at Damascus (22:12). He had already heard that Paul was coming to Damascus to extend his persecution of believers in the name of the Sanhedrin (9:13–14), but his reference to this may be more an expression of amazement than objection. At the Lord's command, he obediently went to Paul.

Ananias warmly greeted him as *"brother* Saul." That adjective alone speaks volumes about the Christian Way, and Paul would have recognized it at once. No doubt this conversation (like most biblical conversations) is condensed. The two would have had much to discuss. Even so, Ananias carried out three main functions. First, he "laid hands" and Paul's sight was restored. This was not an ordination ceremony but a symbolic touch of identification and of spiritual blessing (9:17). Second, he baptized Paul (9:18; 22:16). Third, and most important, he delivered to Paul the Lord's official commission for his ministry (9:15, 16; 22:14–15; and probably 26:16b–18).

Like the conversation, the commission is probably condensed. The varied wordings in the three accounts tend to argue for that. Whether or not that is the case, the main elements are clear: (1) Paul was a chosen vessel (9:15; 22:14); (2) he had experienced and would yet see things that gave him special understanding in the Lord's way (22:14; 26:16); (3) his role would be that of a witness, to bear the Lord's name (9:15; 22:15; 26:16); (4) although that role would involve him as witness to all, Jews and Gentiles alike, there would be special emphasis on a mission to Gentiles (9:15; 22:15; 26:17); (5) suffering would be included in his lot (9:16). One never reads anything in Acts about Paul or anything in Paul's letters referring to his experiences in ministry without realizing that these five aspects of his commission in Christ's service were always with him.

CONCLUSION

It seems unfruitful to argue whether Paul's new birth took place on the road or when Ananias came. Most are satisfied that his submission after Jesus identified Himself (22:10) is adequate evidence of his conversion. Some prefer to see the blindness and recovery of sight in Damascus as simultaneously parallel with his spiritual condition. They would associate his baptism more closely with his regeneration (note 22:16). We are probably trying too hard to formalize God's ways when we press such issues.

Nor need we answer those who attempt to explain Paul's change as something other than genuine conversion. Some critics have suggested that Paul's experience was an epileptic seizure. It is true that epilepsy need not prevent greatness, as Julius Caesar, Augustine, and Dostoevsky (among many others) might testify. The condition might even spur one on to more determined accomplishments. But whoever testified that one seizure totally changed his life and gave him such a vision and purpose as that which made Paul what he was? "Something more than epilepsy is required to account for all that Paul became and achieved. He himself gave one consistent account: in that illuminating flash he saw the glorified Christ."[19]

Even more ridiculous are two other suggestions that must have been made only half seriously, namely, that Paul suffered sunstroke traveling at midday or that he deliberately converted to Christianity to spite the high priest's daughter who had spurned his love. It makes much more sense to deny the Bible outright than to invent such explanations.[20]

We should not forget to view Paul's conversion and commission in the light of what we have discussed in the first two chapters. It is true that one lays aside certain things when he becomes a Christian, but he also takes with him much of what he is.

Paul was a learned Jewish rabbi, zealous for the devout legalism of the Pharisees, even if somewhat broader in his outlook because of his Dispersion background than Simon Peter, for example. He had outdistanced most of his fellows in knowledge and achievement, becoming a respected leader among the orthodox Jews in Jerusalem, probably serving the Sanhedrin. He volunteered to lead official efforts at destroying the faith and influence of those devoted to Jesus of Nazareth, whom they claimed to be risen from the dead and the promised Messiah. Outraged at such claims and altogether occupied by that one mission of arresting the misguided followers of that Way, Paul himself was arrested by the very one whose claims he denied, forced to face the truth he was willfully resisting, and commissioned to become a witness of Jesus' resurrection and redemption (26:18).

Conversion is always supernatural, always an about-face; Paul's may only seem a bit more so than most. Still, remember that Paul did not have to reject his Jewishness to become a Christian. Whatever he had to reject, some of it would take time as he learned and grew. But Judaism, at least in its *biblical* orientation, did not have to be rejected. After all, Jesus was the Messiah of the prophetic Scriptures. One became a true son of Abraham, one became what a Jew really ought to be, by the regeneration accomplished in the atonement and resurrection and outpouring of God's Spirit wrought by Him. When Ananias left Paul on Straight Street that day, that much Paul understood. And he understood that he was now personally commissioned by that Messiah-Redeemer to represent and preach Him. He had come to persecute Jesus' name; he would leave to bear it (cf. Gal. 1:23).

One final point about Paul's commission needs to be made. It was an *apostolic* commission. We might take that for granted, but it should be said. Paul himself may not have immediately grasped the significance of that; but it was not long before he understood, and all his writings insist on it. That the bodily appearance of the risen Christ to him was directly linked with his apostolic credentials is clear in 1 Corinthians 9:1. So is the fact that he "had been entrusted with the gospel to the uncircumcised, just as Peter had been to the circumcised" (Gal. 2:7). Add to that the role of revelations (Acts 26:16) and miraculous powers (2 Cor. 12:12) in his life.

Thus nearly all the Pauline epistles begin with the identification of Paul as apostle. This does not mean that Peter and the eleven were wrong in selecting Matthias to replace Judas (Acts 1:15–26), that God intended Paul to be the twelfth apostle. Nor does it mean, on the other hand, that anyone called to go with the gospel is an apostle. But it does mean that being an apostle signified a special role and authority, and Jesus personally commissioned Paul in that office and sent him forth[21] on the life's mission that would lead to his place as apostle to the Gentiles and human author of the New Testament's crucial interpretation of the meaning of the gospel of Christ.

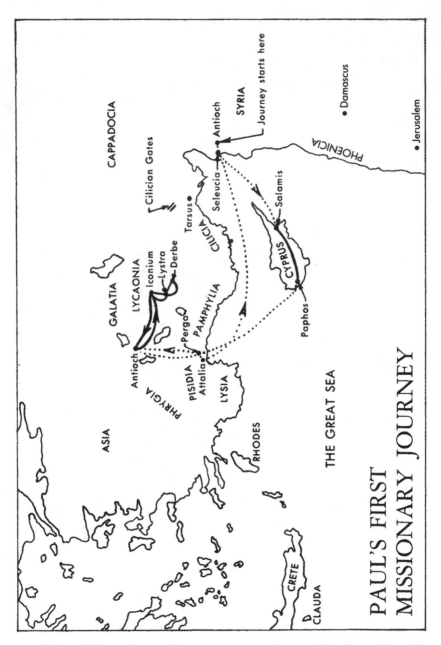

PAUL'S FIRST
MISSIONARY JOURNEY

NOTE: In this and the two missionary journey maps to be shown later, the solid line represents the crusades of Paul's actual ministry while the dotted line represents the travel courses followed to the first cities of those crusades.

From New Convert to Missionary Traveler

Acts 9:19–14:28

When the "scales" fell from Paul's eyes in Damascus, he arose to be baptized in the name he had persecuted and to accept His commission as the starting point of a radically changed life.

It would be difficult to exaggerate the importance of Paul. J. Gresham Machen expressed it thus:

> The Christian movement . . . in 35 A. D. . . . would have appeared to a superficial observer to be a Jewish sect. Thirty years later it was plainly a world religion. . . . This establishment of Christianity as a world religion, to almost as great an extent as any great historical movement can be ascribed to one man, was the work of Paul.[1]

The rest of this text will examine that famous life and ministry. Luke's Acts will be our basic guide, supplemented by introductions to the letters of Paul at the appropriate places in the story. Paul's ministry and missionary travels provide the context for the writing of the letters. All the churches he wrote to, except for the one at Rome, were organized by him and his helpers during the ministry described in Acts.

For convenience we will divide the material into several chapters, with this chapter covering the period from Paul's conversion through the first missionary journey (Acts 9:19–14:28).

At the beginning of each chapter a brief outline of the main events of the period covered will be given, then used as a guide for the chapter. These outlines, combined, can serve as a fairly complete survey of Paul's Christian life. The dates given should be regarded as tentative and approximate. There are several debatable issues about dates; some of these will be mentioned when they arise, but it is beyond the scope of this text to explore the technicalities in detail.[2]

PAUL'S CHRISTIAN LIFE AND MINISTRY, PART I

1. AD 33/34 conversion (see the previous chap.)
2. 33/34 days in Damascus, Acts 9:19–21
3. 33/34–35/36 time in Arabia, Gal. 1:15–17
4. 36 ministry in Damascus, Acts 9:22–25
5. 36 first return to Jerusalem, Acts 9:26–29; Gal. 1:18–20
6. 36–42 ministry in Tarsus, Acts 9:30–31; Gal. 1:21–24
7. 42–43 ministry with Barnabas at Antioch, Acts 11:19–26
8. 44 second return to Jerusalem, for famine relief, Acts 11:27–30; 12:25 (Gal. 2:1–10?)
9. 45–46 first missionary journey, Acts 13:1–14:28

As each of these is examined in detail, the Scripture passages involved should be carefully read.

DAYS IN DAMASCUS (ACTS 9:19–21)

Acts 9:19–25, which describes Paul's ministry at Damascus after his conversion, presents a small problem. At some point during that time, Paul went into Arabia for a while. But Acts makes no reference at all to that sojourn, so we cannot be absolutely sure just where to fit it in. Some put it between the two sentences of verse 19, some between verses 21 and 22, and some between verses 22 and 23.

What matters is that Paul was at Damascus, then in Arabia, and then back at Damascus. It is as convenient to locate the visit between verses 21 and 22 as any other place, and if that is where it should be inserted, the time thus spent in Arabia might explain why Paul "kept increasing" in ability to preach Jesus as Christ (v. 22).

Luke is notoriously indefinite in references to time, and we do not know how long the "several days" (v. 19) were. Galatians 1:15–17 *sounds* like Paul went to Arabia fairly soon after his conversion.

There is no reason, however, that Acts 9:20–21 could not have been true immediately after Paul's conversion. Indeed, verse 21 sounds like Paul's original arrival in Damascus was fresh in others' minds, and knowing why he had come made what he was now saying all the more startling. Paul had heard Stephen and many other Christians argue that Jesus was the Messiah, the Son of God.[3] He had been told their proof texts. He may even have seen lists some had made of scriptures that were regarded as messianic and fulfilled by Jesus. Furthermore, he was well versed in the Scriptures and would immediately have thought of several to use as testifying of Jesus' office and deity.

So the one who came to Damascus to seek out in every synagogue those who believed in Jesus and deliver them up for discipline now visited those same synagogues to announce that Jesus, after all, is God's Son. We have no trouble understanding the amazement that resulted.

TIME IN ARABIA (GAL. 1:15–17)

Although Luke is completely silent about this event, Paul refers to it in his own brief summary of the period in Galatians. Except for informed guessing, we know next to nothing about it. We do not know why he went there, where in Arabia his journey took him, or how long he stayed. Here are brief comments about these questions.

Why He Went

Why did Paul go into Arabia? Two purposes have been suggested. Some think it was a preaching mission; others, that it was a time for withdrawal and reflection.

Where He Went

Where in Arabia did Paul go? Two opinions link with the options just stated. Those who think his purpose was missionary choose a portion of Arabia that was well populated, like the Mesopotamian re-gion east of Damascus. Those who think he went to study and pray are more inclined to suggest a wilderness area like that around Mt. Sinai.

"Arabia" covered a lot of ground. Galatians 4:25 proves that Paul could use the word to refer to the Sinai area.

In fact, there is no evidence one way or another that resolves the question.[4] No doubt Paul would have felt a need, following his conversion and commission, for a period of serious reflection and study. He would want to prepare himself in depth for the preach-ing ministry he was about to undertake. Sinai would have been an understandable choice for such a retreat. After all, it was a holy place, the place where Moses received the law that Paul had been steeped in and zealous for.

Such logic is not proof, but it is enough to give this view the fa-vor of many interpreters. The fact that Paul seems to put the Arabian interlude in a context of consulting with someone other than flesh and blood may lend a measure of support (Gal. 1:16–17).[5]

The Length of His Stay

How long was Paul in Arabia? All we know for sure is that the to-tal time spent in Arabia and Damascus was three years, as Galatians 1:18 indicates, and even that may be an approximation. Because the Acts description of the time in Damascus does not sound long (a very hazardous way to read Acts) and because the "when many days had elapsed" of Acts 9:23 may refer to the time in Arabia, it seems more likely that the greater part of the three years was spent in Arabia. The dates given in the outline in the introduction to this chapter reflect the idea that two years or so were spent in Arabia, but a variety of opinions on the subject can easily be found.

MINISTRY IN DAMASCUS (ACTS 9:22–25)

Paul's Preaching

The increased ability of Paul (v. 22) may have been a result of a lengthy period of prayer and reflection on the Scriptures. Whether or not that is the case, Paul capably presented the truth that Jesus is the Messiah. That is precisely the point of the last clause in the verse. The word "Christ" is the Greek *Christos*, a translation for the Hebrew word for Messiah ("Anointed One"). When we read "Christ" in the New Testament, we should always think "Messiah."

The Jews' Plot

The power of Paul's presentation aroused the hostility of those Jews who rejected what Paul proclaimed, certainly the majority of the Jews in the city. They made plans to capture and kill him, posting watchers at all the gates.

In 2 Corinthians 11:32–33 Paul refers to this same incident. There we learn that people other than Jews were involved. A large population of Nabataeans resided in Damascus. They were governed by an ethnarch who was a local representative of Aretas IV, client-king of the Nabataean Arabs from 9 BC to AD 40. He garrisoned the city to try to apprehend Paul, and so there were more than unofficial watchers at the gates. How the Jews enlisted the Nabataeans' help or whether Paul had in some way offended them, too,[6] we have no way of knowing.[7]

At any rate Paul learned of the effort and made an unusual escape. City walls often include the outer walls of some of the houses, and the believers in Damascus made use of one of these. They hid Paul and then lowered him from a window in that part of the wall that was also the back wall of the house, using a rope and basket.

FIRST RETURN TO JERUSALEM
(ACTS 9:26–29; GAL. 1:18, 20)

One might think that Paul would not stay away from Jerusalem so long, but there is no good reason for doubting that Galatians 1:18 and Acts 9:26 refer to the same incident. After all, had Paul returned soon to Jerusalem, the persecution that he had led might have caught him. Add to that the excitement of the new life he had been handed, and together these may explain why Paul did not see Jerusalem for three years after his conversion. That does not mean there was no communication at all. Paul could easily have sent word to any family or friends he wished to, for travel back and forth was common.

Even so, it would not be hard to estimate Paul's emotions and hopes when returning to Jerusalem for the first time since his whole life had turned around. "The grief of Gamaliel, the indignation of the Pharisees, the fury of the Hellenistic Synagogues, all this, he knew, was before him. The sanguine hopes, however . . . predominated in his mind. He thought that they would believe as he had believed."[8]

The Disciples' Reluctance

Acts 9:26 is very understandable in view of Paul's former role as chief of the persecution. For all the believers knew, he was pretending conversion in order to spy them out; the hiatus since his departure for Damascus might simply represent a change of tactics.

Barnabas's Confidence

By some means we are not told, perhaps by word from a trusted acquaintance in Damascus or even by prophetic revelation, Barnabas had come to put confidence in Paul's testimony. He may even have known Paul earlier and detected the genuineness of his experience.[9] Barnabas always lived up to his name (Acts 4:36).

The Apostles' Acceptance

Barnabas convinced the apostles (v. 27), the leaders of Jesus' disciples (v. 26), that Paul was genuine and that he had already preached Christ powerfully at Damascus. So Paul was accepted and ministered with them (v. 28).

The reference in Galatians makes our understanding of this period more precise on two counts. First, the duration was but fifteen days, which probably encompasses the whole time in Jerusalem, although it might refer only to the portion of the time spent with Peter. Second, "apostles" (Acts 9:27) is a generic term; in fact, only two were involved, Peter and James. We could only speculate where the other apostles were, but it is not hard to imagine a fifteen-day period when all the others were away on individual missions.

Paul's own words (Gal. 1:18) seem to imply that becoming

acquainted with Peter was one of his main purposes during this brief stay. Probably he wanted time with him as one of Jesus' most intimate followers. He would rejoice to hear Peter's own telling of the activities and teachings of the Lord during those uniquely blessed days, although Paul knew that the time with Peter added nothing to his own experience or apostolic commission (Gal. 1:1, 15–17).

Paul's Departure

The suggestion of verses 29 and 30 is that Paul might have stayed longer if it had not been for the hostility he soon aroused by proclaiming Jesus as Messiah. Apparently he attempted to speak in the very same Greek-speaking Hellenist[10] synagogues that Stephen had antagonized (Acts 6:9), perhaps with the intention of carrying on the work of that one whose ministry he had helped cut short. But they were of no mind to listen, and their decision to seek his death was no doubt hastened by their view that he had betrayed his own commitment to preserve their pure Judaism.

The plot to kill him was found out, perhaps in some entirely ordinary way. Even so, there was supernatural intervention, too, as Paul relates in describing this in another place (Acts 22:17–21). Praying in the Temple precincts, perhaps about what he should do, he received a vision of the Lord Jesus instructing him to hasten away. He pleaded his unique reputation as former persecutor and participant in Stephen's death, but the Lord repeated His instruction to go. So Paul made preparations to go, no doubt somewhat disappointed that his witness in the beloved city of Zion had been essentially rejected so soon. Still, the Lord's words about his commission to the Gentile world (Acts 22:21) gave him assurance that there was an important ministry ahead.

Fellow believers in Jerusalem encouraged him. For his protection no doubt, they insisted on accompanying him to Caesarea, there to see him off to the place of his boyhood, Tarsus in Cilicia (v. 30). Caesarea was about sixty-four miles northwest of Jerusalem, down to the sea from the hill country of Jerusalem.

MINISTRY IN TARSUS
(ACTS 9:30–31; GAL. 1:21–24)

Acts 9:30–31 tells us little beyond the simple fact that Paul went to Tarsus and the churches[11] of Palestine had rest awhile. The next time Luke mentions Paul is in Acts 11:25, when Barnabas went to Tarsus to obtain Paul's help. Luke, then, is completely silent about the years in Tarsus.

Paul, however, was not silent, as Galatians 1:21–24 makes clear. "Syria and Cilicia" was the combined name of the province of which Tarsus and Antioch were co-capitals.[12] During this time he stayed away from Jerusalem, no doubt with deep sorrow for that, because it was just "too hot to hold Paul."[13] Thus most of the believers in Judea, especially outside the immediate Jerusalem area, knew him only by name. They were certainly familiar with his story. Every new believer was told about the famous persecuting rabbi who now preached the faith he once tried to destroy.

THE JEWISH SYNAGOGUE IN THE TIME OF PAUL

From his earliest ministry Paul preached Jesus in the Jewish synagogues. Whenever he first evangelized a city, he began at the synagogue, if one was present. In part that opportunity was his because of the structure of the synagogue services.

The need and origin of synagogues arose during the Jews' exile, so that when they returned from captivity the rebuilding of the Temple did not force out this new and convenient addition to Jewish life. Synagogues became, in fact, the center of Jewish community life all across the Roman empire and even in Jerusalem.

Any ten families could organize a local synagogue. Often there was more than one in the same city, so that a given synagogue might reflect a common cultural heritage. Each synagogue elected *elders* who not only governed functions but also wielded a measure of authority (as a local Sanhedrin) in the Jewish community. One of the elders was the chief elder. In addition, there were *receivers*, who received and distributed alms, a *minister/attendant* to assist the chief elder, and a *reciter of prayers* who served as something of a secretary in reference to outside affairs. (Some of these offices may have been later than the time of Paul. Probably later were the *ten unemployed men* who were paid to be in regular attendance so that a congregation was guaranteed.)

The synagogue structure was arranged so that the people faced Jerusalem, being built on a spot never used in a profane manner. When possible, a higher elevation was chosen, and preference was usually given to a place near a water supply. The buildings themselves varied from very simple ones to very elaborate ones. The expense of construction was usually borne by the people involved, although sometimes a special benefactor might bear the cost.

The main piece of furniture was the ark where the sacred scrolls were kept. Veiled in front, it was located at the wall nearest Jerusalem. In the center of the room was a platform with lectern and the chief seats. Men and women sat apart. In early periods the order of service was very simple, consisting of prayer, reading of Scripture, and explanation. Later, the service included: (1) recitation of the Shema (Deut. 6:4–9; 11:13–21; Num. 15:37–41); (2) prayer (perhaps a fixed prayer, framed by the local rabbi); (3) a reading from the Law; (4) a reading from the Prophets (at some point the readings were set and followed everywhere, but it is not sure that this was true in Paul's day); (5) translation (using the Aramaic or Greek Targums); (6) the homily, delivered by one sitting down.

Any competent male Israelite could officiate, read Scripture, or preach, although the latter tended to become the duty of the rabbi. The leaders of worship were not necessarily the elders (who supervised the service and were responsible for the care of the building). The minister brought the scroll to the reader and returned it to the ark. Visitors were welcome, and one who seemed capable might be asked to speak, even to bring the sermon. This is the reason Paul could count on having opportunity to preach Christ in almost any synagogue that had not already been exposed to or divided over the gospel.

The synagogue Sanhedrin also administered discipline. Among the options were flogging and excommunication, either temporary or permanent. Within the building was a board for displaying the names of those excommunicated. The minister may have been the one to administer the scourgings. Paul experienced such disciplines as these in abundant measure (2 Cor. 11:24), probably concentrated during the period of his silent years in Tarsus and its vicinity.

So Paul preached the faith in Tarsus and surrounding places, but that is all we know. We can be fairly sure that this period lasted several years, although the estimates, based on fitting the different periods of his life into the dates we can be more or less certain of, usually range from six to eight years.

We can also be fairly sure that some of the trials referred to in 2 Corinthians 11:23–27 took place during this period, mainly because the ministry that *is* described in Acts does not accommodate all of them. There Paul mentions, for example, five lashings at the Jews' hands (v. 24), none of which is described elsewhere in Acts. Such lashings were a common form of synagogue discipline. No doubt Paul made persistent efforts in the synagogues in his home area to turn his hearers to faith in Jesus as Messiah and Redeemer, and no doubt he was subjected to discipline for his efforts.

But we can only guess about specific incidents. Ultimately he would have been excommunicated from any synagogue he identified with. In all likelihood he was disowned and disinherited by his family, assuming the probability that they, too, rejected the Lord he preached. At the same time, we can also assume that his efforts were not entirely fruitless. No doubt some believed the gospel he announced, and groups of disciples came to exist in various areas, whether organized as full-fledged churches at that point or not. A later reference to churches in "Syria and Cilicia" (Acts 15:41) may ultimately rest on Paul's labors during these years, although we cannot be dogmatic on that point. It is quite possible that even during this period, Paul "included Gentiles in his mission."[14]

We can also be fairly sure that 2 Corinthians 12:1–6 refers back to this period. 2 Corinthians was written in about AD 55, and fourteen years earlier (v. 2) would go back to 41. But inasmuch as Paul could not tell the content of the visions therein described (v. 4), we are not helped much by knowing this. Perhaps the visions made yet one more contribution to Paul's preparedness, as did the whole period of testing and growth, for the great Gentile mission that he had been commissioned for and that was about to begin in earnest.

MINISTRY WITH BARNABAS AT ANTIOCH
(ACTS 11:19–26)

The material in Acts 9:32–11:18 does not relate to Paul specifically. Peter's ministry is the subject. Yet even that helps prepare the way for Paul's missionary outreach, because Peter's ministry included the incident with Cornelius, thus clearly showing that the gospel was for Gentiles too. That point would not be capitalized on until Paul was brought into the work in full force.

The Church at Antioch

Acts 11:19–24 describes the circumstances that led to Paul's reappearance in the record, fully prepared to occupy center stage in most of the rest of Acts. The founding of a thriving church in Antioch of Syria provides the context.

Believers scattered earlier by the persecution went abroad preaching Jesus, at first only to Jews (v. 19). One such migration was northward, down[15] the coastal area through Phoenicia, out in the Mediterranean to Cyprus, and on to the Syrian capital, Antioch. In all these places there would be synagogues they would identify with and witness to. The map at the beginning of this chapter shows all these locations. Antioch (modern Antakya) was the third-largest city in the Roman world (next to Rome and Alexandria), with a large and influential Jewish population,[16] Jews having been there since its founding about 300 BC.

In Antioch special success was met with, and some, themselves Greek-speaking Jews from Cyprus and Cyrene (in North Africa), were so bold as to begin preaching the Lord Jesus to Gentiles. This conclusion is based on the contextual implication here (note the contrast between v. 20 and "Jews alone" in v. 19) and the possibility that the correct word in verse 20 is "Greeks" rather than "Hellenists."[17] Note, too, that they were preaching Jesus as Lord, which would be more meaningful to Gentiles than to preach Him as Messiah.

The results were good, and the community of believers in Antioch, Jew and Gentile, grew—so much so that news of the happenings was soon heard in Jerusalem, and the decision was made to send Barnabas to observe and help. Barnabas was a natural choice. Leaders in the work at Antioch included Cypriots (v. 20), and Barnabas was a Cypriot (4:36). His gifts included giving encouragement. He was dubbed "Son of Encouragement" by the apostles (Acts 4:36), the same word as the gift called "exhortation" in Romans 12:8. No sooner had he arrived in Antioch than he promptly proceeded to exercise his gift in encouraging/exhorting[18] the new believers to persist in their devotion to the Lord Jesus (Acts 11:23).

Paul's Enlistment in the Work

The church at Antioch was growing rapidly (v. 24b), and Barnabas desired qualified help in taking advantage of the open door for the gospel. He saw in Paul of Tarsus exactly the man the situation called for, and so for the second time Barnabas played an important role in Paul's post-conversion experience. He went to Tarsus to seek out Paul and recruit him for the work in Antioch.

That he "found" Paul (v. 26) may suggest some time spent in locating him. Whether or not that is the case, he succeeded in convincing Paul that the marvelous goings-on in Antioch were such that he was needed. Paul accompanied Barnabas back, no doubt excited at what was happening among the Gentiles in Antioch, convinced that here at last would begin in earnest the long-awaited Gentile mission he had been called to.

Thus it was that he and Barnabas ministered together for a whole year (one of Luke's infrequent specific time references) at Antioch. The inference of verse 26a is that Barnabas and Paul[19] were the chief teachers in the church. The clause "met with the church" appears to indicate that by this time the believing community was forced to separate from the synagogues and have its own time(s) and place(s) for meeting.

The passing note in verse 26b is extremely interesting. In Antioch, for the first time and during this period, the term "Christian" (Greek, *Christianos*) was coined. The word itself does not connote reproach, meaning nothing more than one who is a follower of Christ, but it may have been used reproachfully at first. What has been said in the previous paragraph speaks to the need for the believing community at Antioch to have its own identity other than as a segment of the Jewish population, and *Christians* was the term that served the purpose.[20]

SECOND RETURN TO JERUSALEM FOR FAMINE RELIEF (ACTS 11:27–30; 12:25)

At the end of the year in Antioch, a special set of circumstances led Paul to break his self-imposed exile from Jerusalem.

Famine Prophesied

The Christian prophets (here and elsewhere in the New Testament) received communication directly from God and passed it on. Thus they were, like those in Old Testament times, "for-speakers," speaking *for* God, and the message might or might not involve the future.

Some with that gift had come from Jerusalem to Antioch (v. 27), among whom was one named Agabus. That there was soon to be severe famine was revealed to him by the Spirit of God, and he shared the information with the church in Antioch.

Such famine would be widespread, "all over the world" as they viewed it, probably meaning the Roman Empire. The implication is that Judea especially would be hard hit. This would be difficult for the churches in Jerusalem and Judea, inasmuch as believing Jews would have been cut off from normal synagogue help for the poor, and there were many poor among the Christian Jews. Apparently the church in Jerusalem had quite a burdensome number of these to aid.[21]

Luke's historical note in verse 28 is simply meant to give verification of the fact that famine actually took place. Claudius was emperor from AD 41–54, but we cannot document from secular sources the particular famine or date here referred to. Classical writers testify to "a succession of bad harvests and serious famines in various parts of the empire" during Claudius's reign.[22]

Relief Sent

The believers were moved to respond to the need that would be acute in Judea. They gave as they could (v. 29a) and arranged to send their offering to the elders of the church. Barnabas and Paul would take the money-gift. F. F. Bruce suggests this "probably" took place in "about" AD 46 because one of Josephus's notes places a hard famine in Judea at about that time.[23] Given the nature of Agabus's revelation, the relief fund might just as easily have arrived before the actual famine. Nor can we be sure this famine is the one Josephus referred to. To follow Bruce we would have to view Luke as meaning that Barnabas and Paul did not go to Jerusalem until two years after the death of Herod described in the next chapter of Acts.

The incidents recorded in chapter 12 have no direct bearing on Paul's ministry except that Luke indicates it was "about that time," that is, the time of sending of relief to Jerusalem, that Herod first beheaded James, then imprisoned Peter and had his purpose frustrated by Peter's miraculous escape, then later moved to Caesarea and was mortally struck at God's hand. We do not know how long all this took. Probably much of it had transpired before Barnabas and Paul actually arrived in Jerusalem. But the most likely meaning of Luke is that some of it, at least Herod's death, may well have happened while they were in Jerusalem. There appears to be no reason this could not have been the case. Herod met his death in AD 44,[24] and Paul and Barnabas might have arrived in Jerusalem during the probably brief span between Peter's escape and Herod's death.

Regardless of the exact time relationship between Paul's visit to Jerusalem, Peter's escape, and Herod's death, Acts 12:25 takes up the story of Paul never to leave it again. Nothing is said about anything that transpired while Barnabas and Paul were in Jerusalem or how long they were there. Luke relates only that they "fulfilled their mission" there, that is, the ministry of delivering the relief fund, and returned to Antioch.

With them went John Mark, who had just been introduced to the readers in the events related to Peter's deliverance. (It was at the house of John Mark's mother where prayer was being offered and where Peter went after the angel delivered him.)[25] John Mark was also a relative of Barnabas. The word translated "sister's son" (Col. 4:10, KJV) is more correctly translated "cousin." "It is natural to suppose, then, that Barnabas and Paul lodged with his mother Mary during their stay in Jerusalem."[26]

It is possible we might fill in some of Luke's silence about things Paul did during this visit to Jerusalem with famine relief. That is, we could if the view of some is correct that what Paul relates in Galatians 2:1–10 happened then rather than on Paul's next trip to Jerusalem, described in Acts 15. There are points to be made on both sides of the argument. Regardless of who is right, the subject of Galatians 2:1–10 is the same as that of Acts 15, and so it will suit our purpose better to delay discussing the issue until we deal with Acts 15 in the next chapter. In fact, we will delay extensive discussion of the issue until we deal with the epistle to the Galatians in chapter 6.[27]

FIRST MISSIONARY
JOURNEY (ACTS 13:1)

Barnabas and Paul returned to Antioch and took up again the place they had filled in the life of the Christian community there. Acts 13:1 gives all too brief insight into the role that they played.

In addition to Barnabas and Paul, there were at least three others: Simeon, Lucius, and Manaen. Simeon's Latin nickname, Niger, probably indicates a dark complexion.[28] Lucius was from Cyrene (cf. 11:20), surely not the Luke who wrote Acts; possibly he was the same as in Romans 16:21. Manaen (Greek for the Hebrew *Menahem)* had been raised with Herod Antipas,[29] son of Herod the Great. "The title 'foster-brother' was given to boys of the same age as royal princes, who were brought up with them at court."[30] The ministry of these prophets and of the teachers made them natural leaders.

Verse 2 indicates a special time of prayer and fasting, quite possibly set aside because Barnabas and Paul had felt God's summons to undertake a work and were seeking direction. The Holy Spirit in all probability spoke through one or more of the prophets (v. 1) and confirmed that God was leading them forth. At the Lord's direction the two men were consecrated to the special mission that was before them. The laying on of hands here need not necessarily suggest a formal ordination so much as identification with them and delivering them into God's hands for the journey.

Thus began Paul's first missionary journey in company with Barnabas and John Mark, setting out from the city of Antioch in Syria in about the year 45. As we follow their steps, we will indicate the places visited and the events that occurred at each place. That is probably the best (it is the traditional) way to learn the journeys. One should study them with careful reference to the biblical text and to a map (see page 62); the facts have more meaning and are more easily remembered when one sees the journeys in that way.

TRAVEL IN THE WORLD OF PAUL

Paul's missionary work in the Roman Empire of AD 45–60 was possible in part because of the ease of travel. As noted in chapter 1 of this text, the Mediterranean world at that time was a busy world of commerce and travel.

Travel by land. Trade routes existed from earliest times. In Paul's day travel by major routes had been made easier by the fact that the Romans deliberately built good roads to tie the empire together and to provide for the movement of troops and of the imperial postal service. Ultimately the Roman roads included some 50,000 miles of primary roads and four times that much of secondary roads. It was no exaggeration that "all roads led to Rome."

The primary road was built on a foundation of layers of sand and gravel, up to a depth of three feet or more. A bed of concrete (invented by the Romans) might be laid. Whereas some roads might have a gravel surface, the most important ones, especially near cities, were paved with large blocks of stone bound together by mortar. Such a road might be twenty feet wide, although those in mountainous terrain (or lesser roads) might be as narrow as five or six feet. Using the arch as the basic construction form, stone bridges were built across many streams. Stone posts six to eight feet tall marked each "mile" (1620 yards), as measured from the golden milestone in the forum in Rome.

All the journeys of Paul recorded in Acts were along such thoroughfares. The cities where Paul planted churches were for the most part major centers on major routes.

The general assumption is that Paul and his companions usually walked, although it is possible that some land trips might have been made on donkeys. At times Paul and the members of his team would have had to travel alone; at others, they might have arranged to travel with groups that made up informal (or even formal) caravans, a much safer way to travel. On foot travelers might cover twenty miles or more in a day at the rate of three miles or so per hour.

Inns for travelers existed, although such establishments were not always secure; even the innkeeper might not be trustworthy. When possible Paul and his companions would have been more likely to lodge with fellow believers, perhaps even (on first arrival in a new place) with fellow Jews.

Travel by sea. The Mediterranean world was busy with ships plying their trade from one port of call to another. Such ships—like the grain fleet of Egyptian Alexandria, for example—might easily accommodate the 276 people mentioned in Acts 27:37 or even the 600 with whom the historian Josephus traveled on an occasion not much later than this. In Paul's day arranging for passage on such trade vessels was relatively common and at reasonable fares. One might even sign on for certain duties in exchange for passage.

As sailing vessels, these ships were at the mercy of the winds. Shipwrecks were not uncommon (2 Cor. 11:25). The winter months were the most dangerous; the summer, the best time. From mid-November through February all sailing stopped, with a couple of months on either side of this period considered somewhat risky. These factors are involved at several points in Paul's missionary travels.

On land or sea Paul's missionary journeys, although relatively ordinary in his day, were tiring and often dangerous (2 Cor. 11:26).

Seleucia

Seleucia (13:4), the port city of Antioch, is mentioned only as the place where the missionaries booked passage on a ship scheduled to stop at the island of Cyprus (the Old Testament Kittim), some ninety miles out in the Mediterranean. Barnabas, a Cypriot, was interested in the people of his home area.

Salamis

Salamis (13:5), the leading city on the eastern side of the island and a mercantile port, is mentioned only briefly as a place where Barnabas and Paul preached in the synagogues. All we can do is assume that such passing references as these imply short and relatively uneventful stays, but that is a risky assumption. Luke did not try to tell everything. This is the place where Luke inserts the fact that John Mark was along to assist them. Some think this means he did the baptizing of their converts.[31]

Paphos

Paphos (13:6–12), the capital, was on the western side of Cyprus; Barnabas and Paul went there by land. Two intertwined incidents of special interest happened there.

The blinding of Bar-jesus (Elymas). Bar-jesus[32] was Jewish and thus a sorcerer against the law and practice of his people. "Elymas" may represent the Semitic equivalent of the word "sorcerer" (Greek *magos*). He "claimed falsely to be a medium of divine revelations."[33] He must have had some standing as an adviser to the proconsul. The sorcerer resisted the gospel and urged his master to do the same. Paul,[34] given special insight by the Holy Spirit, denounced the man and pronounced a judgment of temporary blindness on him.

The belief of Sergius Paulus. Sergius Paulus, proconsul[35] of the island province, was Roman, probably "the Quintus Sergius Paullus whose name has been deciphered in fragmentary form on a Greek inscription"[36] there. His interest aroused by reports of what Barnabas and Paul were saying in the city (with some stir, no doubt), he sent for and listened to them. In spite of the efforts of Bar-jesus and in part because of the astonishing miracle, Sergius Paulus "believed." Some interpreters insist this does not mean the full-fledged faith of conversion, but this word at least usually means that in Acts. There is possible evidence that the man's daughter and grandson were Christians.[37]

Perga

Perga (13:13), a port city on the southern coast of Asia Minor in the district of Pamphylia, was reached by passage on another ship that had docked at Paphos. Here John Mark left Paul and Barnabas and arranged passage for Jerusalem and home. We are not told why, only that Paul did not view it kindly (Acts 15:37–39). Some speculate that he drew back from the toil or danger anticipated; others, that he was jealous because of Paul's increasing prominence over his cousin Barnabas.

Antioch of Pisidia

Antioch of Pisidia (13:14–52), a Roman colony, is called that to distinguish it from Syrian Antioch. No doubt Paul and Barnabas had a tiring journey across the highlands to reach it. It was actually in Phrygia at the border of Pisidia, both of these being districts of the large province of Galatia. There were also dangers. The rough country was well known as a haven for bands of robbers (cf. 2 Cor. 11:26), although travel had been somewhat safer in that region since "the final pacification of the wild Isaurian and Pisidian highlanders in the last decade BC."[38]

First Sabbath in the synagogue: Paul's first recorded sermon. Verses 14–16 provide a good picture of what Paul and Barnabas typically encountered in the Jewish synagogues from place to place, and so we examine it here as representative of what happened over and over in Paul's efforts to win the Jews in various cities.

The synagogue service was simple. Prayer was followed by standardized Scripture readings, one passage from the Law[39] and another from the Prophets.[40] Then, as arranged by the synagogue's "rulers," someone gave an address. A traveling Jew from abroad would be welcome and might be invited to give the address,[41] especially if there were indications he was capable.

That is what happened here. No doubt the rulers had learned prior to the service that these were knowledgeable men. Thus they were glad to extend the courtesy of inviting them to speak. Paul readily accepted.

The point to remember is that this was Paul's basic method in every city he entered, on this journey and others. He first went to the Jewish synagogues and made an effort to persuade them that Jesus is Messiah and Redeemer. Almost as a matter of course he could expect to have opportunity to address any synagogue anywhere (not in Judea, of course), as he did here in Pisidian Antioch.

Paul's address (vv. 16–41) is obviously typical of what he would say in synagogues at every opportunity. That it is the first one *recorded* by no means implies it was his first. By some means unknown to us, there was probably an especially good memory or record of this one that Luke had access to and included as typical.

The essence of Paul's message is:

The early history of Israel: from the redemption from Egypt (v. 17), through the wilderness wanderings (v. 18), the conquest of Canaan (v. 19), the period of the judges (v. 20), the kingdom of Saul[42] (v. 21), to the kingdom of David (v. 22).

The coming of Jesus as David's seed and Israel's Savior (vv. 23, 26), announced by John the Baptist (vv. 24–25), rejected and put to death in Jerusalem (vv. 27–28), thus fulfilling Scripture (v. 29).

The resurrection of Jesus (v. 30), as duly witnessed (v. 31) and as fulfilling the promises of the Scriptures (v. 32) in Psalm 2:7 (v. 33), Isaiah 55:3 (v. 34), and Psalm 16:10 (v. 35), which was not fulfilled in David (v. 36) but in Jesus' resurrection (v. 37);[43] the preaching of Jesus, therefore, for forgiveness of sins (v. 38) and for the justification that the law of Moses could not perform (v. 39), and as one who must not be rejected under pains of prophetic warnings against unbelief (vv. 40–41).

The good results of the first Sabbath's effort in the synagogue are indicated in verses 42–43. Two things are clear: that there was enough excitement and demand to cause an appointment to be set for Paul to speak again the next Sabbath (v. 42) and that a significant number both of Jews and proselytes believed Paul and put faith in Jesus as their Messiah and Savior (v. 43).

A word is in order here about proselytes and those called in the New Testament *devout* or *God-fearers*. These were Gentiles who had converted to Judaism and identified with synagogue life and worship. They represented different levels of response. Some were full-fledged proselytes. If males, they had submitted not only to self-administered baptism but also to circumcision, which may explain in part why there were usually more women than men proselytes. Others were more loosely identified (the God-fearers), worshiping in the synagogue service but not fully received as Jews. They were sometimes called "proselytes of the gate."

As verse 43 indicates, many of these identified themselves with Paul and Barnabas; they had been included in his address (v. 16). Proselytes were among the best prospects for what Paul preached, prepared as they were for the gospel as fulfillment of Old Testament teaching and not bound by centuries and generations of Jewish tradition. No doubt they made up significant portions of the membership of the churches Paul established everywhere.[44] They also served as an important bridge to the "heathen" Gentiles, who were their families, friends, and neighbors, in every city.

Second Sabbath in the synagogue: turning to the Gentiles. When Paul and Barnabas arrived for the next Sabbath's appointment, a large and excited crowd was on hand, no doubt composed of nearly every Jew in the city, the proselytes, and many of their heathen Gentile contacts. The majority of the Jews by now had decided against the claims of Jesus and Paul as usual, and they argued against everything Paul said.[45]

It was clear that the synagogue would be closed to Paul from then on, that he and all who followed him would not be welcome. Therefore Paul and Barnabas boldly rebuked the Jews' unbelief and announced they were turning to the Gentiles in fulfillment of God's call and Isaiah's prophecy (49:6). The Gentiles present rejoiced in this, and many came into possession of eternal life by faith.

This is not to be understood as a turning point in Paul's ministry or in Acts. Instead, it is just one more of the things in Antioch that was part of the typical pattern of Paul's ministry. Entering a city for the first time, Paul always started at the synagogue and labored there as long as he was tolerated, which was not usually much longer than here in Antioch. Excluded from the synagogue, he would then begin assembling the Jews and proselytes who believed along with heathen converts in their own congregations. At every place, then, the time came when he left the synagogue and turned to the Gentiles in the city. No doubt, he said words similar to those in verses 46–47 in nearly every city, although Luke does not recite them often; such a speech, however, does mark the end of Acts where Paul is speaking to the Jews in Rome (Acts 28:25–28). Compare the description of action in Ephesus, where Paul was tolerated an (apparently) unusually long period of three months in the synagogue before the inevitable separation came (Acts 19:8–9).

Expulsion from Antioch. Verse 49 implies an indefinite period of time when Paul and Barnabas ministered the Word of the Lord in and about Pisidian Antioch. But unbelieving Jews were not content that the missionaries should be tolerated in their city any more than in their synagogue. So they talked and stirred up influential women and men, probably accusing Paul and Barnabas of being trouble-makers whose continued presence would lead to serious disturbance of the peace. They succeeded in getting them publicly escorted to the borders of the district, and warned them to stay away. "There is no suggestion that this was done by magisterial action."[46] Paul and Barnabas performed the symbolic shaking of dust from their feet (Luke 9:5; 10:11) and headed down the road to the next city.

Iconium

Iconium (14:1–6), modern Konya, was some ninety miles to the east in Galatia, just in the Phrygian district and near Lycaonia. Luke's description of the missionaries' visit to that city amounts to little more than saying that the typical pattern of Paul's ministry was displayed there.

A relatively fruitful ministry began, as usual, at the synagogue. The initial synagogue ministry, however long it was tolerated, led to the conversion of a great number of Jews and Gentiles. Thus there was "a long time" (another of Luke's unspecific time measures) of bold speaking witnessed by miracles performed through Paul and Barnabas.

A resistance on the part of many led to an unsuccessful effort to stone Paul and Barnabas, resulting in their departure. As always, unbelieving Jews stirred opposition among Gentiles and poisoned their minds against Paul and Barnabas. In consequence, the city was tense and divided, and the hostility led to an effort to assault and stone them; the language suggests that it was not a regular legal proceeding, even though rulers were party to the plan.[47] But Paul and Barnabas learned what was afoot and left on the road that led to Lystra and Derbe.

Lystra

Lystra (14:6–20), still in provincial Galatia and another Roman colony, was in the district of Lycaonia, just eighteen miles south, and Paul and Barnabas pursued a preaching ministry there. Luke's silence about any synagogue ministry there and at Derbe, mentioned later, may indicate that there was not a large or organized Jewish population in these up-country towns. At any rate, other than the general description of verse 7, three incidents are specifically detailed, which apparently took place some little time after the missionaries' arrival in Lystra.

A cripple's healing obviously created a sensation. The man was lame from birth (v. 8). As he listened, Paul detected his faith in the Christ he preached (v. 9) and commanded his healing (v. 10). The result excited the people.

An effort to worship Paul and Barnabas was barely stopped by them. Seeing the miraculous healing, the heathen Lystrans jumped to the conclusion that Paul and Barnabas were Greek gods come to visit them. There was a local legend that Zeus and Hermes had visited there as men before. The (probably) older and quieter Barnabas was identified as the chief of the Greek pantheon, the father figure Zeus. Paul, who did more of the public preaching, was identified with Hermes, Zeus's son and the messenger of the gods.[48] Obviously such notable guests deserved sacrifices in their honor. There was a temple to Zeus

in front of the city, and the priest of the cult made appropriate preparations, getting the sacrificial oxen decked out with festive garlands.

When Paul and Barnabas learned what was about to take place,
they were horrified. (According to v. 11, the people had been speaking the native Lycaonian language, which they did not understand,
instead of the common Greek that all of them would have understood.) They ripped their outer garments, a sign of great emotions,
and cried out to stop the misguided effort. As verse 18 puts it, they
barely managed to avoid being honored in sacrifice as gods.

The words of verses 15–17, uttered in the rush to stop the un-
thinkable, typify Paul's presentation of the gospel to a Gentile/Greek
audience (in contrast to 13:16–41 above, delivered in the synagogue
in Pisidian Antioch). Although abbreviated and incomplete, the content is quite similar to the message later preached on the Areopagus
in Athens (Acts 17:22–31).

The message focuses on the living God who created all the physi-
cal universe. This God has permitted men of all nations to go their
own ways, but He is witnessed in the goodness of His provisions. He
is not to be identified with any of His creation, and so all idolatry is
vain (empty) and should be turned from. It is obvious that sacrificing
to Paul and Barnabas would violate their message. However, "even
saying these things, with difficulty restrained the crowds" (v. 18).

If the message was completed, it probably took a form similar to
Acts 17:30–31, stressing God's command to repent, judgment, and
the death and resurrection of Jesus.

Paul was stoned, near death, and miraculously restored. This came
about as a result of the hostility of Jews from Antioch and Iconium,
who learned that Paul and Barnabas were in Lystra and came there
to persecute them. What they had failed in at Iconium (14:5) they
succeeded at here. A mob was aroused, and Paul was attacked with
stones and dragged insensible to the refuse dump outside the city.[49]
Indeed, they thought him dead, but when the believers gathered
around he got up and accompanied them back into the city. The next
day the two preachers left for Derbe.

We need not be overly concerned with why only Paul was stoned. Probably Barnabas and Paul were not together when the mob's anger peaked and he, the spokesman, after all (v. 12), was seized. One point may be worth noting, what Bruce calls the "grim irony in the quick reversal of the local attitude to the two apostles."[50] Having stopped the attempted sacrifice may well have made unspoken contribution to this later rejection.[51]

We should also mention something Luke does not mention: Apparently young Timothy was converted under Paul's ministry during this visit to Lystra. On Paul's next journey he visited Lystra again, and Timothy became a traveling companion and coworker (Acts 16:1–3). This will be discussed in the next chapter. For now it is significant to read what Paul much later wrote to Timothy, recalling persecutions and afflictions "at Antioch, at Iconium, and at Lystra"—note the precise order—that Timothy knew about (2 Tim. 3:10–11).

Derbe

Derbe (14:20–21) was also Lycaonian, about sixty miles from Lystra to the southeast.[52] All we are told is that they "preached the gospel to" (evangelized) that city and made many disciples, typical of the entire journey. This was the farthest point of the first missionary journey, and when Paul and Barnabas left there, they headed back to revisit the churches established on the mainland during the preceding months.

Lystra, Iconium, and Pisidian Antioch

Lystra, Iconium, and Pisidian Antioch (14:21–23) were revisited in reverse order, with edification of the young churches as a goal. The missionaries encouraged and exhorted them to be steadfast in faith. They also guided in the selection of elders,[53] who would have responsibility for spiritual leadership in the churches. Probably they were following the pattern of organization they were already familiar with in the Jewish synagogue.

Note that Paul and Barnabas were returning to cities they had been violently driven from. W. M. Ramsay's suggestion that new magistrates were now in office in these cities[54] does not mitigate the missionaries' bravery in this course of action.

Perga

Perga (14:24–25) in Pamphylia was also revisited. This time they definitely spent some time preaching the Word there (cf. 13:13–14).

Attalia

Attalia (14:25–26), another Pamphylian port (modern Antalya) near Perga, was the place from which they sailed for home. Probably they had not found desired passage from Perga.

Antioch in Syria

Antioch in Syria (14:26–28) was home base, and Paul and Barnabas returned there with the satisfaction of work completed (v. 26). They reported all that happened, including especially that many Gentiles had become Christians (v. 27). The church no doubt welcomed the report and rejoiced to have the esteemed Paul and Barnabas back with them.

We have no way of calculating with any precision the duration of the first missionary journey. Estimates vary from one to four years.[55] Luke concludes the account by taking note of the "long time" at Antioch following the journey.

THE PATTERN OF PAUL'S MINISTRY

We have seen enough in this chapter to discern the basic method and pattern of Paul's ministry not only during the first journey but always thereafter. That pattern can be summarized as follows:

- Witness to Jews (and proselytes), using the synagogue (if there was one) as long as tolerated there, resulting in faith in Jesus on the part of many, though never a majority

- The inevitable ostracism from the synagogue and "turning to the Gentiles," drawing believers from Jews, Jewish proselytes, and heathen Gentiles into their own assemblies

- Suffering at the hands of unbelievers, usually stirred up by hostile Jews

This is not meant to say that there was never any variation from routine. But these three elements characterized Paul's efforts to evangelize almost any city he entered. The principle exception would be in a place where there were few Jews.

This method, not available to us, of course, was extremely practical. The Jewish population provided Paul a ready-made contact with people of his own background, whom he could appeal to on common ground. Besides, he always carried a burden for his "kinsmen according to the flesh" (Rom. 9:3). The synagogue gave him contact with Gentile proselytes to Judaism, an especially fruitful soil for the gospel. The proselytes in turn gave him access into the Gentile community via their friends and families.

PAUL THE LETTER WRITER

So far as we can tell, Paul did not write any letters to churches during his first missionary journey. The next chapter, however, will treat Paul's second missionary journey; and by the time that journey was done, he had begun writing the letters that are found in our New Testament. From our vantage point there is no doubt that his letters were as important to the church as his tireless labor in spreading the gospel. Paul's letters, in fact, have always been the most dominant influence in the shaping of the theology of the Christian way.

LETTER-WRITING IN THE TIME OF PAUL

The materials used in New Testament times. Many kinds of writing materials were in use in Paul's day, including wood, clay, or stone tablets. For letters, however, something more portable was required. Sometimes clay shards (ostraca, pieces of broken pottery) were used, especially by the poor, but these would not have done for Paul's letters, all of them longer than typical letters (except for Philemon).

He *could* have used parchments (2 Tim. 3:14). These were animal skins, especially of sheep, goats, or calves. The simpler ones would have been usable on one side only, the finer ones—vellum—prepared for writing on both sides. The skins were scraped, cured, softened, and rubbed smooth with powdered pumice, thus making a fine and long-lasting document.

More likely, he used papyrus, which was less expensive and readily available. It was made from the papyrus reed that flourished especially in the marshes along the Nile in Egypt—probably the material used for the little boat that baby Moses was preserved in. The reed was sliced into strips. These were placed in two crosswise layers and moistened with sticky water. The plant's natural juices tended to aid the adhesion required. Then the sheets were pressed or pounded together, dried and rubbed. A fairly good, tough "paper," in varying sizes, was the result. The sheets could then be pasted together to make rolls. In 2 John 12, this is assumed to be the common material for letter-writing.

The pen used was most likely the kind made from the hollow, jointed stalk of a reed. The dried reed was sliced diagonally, then the pointed end was shaved even finer, split, and stubbed off. The word used in 3 John 13 is literally "reed," apparently referring to this kind of instrument. Ink (mentioned in both the references just cited) might have been made from any number of materials. Probably it was a lamp-black (soot) and gum mixture, kept dry until time for use. There were, however, other formulas for ink, either dry or liquid.

The production and sending of letters. The use of scribes to take letters by dictation was common in Paul's day. Many could even use "shorthand," which "was in use among the Romans at least from the time of their occupation of Palestine, and among the Greeks [from] a considerably earlier time."[56]

There is no question that Paul used this method, probably for all his letters. There are frequent references to this in his letters. On one occasion the scribe is identified by name (Rom. 16:22); on others, Paul signs off in his own hand at the end (2 Thess. 3:17, for example).

The dictation process was relatively slow. A scribe could hardly keep up with one whose thoughts raced along as Paul's obviously often did. That fact may account for some aspects of Paul's style, indicated in this chapter. Longer letters, especially, would not be dictated at one sitting and might carry over several interruptions.

There was an imperial Roman post, but it was for official business only. Private letters had to be sent by private arrangement. In some cases, Paul's letters provide enough information that we can tell who carried them; often we cannot.

This seems an appropriate place, therefore, to provide a general introduction to Paul's letters as a group. Some attention now to the general characteristics of the thirteen Pauline epistles should help the student prepare to study them individually.

The Form of Paul's Letters

The letters of Paul were real letters. We often call them epistles, but an epistle sounds like something very imposing and formal. Paul's letters should be thought of as letters in real life. The following points will help make this clear.

Paul used the ordinary letter-form of his day. In our day we all follow a common letter-form, with the writer's address and date in the upper right-hand corner, the address (if formal) and opening next, then the body, and the complimentary closing and signature at the end. Many people never consider that Paul would have written in just that way had he been writing in our day. Try reading his letters with that in mind. Suppose 1 Thessalonians, for example, started out, "Corinth/50,"[57] then went on to say, "Dear church of the Thessalonians," and closed with "grace and peace in Christ, Paul." If it did, we would feel the personal impact more keenly.

The point is, Paul wrote in exactly the form that was as common and personal in his day as our letter-form is to us. He used the same form that anyone else would have used in writing a friend, a member of the family, or even an official. That is impressed on us as a result of the hundreds of papyrus letters that have been discovered, especially in Egypt, dating to the time of Paul. Many of them are about everyday matters. Like Paul's, all of them begin with the name of the person writing the letter (one did not have to finish a letter before learning who it was from), followed by the name of the addressee and some words of greeting or well-wishing; then comes the body of the letter and a concluding "blessing."

The student who wishes to feel this more intensely will do well to read several of the letters of that time (as contained in *Selections from the Greek Papyri*,[58] for example). Here are a couple of interesting ones.

> Theonas, to Theon his father, greeting.
>
> You did well: You didn't take me with you to the city! Since you don't wish to take me with you to Alexandria, I will not write you a letter or speak to you or wish you good health. . . .

Send for me, I plead with you. If you don't send, I will not eat; I will not drink. So there!

I pray that you are well.[59]

Hermocrates to Chaeras his son.

Before everything else, I pray that you are well. I urge you to write concerning your health and what you counsel. . . . I wrote you . . . and you neither wrote back nor came; and now, if you do not come I risk losing the parcel of land that I have. . . .

Your sister Helene sends you greetings, and your mother reproaches you because you did not write her back. ... I pray that you are well.[60]

Such letters would generally have a notation about address on the reverse side, such as "Deliver to Theon, from Theonas his son," or "Deliver from Hermocrates to Chaeras his son." Short letters might have remained flat or folded; longer ones were probably rolled up.

Paul's letters were personal. They were written to specific individuals or groups he was well acquainted with. It will not do to think of Paul's letters as formal epistles, artfully contrived as a means of teaching systematic theology or writing persuasive essays. They were not written for literary purposes or as a platform for public address.

This insistence does not deny that God's own Spirit inspired Paul to write in such a way that his New Testament letters are God's revealed Word for His church of all ages. That is true. Even so, the feel of Paul's letters will not be right unless one realizes that Paul, the very real man we have met in the preceding chapters, wrote his epistles as personal letters to very real people he loved and ministered to. The Thessalonians, the Corinthians, the Philippians, and others were believers he knew personally. Even Romans should not be thought of as a systematic treatise but as a letter. Even so, the letters were meant to be read aloud to the congregation.

Paul's letters were "occasional." At one with the preceding is the observation that Paul's letters were written out of the occasion of specific circumstances. They came about as a result of particular incidents and were written to accomplish certain purposes that were appropriate in reference to those developments. When Paul wrote the Thessalonians, for example, Timothy had just returned to him from a visit with them and reported on their spiritual needs. When he wrote the Philippians, they had sent a gift by one whose serious illness had delayed his return and who had then recovered and was ready to go back. And so on.

We must study Paul's letters with an appreciation for the real-life people and situations they represent. Only then can we interpret properly what they have to say as God's Word for us. They were true letters. If there is any difference between them and other personal letters of Paul's time, it is only that most of them are considerably longer than typical ones, simply because of the importance of the content. Paul would take advantage of any messenger's trip to say everything that needed to be said to the believers he was writing.

The Language of Paul's Letters

Paul wrote in the vernacular Greek of his time. The period from about 300 BC to AD 300 in the history of the Greek language is called the *Koine* ("common") period because Greek was more or less the common language of the Greco-Roman world, especially in the eastern provinces. All the New Testament is in Koine Greek.[61]

Earlier, scholars had no Greek writings exactly like those of the New Testament (and the Greek Old Testament, the Septuagint). Most of the things preserved from the Koine period were literary and of a style different from that of biblical Greek, more like the earlier Classical Greek writers. Consequently, many thought that biblical Greek was a special case, perhaps because of inspiration (a "Holy Ghost" kind of Greek) or because the writers were heavily influenced by the Hebrew/Aramaic tradition or because the writers were poorly educated. But then came a flood of discoveries of papyrus documents written by ordinary people of that period. They were found especially in Egypt, where conditions for preservation were excellent. Soon the language was compared and Bible scholars realized that Paul and other

New Testament writers wrote in the vernacular of the time, in the everyday language of everyday people.[62]

This awareness complements the points made above about the common letter-form Paul used. Paul was not trying to be literary but wrote real people in their everyday language. This fact also adds to our appreciation that the Word of God was written to be understood; the content and not the language is what makes it the "holy" book. It speaks best in the language people really use.

The General Character of Paul's Letters

There is no need here to give attention to specific subjects dealt with in Paul's letters; that will come as each one is introduced in the remaining chapters. For now, we look briefly at a few characteristic things that will be helpful to keep in mind as the background of each letter is studied.

The subject matter is varied. That would be expected from the occasional nature of the letters indicated above. The different churches and individuals (Timothy, Titus, Philemon) written to had various needs and problems. These in large measure governed Paul's choice of subjects. One should always try to discern the needs and problems that led to the writing of the individual letters.

Furthermore, these varying circumstances also control the overall character of the letters. Some are very personal, like Philemon or Philippians. Others are more wholly given to doctrine, like Romans or Ephesians. For some, the teaching is more ethical and practical, like 1 Corinthians.

There is a loose pattern that characterizes several, but not all, of Paul's letters, and that is helpful to observe when it exists. That is, Paul often deals in the first part of a letter with doctrine and then follows with practice. Ephesians, Colossians, Galatians, and 2 Thessalonians are good examples. Even when this oversimplification does not apply, it is important to see that Paul never isolated doctrine from behavior. He gave full attention to both, and all his letters have both elements in good balance.

The style is intensely emotional. Paul did not write calculated essays, but—to repeat—personal letters about things he was really involved in. Both his organization and his writing style demonstrate this.

Paul probably did not organize his letters by a preplanned outline. Even Romans does not fully approach such a formality. He wrote according to what was pressing on his mind, and one thing led to another. His writings show a sound logic in this, even if at times one subject interrupts another. Artful, catchy outlines, therefore, do not usually convey well the spirit of Paul's letters. (The outlines used in this text will be aimed at following the natural divisions of thought as changes are made from one subject to another.)

Paul's style of writing shows his enthusiasm and depth of feeling. He frequently gets carried away. The sentences are often very long, and some are never finished in a technically grammatical way. His words and expressions, however, often rise to wonderful heights, approaching the finest poetry, as in 1 Corinthians 13, for example.

The basic system of theology is fixed. This observation is not meant to deny growth in Paul's understanding of spiritual truth. It is meant to deny the evolutionary growth of his foundational theology.

Some students of Paul and of the early church in general have thought they could trace the gradual development of key Christian doctrines in the New Testament writings. Thus they might suggest that the idea of the deity of Jesus or of His bodily resurrection or of the atoning nature of His death, for examples, only gradually came to be part of Christian belief. But Paul's very earliest letters (whether we start with 1 Thessalonians or Galatians) show a settled, basic system that was common to him and his readers.

A few major "battles" recur. In spite of the varying circumstances and subject matter discussed above, there were some problems that required attention again and again. These show up directly or indirectly throughout his letters. Three of the most important are as follows.

First, Paul had to resist a Judaizing corruption of the gospel. The next chapter will clarify the background for understanding this. (See especially the discussion of the Jerusalem Council.) Because the first Christians were naturally devoted to Judaism, it was easy for some to confuse the keeping of the Mosaic law with the gospel in such a way as to threaten the teaching of justification by faith. Paul frequently encountered such misunderstanding, but he had no tolerance for a mixture of works with the gospel of salvation by grace. He is always on guard against this in his letters.

Second, Paul had to correct pagan immorality and idolatry. Most of his converts in the churches came either originally (as proselytes to Judaism) or immediately from heathenism. They had an outlook entirely different from that of the Jews. Various kinds of immorality were a way of life for many of them. They did not have the biblical background we often take for granted. In several of Paul's letters, then, we find him grappling with problems that reflect this situation, things he might have had to say very little about if all Christians had been Jews originally.

Third, Paul often faced attempts to undermine his authority. He was not one of the original twelve, and that made it easy for anyone who opposed him to deny his authentic apostleship. That frequently happened, and passages in his letters can often be seen as direct responses to such attacks. Even when no specific opposition is being answered, however, Paul often includes passing references to his apostolic position to safeguard the authority of his instruction.

The Chronological Arrangement of Paul's Letters

In the following chapters Paul's thirteen letters will be introduced in connection with the events that were taking place when he wrote them. For now, it will be helpful to provide a chronological listing, showing the groupings that will be used. (The canonical order of Paul's letters apparently reflects length, going from the longest to the shortest, except where two letters were written to the same readers.)

For purposes of quick reference and study, the following chart lists the thirteen letters in four groups, corresponding to four periods in his ministry. The place and approximate date of writing is given for each. Also given is a very general characterization by which each group is often known.

PAUL'S LETTERS
ARRANGED CHRONOLOGICALLY

Group One: written during the second missionary journey (see chap. 5)

1. 1 Thessalonians, from Corinth, AD 50
2. 2 Thessalonians, from Corinth, 50/51

These are sometimes called the *eschatological epistles* because of the special interest in the second coming: "eschatology" (Greek, *eschatos*, "last") is the study of last things.

Group Two: written during the third missionary journey (see chap. 6)

3. 1 Corinthians, from Ephesus, 56
4. 2 Corinthians, from Macedonia, 56
5. Galatians, from Macedonia or Achaia, 56 (see below)
6. Romans, from Corinth, 56 or 57

These are sometimes called the *doctrinal epistles* as a group, or Paul's major or capital epistles. As a whole, they are the longest of Paul's letters. They give the most attention to doctrinal matters, especially Romans and Galatians. Actually, the Corinthian letters are more practical and personal, and so the doctrinal characterization is not absolute.

Group Three: written during Paul's first Roman imprisonment (see chap. 7)

7. Colossians, from Rome, 61
8. Ephesians, from Rome, 61
9. Philemon, from Rome, 61
10. Philippians, from Rome, 62 (see below)

These are generally called the *prison epistles;* they are also sometimes characterized as Christological because the doctrine of the person and work of Christ is prominent in them.

Group Four: written during the time of Paul's release and second Roman imprisonment (see chap. 8)

11. 1 Timothy, from Macedonia, 64/65
12. Titus, from Macedonia, 64/65
13. 2 Timothy, from Rome, 66

These are called the *Pastoral Epistles*; they are sometimes characterized also as ecclesiastical, because of their emphasis on church administration.

There are a few major questions about this chronological arrangement. These are mentioned briefly now, but they will be dealt with more thoroughly later.

The dating and placement of Galatians. Several scholars would place this epistle first on the list. They believe Galatians was written before the Jerusalem Council, perhaps from Antioch. It is the hardest of Paul's letters to date. Its doctrinal affinity with Romans makes it convenient to study them together, however, regardless of when and where Galatians was written.

The dating and placement of Philippians. Some would place its composition in Ephesus during the third journey. This view is predicated on an Ephesian imprisonment. The view represented above is the more common one.

The dating and placement of the Pastoral Epistles. The listing above assumes that Paul experienced two Roman imprisonments. Not all scholars agree to this. (See the lengthy discussion in chap. 8.)

The question of Hebrews. The epistle to the Hebrews has not been listed. There are too many considerations against Pauline authorship for it to be included in this text. On this matter the student is referred to the many good commentaries on Hebrews and the more general New Testament introductions. Suffice it to say here that the form of its content is entirely different from the thirteen letters, and it nowhere claims to be the work of Paul.

The question of lost letters of Paul. Are all Paul's letters found in the New Testament? The answer is that they are not. Undoubtedly Paul wrote at least some that are not included in the canon of Scripture. We will see later that there are indications of this in the letters that we do have.

Speaking about Philemon, J. B. Lightfoot said, "It is only one sample of numberless letters which must have been written to his many friends and disciples . . . in the course of a long and checkered life."[63] That may be putting it a little too strongly, for one can hardly conceive that many of Paul's letters perished. Even so, every letter that God intended for the church's permanent instruction, all "God-breathed" Scripture (cf. 2 Tim. 3:16), was no doubt providentially preserved. Such is our confidence in Him.

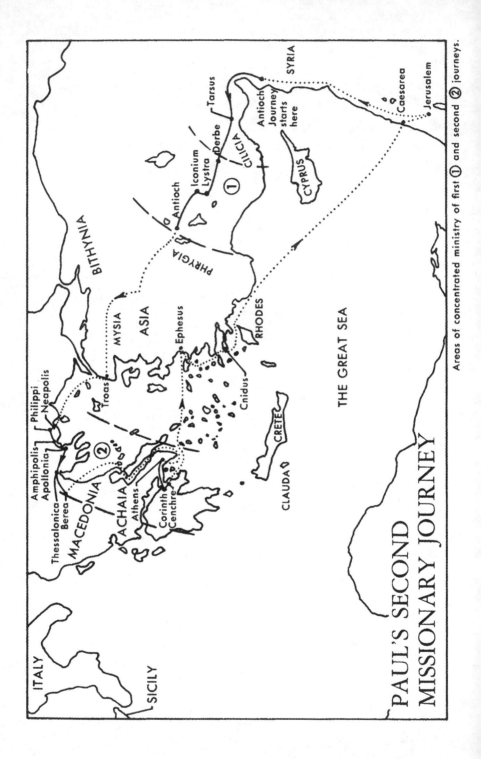

PAUL'S SECOND
MISSIONARY JOURNEY

Areas of concentrated ministry of first ① and second ② journeys.

5

THE GENTILE
MISSION EXPANDS

ACTS 15:1–18:22

Paul and Barnabas returned to Antioch after the first missionary journey in about AD 46. A lengthy period at Antioch followed (Acts 14:28), with the two men probably filling once again the role of leading teachers, as earlier (11:26; 13:1).

Paul, no doubt, waited for whatever new directions he might receive for the pursuing of his commission. Indeed, a new stage in his ministry was in the making. As we examine this period, we will use the same procedure we used in the preceding chapter.

PAUL'S CHRISTIAN LIFE AND MINISTRY, PART II

1. AD 47/48 third return to Jerusalem: the Jerusalem Council, Acts 15:1–29 (Gal. 2:1–10?)
2. 48/49 return to Antioch and separation from Barnabas, Acts 15:30–39
3. 48/49–52/53 second missionary journey, Acts 15:40–18:22

Again, as each of these is examined, the Scripture text should be carefully read.

There is one very important question about this period in Antioch between the first missionary journey and the Jerusalem Council. Did Paul write Galatians during this time? Some interpreters think so. If he did, then Galatians is the earliest of Paul's letters, written in about AD 47 from Antioch in Syria. No less a Pauline

scholar than F. F. Bruce holds this view. He thinks that Judaizing believers from Jerusalem came to Antioch some time before or shortly
after Paul and Barnabas returned there at the end of the first journey.
These Judaizers learned about the churches Paul and Barnabas had
planted in Galatia and proceeded there (as in Antioch) to try to bring
the Gentile converts under the Mosaic law. Word reached Paul, and
he wrote Galatians to deal with the problem.

This possibility need not be dealt with here. (It will be discussed
in detail in the introduction to Galatians in chap. 6.) My own inclination is to date the writing of Galatians to about AD 55 on the
third journey. Certainly, Galatians is the most difficult of all Paul's
letters to date.

THIRD RETURN TO JERUSALEM:
THE JERUSALEM COUNCIL (ACTS 15:1–29)

Acts 15 opens without indicating a precise time. The problem
referred to may have begun while Paul and Barnabas were away, their
return contributing to the tensions; or the visitors referred to may
have come to Antioch after the missionaries' return, during the "long
time" referred to in 14:28. Either way, the chapter describes one of
the most important crises in the early church. "It is as epoch-making,
in [Luke's] eyes, as the conversion of Paul or the preaching of the
gospel to Cornelius."[1]

The Problem

The visitors were Jewish Christians from Judea, come to see this
great church; perhaps, to correct it. We call them Judaizers. Their error can be better understood when we see it from their perspective.

It was easy for the first Jewish Christians to see their faith as
the true Judaism. After all, they were God's chosen people to whom
a Messiah had been promised. When they accepted Jesus as the
Messiah, they saw no reason to forsake their unique *Jewish* ways. For
was not Christianity really the Jewish faith?

Furthermore, even before Christ had come, the Jews had means
of converting Gentiles: as proselytes.[2] Their logic, as inadequate as it

was, said they were still making proselytes to the (true) Jewish faith. Such proselytes had always been required to adopt a fully Jewish life-style, observing circumcision and the rest of Moses's law. Surely, then, Gentile believers in the Jews' Messiah should still be required to do so.

What verse 1 means, then, is plain: in the Judaizers' view, a Gentile, to be a Christian, had to become a Jew.

Some think there was a political as well as a theological reason for the desire that Gentiles be circumcised. The period was one of increasing patriotism among the Jews. With Herod's death in AD 44, Judea had once again become a Roman province, under procura-tors (see the historical insert in chap. 2). The activity of Zealots, who were hostile both to the Romans and to any Jews suspected of being collaborators with the hated Gentile overlords, was kindled afresh. Therefore, some in the church might easily have found it expedient to insist that any Gentiles they associated with must become Jews.[3]

Dissension and Decision

We have no trouble imagining the turmoil created by the Judaizers' views. Formerly, Gentile converts had been regarded as Christians without adopting the Mosaic structure. Now their standing was threat-ened. Paul and Barnabas discerned and resisted the error, and tension spread in the Christian community. The decision was made for Paul, Barnabas, and others to go to Jerusalem to discuss the issue.

Why was Jerusalem chosen? It was not because the Jerusalem church ruled the churches elsewhere. Rather, that is where the Judaizing Christian teachers had come from. Second, Jerusalem is where the original apostles were, and the issue was so important that it would affect the future of the church everywhere. Third, "there was grave danger of a complete cleavage between the churches of Jerusalem and Judaea on the one hand and the church of Antioch and her daughter churches on the other hand."[4]

Arrival in Jerusalem

Paul and those with him proceeded to report to the assembled church (v. 4). Immediately the problem surfaced (v. 5). No doubt the Judaizers who had created the stir in Antioch had returned with Paul's company or had come on ahead to await them.

Luke tells us that these Judaizing Christians were Pharisees before (and after) they put faith in Jesus. That background contributed to their rigid zeal for the law. They were insistent that Gentile Christians must submit to the full observance of the Mosaic law.

The Jerusalem Council

Verses 6–29 probably give us a condensed account of a series of meetings. Perhaps the matter was first discussed in a small group with the apostles and elders (v. 6) and later involved the whole assembly (v. 22). Even if that is the case, it is difficult to mark the exact place(s) where transition is made from a meeting at one level to another. Regardless, the main developments are clear, as follows:

—much disputing (or "debate"), v. 7a
—Peter's contribution, vv. 7b–11
—the testimony of Barnabas and Paul, v. 12
—James's opinion, vv. 13–21
—the church's decision (and delegates), v. 22
—the letter to Gentile brethren, vv. 23–29

Peter's contribution to the discussion is noteworthy. He reminded the council of his own experience with Cornelius (vv. 7–9; cf. Acts 10:1–11:18) nearly ten years earlier and showed that he understood clearly the lessons involved: (1) the law had been an unbearable yoke to Jews; (2) both Gentiles and Jews must be saved by grace.

James's role is not absolutely clear. This was probably James, the brother of the Lord, and he may have been presiding officer at the sessions. References in Acts and Galatians appear to place him as the chief elder of the Jerusalem congregation.[5] His opinion was in favor of Gentile freedom from the Mosaic law, and his quotation from the Old Testament (Amos 9:11–12) illustrates his understanding of Gentile salvation.

James's suggestion that a letter should be written to Gentile

Christians (v. 20) was adopted by the entire body. Two of their number, Judas Barsabas and Silas, who was soon to have a prominent role with Paul, were named to return with Paul's company and confirm the written letter, contained verbatim in verses 23–29. It clearly denies that the Jerusalem church had sent the Judaizers to Antioch to teach that Gentile converts must observe the Mosaic law. It also recommends to Gentile converts the four constraints James had suggested (vv. 20, 29), sometimes called the Apostolic Decree(s) (cf. Acts 16:4).

The appropriateness of the four prohibitions is widely debated. Obviously, Gentile converts should abstain from (1) idolatry and (2) fornication. But how about (3) things strangled and (4) blood? These restrictions, apparently based on Leviticus 17:10 14, seem more ceremonial and temporary in nature than permanent and moral. Consequently, some interpreters criticize the council as falling short of a Christian understanding.

J. Gresham Machen's suggestion makes good sense. The Council meant for Gentile believers to voluntarily limit their liberty regarding these two nonmoral issues. They recognized that believing and unbelieving Jews alike would be apt to find such practices particularly offensive and a hindrance to fellowship and the gospel.[6] Understood in this way the meaning would be very much like Paul's own attitude in 1 Corinthians 9:19–22.

Whatever view one takes of this, the main point is clear: the outcome of the council was definitely on the side of Gentile freedom from the Mosaic system. A Gentile could be a Christian without becoming a Jew.

One question about the Jerusalem Council that was raised in the previous chapter remains to be answered. Is Galatians 2:1–10 referring to the same conference, or is it to be identified with the earlier visit for famine relief? Because the answer to that question does not materially affect our understanding of the Acts record, we will wait to deal with it in chapter 6, where Galatians is introduced. (It is clear that if Galatians was written before the Jerusalem Council, as some think, then Gal. 2:1–10 refers to the earlier visit for famine relief.)

RETURN TO ANTIOCH, SEPARATION FROM BARNABAS
(ACTS 15:30–39)

Armed with the confirmation of their position, Paul, Barnabas, and those who had gone with them (15:2) departed Jerusalem for Antioch. With them were the two, Judas and Silas, selected to represent the church in Jerusalem (v. 22). They carried with them the letter (vv. 19–20, 23–29).

Arrival in Antioch

Verses 30–31 refer to the gathering of the believers in Antioch when Paul and his companions returned. We have no trouble identifying with their joy and encouragement. The gospel of justification by faith apart from the Mosaic law had been fully recognized as the truth.

Ministry of Judas and Silas

These two did more than confirm "by word of mouth" (v. 27) the decisions of the Jerusalem Council; they carried on a prophetic ministry of their own. After they had "spent time there" (Luke's indefiniteness, again), they were given leave to return to Jerusalem, but Silas stayed on. He would soon become Paul's traveling companion, replacing Barnabas.

Separation from Barnabas

After "some days" Paul raised with Barnabas the question of returning to visit the churches established on the first missionary journey. Barnabas was as ready as Paul. Furthermore, his cousin John Mark was again with him, probably having gone back with them from Jerusalem after the Council. Barnabas's will was to take him along.

Paul was not so inclined. John Mark had quit them on the first journey, and Paul was not convinced that he deserved another chance. They decided to make two teams. Barnabas would take his cousin and go to his native country. Paul would take Silas and go across Cilicia to the Galatian churches.

It is probably not profitable to discuss which man was right. Perhaps both were. At any rate, Mark did redeem himself, as Paul's later epistles confirm (Col. 4:10; 2 Tim. 4:11). Tradition is that he became a coworker of Simon Peter and wrote the second Gospel.

It is possible that Galatians 2:11–14 may suggest another reason for tension between Paul and Barnabas at this same time. But that depends on the whole question of the date of Galatians, to be discussed in chapter 6.

RELIGION IN THE GRECO-ROMAN WORLD

Far from being irreligious, Paul's world was full of religions. At every turn in his work to spread the gospel, Paul encountered one after another of these. His own native faith, Judaism, flourished in Jewish communities all across the empire, and many Gentile proselytes attached themselves to the synagogues. (See chap. 2 for treatment of Judaism.) Beyond Judaism there were numerous Greek, Roman, and Eastern religious influences. Here is a sampling.

Greek and Roman mythology. Probably the best known feature of religion in Paul's day is the ancient pantheon, the gods and goddesses who were much like supermen and around whom an extensive mythology was woven.

Among the Greeks some of the most important were *Zeus,* the father figure and ruler of Mt. Olympus (Acts 14:11); *Hera,* his wife, goddess of marriage and families; *Apollo,* son of Zeus who killed the serpent Python and received the gift of prophecy manifested at the Delphic oracle (Acts 16:16); *Aphrodite,* goddess of love and beauty; and *Hermes,* the messenger of the gods (Acts 14:12).

Generally corresponding to these, in the Roman system, were *Jupiter, Phoebbus, Venus,* and *Mercury. Mars* (Greek *Ares*) was the Roman god of war (Acts 17:19).

The legends and names of some member(s) of the pantheon were often intermingled with local myths and deities, so that all sorts of versions existed. A given city might be devoted to the worship of a particular deity; there was a temple to Zeus in Lystra, for example (Acts 14:13), and *Artemis,* the famous goddess of Ephesus, was a local fertility goddess only vaguely similar to the Greek Artemis (Acts 19:23–35). Even Sumerian, Assyro-Babylonian, and Egyptian deities were regarded (and often mingled) with Greek and Roman gods.

Greek mystery cults. By the time of Paul most people no longer believed in the old gods in the original, naive fashion, even though the forms of recognition and worship were still prominent. In many areas, "mystery" forms of the religion had developed, with secrets and rites limited to those initiated into the particular cult. Among these were (1) *the cult of Eleusis* (just west of Athens), celebrating its annual festival—the Eleusinian rites—in September (Nero's application for admission to this cult was rejected); (2) *the cult of Dionysius* (god of wine), made up mostly of women who celebrated in drunken, ecstatic dances; and (3) *the cult of Orpheus,* whose adherents practiced forms of cleansing and abstention from meats in order to escape the cycle of reincarnation. There were others. Most of these cults emphasized exuberant and passionate celebrations; many involved sexual orgies or gory rituals that included bloody animal sacrifices.

Near Eastern mystery religions. These were similar, having probably influenced the Greek cults. Some of the most important of these were: (1) *the cult of the Sibyls,* successors of the original priestess Sibyl, who uttered ecstatic gibberish that was translated into prophetic oracles widely circulated and highly regarded by many; (2) *the cult of the "Great Mother" goddess Cybele* in Asia Minor (perhaps involved in Acts 16:17; see page 116); (3) *the cult of Artemis of Ephesus* ("Diana" of the Ephesians, Acts 19:24; kjv); and (4) *the cult of Isis and Serapis*, Egyptian deities. Most of these were popular in various places across the Greco-Roman world.

In addition to these, some of the Phoenician, Syrian, and Persian deities had come to be influential in other parts of the empire. Many local forms of worship and cults were very syncretistic, representing influences from various sources.

Roman civil religion. Formally or informally, any religion that was to be publicly practiced had to be tolerated by the Roman authorities. So long as a religious practice did not tend to disturb the peace or foment rebellion, such tolerance was not hard to obtain. Beyond that, however, there was, in varying degrees at different times, a religion of the Roman state.

At first Roman rulers disdained deifying themselves in the manner of many eastern rulers. As time went by, however, some adopted the practice of seeking divine honors; no doubt it proved a convenient way of enforcing unity and loyalty within the far reaches of the empire. Julius Caesar was declared divine by the Roman Senate after his death, and that may have set the stage for some of his successors, leading to what is called emperor worship—the imperial cult. Augustus encouraged, especially in the eastern provinces, the dual worship of Roma and Augustus.

Tiberius and Claudius did not promote this practice. Caligula, on the other hand, demanded divine honors and insanely punished people in places where there was resistance. Nero vainly erected a colossal statue of himself, with his face as the face of the sun god, in Roman Britain. In many places emperor worship was made part of the local worship of other deities. From the time of Augustus the Jews were exempted from emperor worship, but two daily sacrifices "for Caesar and the Roman nation" were offered in the Temple in Jerusalem.

One manifestation of the imperial cult was the use of certain names and titles of the emperor: words like Lord, King, and Savior, even God or Son of God. No doubt the use of these titles for Jesus could become occasion for tension in some areas, as probably occurred in Philippi and Thessalonica (Acts 16:21; 17:7).

Later emperors, like Domitian and Trajan, used Christians' refusal to worship the emperor as a basis for intense persecution of the church, but this was evidently, at least officially, not involved in Nero's persecution.

THE SECOND MISSIONARY JOURNEY
(ACTS 15:40–18:22)

The second journey began sometime in the period AD 48–50 and took three years or longer. Paul's companion was Silas,[7] one of the two selected by the Jerusalem church to visit Antioch after the Council.

As in the previous chapter, we will follow the journey carefully, indicating the places visited and the events at each place. Again the biblical text should be read and a map consulted (see page 102).

Syria and Cilicia

Syria and Cilicia (15:40–41) is the full name of the combined province. Clearly, there were other churches than the one in Syria's capital city of Antioch. As we noted earlier (chap. 4), some may even have been founded during Paul's silent years in Tarsus. Luke tells us only that Paul and Silas visited and strengthened these churches.

Derbe

Derbe (16:1) was the first of the Galatian churches Paul and Silas would reach, going overland through the Cilician gates. No events are described, but 15:41 would apply here and anywhere else they were visiting previously established churches. So would 16:4–5, commented on below.

Lystra

Lystra (16:1–5) was next on the route, obviously Timothy's home. Timothy had apparently been converted on the previous journey and was now ready to become a coworker and fellow traveler of Paul's. Three facts stand out about this young man: (1) he was half Jewish (his mother and grandmother being named in 2 Tim. 1:5); (2) he had established a good reputation among the Christians in Lystra and nearby Iconium; and (3) Paul had him circumcised before taking him along for the ministry that lay ahead.

Some would criticize Paul as inconsistent for this act, but that criticism reveals a serious defect in understanding Paul's practice. As son of a Jewess, Timothy would be an offense to Jews if uncircumcised. Although Paul determinedly resisted the circumcision of Gentile converts,[8] he readily agreed to the circumcision of Jewish believers. As we have seen in discussing the Jerusalem Council, the question of whether a Gentile must become Jewish to be a Christian was plainly answered no. But a Jewish Christian should live the Jewish lifestyle lest his witness to unbelieving Jews be hindered.

This is 1 Corinthians 9:20–21 in practice. The consistent practice of Paul in Acts is that the Jewish Christian continues to live as a Jew (yet knowing that justification is by faith); the Gentile Christian does not adopt the Jewish lifestyle. That difference will explain the apparent inconsistencies of Paul's (and the others') practice.

Verses 4–5 describe, no doubt, what happened at all the churches revisited. The provisions of the decision of the Jerusalem Council would be helpful not only in Antioch but wherever there were both Jewish and Gentile believers. Silas's presence was especially important in this matter.

Phrygia and Galatia

"The Phrygian and Galatian region" (16:6) is a composite description, Galatia being the official name of the whole Roman province and Phrygia the ethnic name for the region that included some of Galatia and some of the province of Asia to the west. In all likelihood a revisit to Iconium and Antioch are included here. It may be, as some think, that Paul, Silas, and Timothy also traveled into new territory in northern Galatia and founded churches there, but we cannot be sure. Some maps of Paul's journeys show the routes of both the second and third journeys to include northern Galatia. (See the discussion in the introduction to Galatians, chap. 6.)

Asia, Mysia, and Bithynia

Asia, Mysia, and Bithynia (16:6–7) were bypassed. Paul probably had Ephesus, capital of the province of Asia, in mind, but the Holy Spirit directed them not to take the road that would lead there. Instead, they headed north to the borders of Mysia, thinking perhaps that they should go into Bithynia along the northern coast of Asia Minor on the Black Sea. Again the Spirit directed otherwise, and they went on to the northwestern coastal city of Troas. Bruce is probably accurate in saying that they went through "Phrygia Galatica" (including Iconium and Pisidian Antioch) to Philomelium, intending to enter Bithynia; then, "since they could not take the north road into Bithynia, they turned west, skirted the territory of Mysia, and reached the Aegean coast at the port of Alexandria Troas."[9]

How did Paul and his two companions receive these directions from God's Spirit? Most likely by some kind of revelation. Paul and Silas certainly had the prophetic gift; Timothy may have also.

Troas

Troas (16:8–10) was a free city near the ancient Troy, the northernmost port on the Asian side of the Aegean Sea. There Paul and his companions awaited directions from the Lord. The church in Troas, which we meet on the next journey, may have been begun during this visit. Two items are particularly worth noting.

The Macedonian call was given to Paul. In a night vision Paul saw a Macedonian calling for help; he understood at once what he should do. Macedonia was a Roman province in the northern part of the area we now call Greece. It lay in sight of Troas, across that edge of the Aegean. No doubt Paul had looked across to it the day before and prayed about whether he should venture there. The vision provided his answer.

Luke joined Paul and his two companions in Troas. That is indicated by the first occurrence of the pronoun "we" in Acts, showing the author's own involvement. This begins the first of the "we" sections in Acts (16:10–40). Luke was probably a Gentile, perhaps from Philippi. He may have already been a believer when Paul, Silas, and Timothy made his acquaintance in Troas, or they may have led him to the Lord. Either way, the meeting must have occurred before the Macedonian vision; Luke may well have shared with Paul a burden for his hometown of Philippi in Macedonia (if, indeed, it was his hometown). Some even speculate that Luke's was the face of the man in the vision.

Samothracia

Samothracia (16:11) was an island on the route. Apparently the ship on which they had arranged passage stopped overnight there.

Neapolis

Neapolis (16:11), modern Kavalla, was the Macedonian port where the ship docked. The four men apparently did not tarry there.

Philippi

Philippi (16:12–40) was their destination, about ten miles inland. The city was a Roman colony (see chap. 1), prominent in its particular division of Macedonia.[10] Five important events happened at Philippi.

The conversion of Lydia. Verse 13 refers to their first Sabbath in the city. As we saw in the previous chapter, Paul's pattern called for him to approach first the Jews in their synagogue. The reference to "a place of prayer" may mean that there was not a regular synagogue there. Some think this was a smaller building, a house of prayer, that was not an official synagogue. (But the Jewish writer Philo consistently used just this word to mean a regular synagogue.)[11] This may imply that there was not a large Jewish population in Philippi, a fact not surprising in a Roman colony. The reference to women who gathered tends to confirm this. The fact that the meeting place was outside the city may indicate Philippian intolerance of Judaism as an alien sect.

Lydia was one of these women, a Gentile proselyte to the Jewish faith. She was a businesswoman who dealt in a special kind of purple dye "derived from the juice of the madder root"[12] produced in Thyatira, a city of Asia Minor in the area of the earlier kingdom of Lydia (whence her name). It appears that Thyatira was her hometown, and she may have originally become a God-fearer there. "There was a Jewish colony in that city."[13]

Lydia's conversion was followed by that of her "household," a word broad enough to include not only family but slaves. She must have had a spacious house, and she pressed the team to stay there while in Philippi.

The exorcism of the fortune-telling demon. The slave girl (v. 16) is said to have had a "spirit of divination," which refers to those inspired by Apollo, the god who gave oracles and was worshiped at Delphi, also called Pytho. This supernatural force enabled her to make revealing and prophetic utterances. Her masters realized great profit from her powers.

It is difficult to account for her actions (vv. 16–17). Perhaps this is similar to those times in Jesus' life when demoniacs encountered Him and were forced to speak the truth about Him, as in Luke 4:33–34, for example. Or perhaps *her* use of "Most High God" reflected a syncretistic concept that fused together several pagan ideas: Cybele, the great Mother-goddess, Sabazios, and even the Jehovah of Hellenized Judaism.[14] At any rate, Paul was grieved and cast the demon from the girl. No doubt she became a Christian.

The beating and jailing of Paul and Silas. The owners of the slave girl were concerned about their pocketbooks (v. 19). They seized Paul and Silas (Timothy and Luke were probably elsewhere at the time) and dragged them before the civil magistrates,[15] accusing them of being Jews who were disturbing the peace of the city. As we have seen, Jews might well have been unpopular in Philippi, and disturbing the peace was serious business in the Roman Empire, especially in a colony.

There is probably more to it than that. The "customs which it is not lawful for us to accept or observe, being Romans" (v. 21) apparently implies that the Jewish religion of Paul and Silas was an alien religion. If so, this could mean that the accusers were aware of the recent efforts of the emperor Claudius to discourage the spread of Judaism.[16] (See the discussion of Corinth below.) But that was probably a weak charge. Generally the emperors were indifferent toward foreign cults unless the practices of some particular one created special problems,[17] and Judaism was not such a religion; nor, apparently, had Claudius actually outlawed Jewish proselytizing. Indeed, Judaism enjoyed the status that would later come to be called *religio licita*,[18] an officially permitted religion.

It may also be that the titles of Jesus used by the Christians—like Lord, Savior, Son of God, and King—were involved. (See the discussion below on the charges at Thessalonica.) Roman emperors often took such titles to themselves, some in a token way and some more seriously. The accusers of Paul and Silas, although they hardly distinguished their teaching from any other brand of Judaism, might have hoped to find in these titles a way to make a charge against them. At any rate, what they were saying was: "Here we are, Roman citizens, in this proud colony of Rome, and we do not dare risk disloyalty to Caesar by following the strange teaching of these Jews."

This approach produced the desired effect. The crowd burst out in angry uproar. The magistrates commanded that the missionaries' backs be laid bare and beaten "with rods."[19] These were the bundles of rods carried by *lictors,* official attendants of such magistrates, and used for discipline. After receiving "many blows" (v. 23), Paul and Silas were delivered to the jailer, who was charged to keep them safely. He fastened their feet in stocks in the innermost part of the prison.

We can only speculate why Paul and Silas, both Roman citizens (v. 37), did not make use of their status to avoid the beating, which could not legally be inflicted on a citizen without formal trial. Perhaps they deliberately decided not to claim an exemption that other local noncitizens, Christian or Jew, could not claim.[20] Regardless, Paul's feeling about the treatment received was that he had been insultingly humiliated; see his reference to this in 1 Thessalonians 2:2.

Earthquake; conversion of the jailer. Undaunted, Paul and Silas were praying and singing, with other prisoners listening to them. Sometime around midnight an earthquake shook the prison and jarred loose doors and stocks, though apparently not the outside gates of the compound. Having been wakened, the jailer concluded the worst and was about to commit suicide,[21] for at the very least he would have been disgraced by the prisoners' escape.

When Paul called out to stop him, the jailer brought him and Silas forth and proceeded to inquire about salvation. It appears that he had heard enough to provide a background for that. Paul and Silas told him about faith in Jesus Christ as the Lord. He desired to hear more and took them to his quarters (still within the prison compound, no doubt) so that all his family could also hear. He washed their backs, and they in turn baptized the jailer and his family, "having believed in God with his whole household" (v. 34).

Release from jail. The next morning the magistrates sent the lictors (KJV, "serjeants") to release Paul and Silas. Paul objected to the violation of their citizens' rights and required that the magistrates come in person. "So much was at stake for Paul's future contact with Roman officialdom that . . . Paul sensed the importance of leaving Philippi with the record set straight."[22] Hearing that Paul and Silas were citizens, the magistrates were troubled[23] and came to urge them to depart, not only from the jail but from the city as well. Paul and Silas obliged, but not before they visited Lydia's house and the believers again.

Amphipolis and Apollonia

Amphipolis and Apollonia (17:1) were two cities on the route westward, the Egnatian highway,[24] that Paul and his companions were traveling. Whether they evangelized these places we are not told. Note that "we" is now "they." It is clear that Luke remained in Philippi when Paul, Silas, and Timothy moved on. The next "we" section of Acts will begin when Paul passes back through Philippi at a later date, on the third missionary journey (Acts 20:6).

Thessalonica

Thessalonica (17:1–10), also on the Egnatian highway, was the next important stop, about ninety miles from Philippi. Now known as Saloniki, it is still, as then, the leading city of the area. Like Tarsus, Thessalonica was *civitas libera* (a free city) and the seat of the provincial administration. Here the following should be noted.

Paul's synagogue ministry. Verses 1–4 describe a three-week period when Paul was tolerated in the synagogue. A review of the previous chapter will refresh one's memory of the typical pattern of ministry Paul employed when entering a new city with the gospel. That typical pattern was followed here with the usual results (v. 4).

Verse 3, especially, serves as an excellent summary of Paul's usual approach to Jews, with a three-step presentation, showing first (from the Old Testament) that the Christ/Messiah was to die, second (also from the Old Testament) that the Messiah would rise from death, and third that Jesus of Nazareth fulfilled these prophecies and is Messiah.

Assault on Jason's house. Jason,[25] apparently, was host to the team. When unbelieving Jews, no longer tolerating Paul in the synagogue, aroused "a gang of idlers around the city marketplace"[26] against the preachers, they stormed into Jason's house to seek them. Not finding them there, they took Jason and other converts to the civil rulers[27] and charged them with harboring those who were upsetting things everywhere; no doubt, word of what had happened at Philippi had reached Thessalonica. The charge of creating subversion in the world as Jews might well have been a touchy issue. Claudius had cautioned the Jews in Alexandria against things that might make him suspicious of their "fomenting a general plague throughout the whole world," and the wording of the charge here sounds very similar.[28]

So Jason and the others were required to put up property or money as a guarantee of keeping the peace: "giving security for the good behaviour of his guests."[29] A common method of assuring order was "the threat of imposing fines or of seizing property, and at times a peace bond was required."[30] Because of the risk involved, all decided that Paul and Silas (probably Timothy, too, even though he is not named[31]) should leave the city.

Both in Philippi and in Thessalonica Paul and his helpers were accused before local (municipal) authorities, not before the provincial governor: "Paul exploits the fact that there was no inter-city jurisdiction or authority except that of the Roman governor. If the proconsul or legate is not apprised of a political affair, a trouble-maker can continue his career indefinitely by moving from city to city."[32]

Note that the accusations (v. 7) were very similar to those at Philippi (16:21). Calling Jesus King could conceivably be interpreted as seditious disrespect for the Roman emperor. Furthermore, Paul's prophetic preaching about Jesus' return and kingdom and such things could easily foment political strife. Augustus and Tiberius had both issued decrees forbidding prediction.[33] But the court of a free city "lay outside the Roman jurisdiction; hence the city magistrates were not compelled to take serious action."[34]

Berea

Berea (17:10–14) was farther west, off the Egnatian Way,[35] and the pattern of Paul's ministry there was again typical. The only exception is that those in the synagogue are described as "more noble-minded" than those in Thessalonica; their searching of the Old Testament Scriptures was evidence that they carefully tested Paul's claims about messianic prophecies fulfilled by Jesus (as in 17:3 above). A serious opposition might not have come at all if angry Jews from Thessalonica had not come to stir up resistance. Even at that, the decision was made that some of the converts should escort Paul from Berea. Silas and Timothy may have been elsewhere in the city when the emergency departure occurred.

We may note that in all three Macedonian cities particular mention has been made of women of influence (16:14; 17:4, 12). The picture matches that of the secular historians: "The women [of Macedonia] were in all respects the men's counterparts; they played a large part in affairs, received envoys, . . . founded cities, . . . commanded armies, . . . and acted on occasion as regents or even co-rulers"[36] (cf. Phil. 4:2–3).

Athens

Athens (17:15–34) might have been reached by sea or land; the text is not clear (vv. 14–15). The city was in Achaia, the southern province of what we now call Greece. It represented the epitome of Greek culture in architecture, sculpture, literature, oratory, and philosophy. Those who accompanied Paul safely there soon returned home to Berea, carrying word to Silas and Timothy to join Paul as soon as possible. That Paul was "waiting" (v. 16) for them there may mean that "Athens was not exactly on Paul's missionary programme,"[37] but not necessarily. Here we may consider two activities.

Ministry in the marketplace. Even if only waiting, Paul could not ignore the obvious spiritual needs in Athens. Much of the marvelous architecture and statuary was idolatrous. So he both followed and expanded his regular pattern, speaking in the Jewish synagogue on the Sabbaths and in the marketplace (Greek *agora*) every weekday. We do not know how long this period lasted.

Address on the Areopagus (Mars Hill). This came about because of some philosophers Paul encountered in the agora. The Epicureans[38] taught that pleasure is man's highest goal. The rival school of the Stoics[39] emphasized brave self-control and self-sufficiency. Hearing Paul, they were curious about the new gods he seemed to be speaking about; probably they understood *Jesus* and *Anastasis* (Greek for "resurrection," v. 18) as names of deities. Verse 21 explains their attitude. Anything new intrigued them.

These philosophers insisted that Paul go before the court of the Areopagus, "which exercised some jurisdiction over visitors like Paul,"[40] especially when matters of religion were involved. (*Ares* is the Greek god, *Mars* the Roman equivalent; *pagus* is the Greek word for "hill.")

The "address" (vv. 22–31), today inscribed in bronze at the foot of the Areopagus, is probably quite typical of Paul's usual approach to heathen audiences[41] except perhaps for the unique opening and the citations from Greek poetry. Without going into technical detail, we can note the main elements:

> —opening: the "unknown god"
> —God as creator: not dwelling in or being represented by anything man-made, giving life to all
> —the oneness of humanity under the providence of God and man's obligation to seek Him
> —the nearness of God as progenitor of man, testified to even in Greek poetry
> —the sinful ignorance involved in idolatrous worship and God's by-passing of judgment in the past
> —God's command, now, to repent, with the appointment of a time for judgment
> —the ordained role of Jesus as appointed judge, raised from death[42]

The altar "to an Unknown God," that Paul used as a text, need not imply that the Athenians realized there was a God they did not know. Someone had probably realized some great benefit, and unsure which member of the Pantheon to credit as benefactor, he had erected this altar to thank whatever god was responsible. Paul obviously turned the words to a different and advantageous meaning: there really was a God they did not know.[43]

Paul's approach, stressing creation, would take advantage of natural revelation; the Athenian idolaters and philosophers would have been largely ignorant of and indifferent to the Jewish Scriptures. Paul wished to stress God's authority over all men and His right to be sought as the One who gives life to all. The poetry cited (v. 28) is from lines attributed to Epimenedes of Crete ("In thee we live and move and have our being") and to Aratus, from Paul's own country of Cilicia ("We are also his offspring").[44]

With the reference to God's bypassing of judgment in the past, compare Romans 3:25. Paul's use of the command to repent and of threatened judgment was intended to prepare for conviction of sins.

The reference to the resurrection of Jesus would naturally have led to further explanation of Jesus' redemptive work, but Paul's address was scornfully interrupted at this point.[45] Most Greeks would regard bodily resurrection as completely undesirable and not just incredible.

In spite of the scorn, some Athenians put faith in Christ, including one of the members of the Areopagus, Dionysius by name,[46] and a woman named Damaris, whose background is not indicated. (She may have been a Jewish proselyte whose conversion resulted from the ministry in the synagogue.) We may not be justified in reading into this (vv. 33–34) that the results in Athens were very meager. Luke never tries to give us all the details.

One loose end remains to be tied before we follow Paul's movement from Athens to Corinth. He was actually waiting for Silas and Timothy (vv. 15–16). Luke does not tell us that they came to him in Athens, but he does indicate that they came to him in the next city, Corinth (18:5). On comparison with 1 Thessalonians 3:1 it is clear that Silas and Timothy did come to Athens, were dispatched back to Macedonia, and then came again to Corinth (as in Acts 18:5). This will be discussed in the introduction to 1 Thessalonians later in this chapter.

CORINTH: A GRECO-ROMAN CITY

More or less typical of the cities of Paul's world was Corinth in about AD 50 when Paul first visited there. It serves as an especially good example of the mingling of Greek and Roman cultures in city life during that period in history.

Corinth was originally a Greek city-state, destroyed by the Romans in 146 BC. For a hundred years following, she was not rebuilt, populated only on a small scale. In 44 BC, by order of Julius Caesar, a Roman colony was established at the old site, and the city once again flourished.

Although most colonies (see chap. 1) were founded for veterans (as with Philippi, for example), Corinth's colonists "were drawn from the poor, most of them *libertini*, freed slaves. This means, in turn, that the first settlers were not in fact 'Romans' but persons from the eastern Mediterranean, probably for the most part Syrians, Egyptians, and Jews."[47] By the time of Paul, then, the population—in the tens of thousands at least—was very heterogeneous, representing Greeks, Romans, and eastern peoples. Latin was the official language, but Greek was the language of the streets and homes.

Corinth was commercially strategic, located on the isthmus between mainland and Peloponnesian Greece. Thus it had a western port (Lechaeum) two miles on the northwest and an eastern port (Cenchrea) six miles in the other direction. Smaller vessels could actually be hauled overland from one to the other, and the cargoes of larger vessels were likewise transported.

To some degree the city was laid out in the style of Rome (see the insert in chap. 7), but some of the features of the old Greek city were retained. A forum—open marketplace and administrative center—was at the heart, located just south of the old city's most prominent temple (either to Apollo or Athena). As in most Greco-Roman cities, many public buildings graced the landscape, including a judgment seat (*bema*), porches (*stoas*) for public gatherings, a great number of temples for various gods and goddesses (as well as one for the imperial cult), public baths, fountains, basilicas, gymnasiums, an amphitheater, and the like.

Local government was under a city council, presided over by two magistrates (*duoviri*) who were elected annually. Corinth was probably the capital of Achaia and thus would also be the residence of the governing proconsul sent by the Roman Senate.

One important feature of life in and about Corinth was the Isthmian Games staged every other year, dedicated to Poseidon, god of the sea. There were competitions in music, speech, and drama, as well as athletic contests. One can imagine Paul . . . making his way through the jostling, boisterous crowds at Isthmia, perhaps even trying to find a hearing for the gospel there."[48]

Various religions were practiced in Corinth, including (1) adherence to the deities and cults of Greece, such as Apollo, Athena, and Aphrodite. There was a sanctuary for Asclepius (god of healing) where people came seeking recuperation and cures. The cults of Demeter, Kore, Palaimon, and others, were active; (2) the Roman imperial cult, represented by a temple that was probably built during Claudius's reign; (3) Judaism.

Jews may have been among the original colonists, and no doubt Jewish population was swelled by edicts (in AD 19 and 41) expelling Jews from Rome temporarily. There were areas where the Jews were concentrated, and any synagogue(s) would be in such localities. (See further the insert on religion elsewhere in this chapter.)

Corinth

Corinth (18:1–18), not far to the west, was Paul's next stop. It was the capital of the province of Achaia, also a Roman colony. On the isthmus connecting Peloponnesian Greece with the mainland, its two harbors gave access to west and east and helped guarantee its commercial prosperity. Worship in the temple of Aphrodite involved temple prostitutes, and sexual license was remarkable.

Residence with Aquila and Priscilla. This Jewish couple had recently been expelled from Rome by edict of Claudius Caesar, and they relocated in Corinth. There was "an extensive Jewish community in Rome,"[49] going back at least to Jewish captives taken there by Pompey in 61 BC.

Expulsion from Rome happened to Jews more than once in Roman history (in AD 19 by Tiberius, for example). This occasion was one in Claudius's ninth year (AD 49 or 50).[50] Not that Claudius was a persecutor of Jews. He had, in fact, befriended them. Under the reign of his predecessor, Caligula, Jews had suffered, especially in Alexandria; in Judea they had borne the threat of having Caligula's image set up in the Temple. Claudius put all that to a stop and ordered that the customs of the Jews be respected as before.[51]

Still, Claudius had allowed Judea to revert from client-kingdom to province, and that was not appreciated by the Jews. Why he expelled them from Rome is not quite clear. Suetonius said: "Since the Jews constantly made disturbances, at the instigation of Chrestus, he expelled them from Rome."[52]

We cannot be sure whether this is a reference to Jesus Christ (many think so), or to "Messiah," or even to someone else altogether.

Whether Aquila and Priscilla were already believers or were converted soon after Paul entered Corinth we are not told. Their craft was the same as Paul's. They made tents and other leather goods, no doubt from the *cilicium* manufactured in Paul's home province. That made it appropriate for Paul to live and practice his trade with them, working to support himself. This couple became fast friends with Paul and were coworkers in the gospel from this point on.

Synagogue ministry. Verses 4–6 describe this typical period, probably short lived, when Paul was tolerated in the synagogue in Corinth. As always, when he was not welcome there any longer, he declared his turning to the Gentiles in the city (v. 6; cf. 13:45–47). Silas and Timothy returned from their missions in Macedonia (see the discussion above) during this period. Verse 5 means at least that their return and report greatly encouraged Paul[53] and gave him new energy for witness. It may be that a financial gift was brought (perhaps by Silas from Philippi[54]), relieving Paul of the need to work. That would give him more time for preaching.

Ministry in Justus's home. In the usual pattern Paul found another place where his ministry could be centered. Justus was a Gentile whose house was next door to the synagogue, a Jewish proselyte before he was converted under Paul's influence.[55]

Paul's ministry was unusually blessed by the conversion of Crispus (v. 8a), the faith of many (v. 8b), the vision given to Paul (vv. 9–10), and the lengthy tenure in the city (v. 11). Crispus, the ruler of the synagogue, was a notable convert (cf. 1 Cor. 1:14).

The vision described in verses 9–10 would strengthen Paul in the face of opposition, assuring him that there were many who would be converted in Corinth. Both Calvinists and Arminians readily acknowledge that God has lovingly identified as His own, from eternity, those who put faith in Him.

The eighteen months referred to (v. 11) may be reckoned to begin either when the vision was received or earlier, when Paul entered the city. Either way, this is the longest time so far that Paul has spent in any one city.

Correspondence with the Thessalonians. Luke says nothing in Acts about Paul's letters; consequently, we are not surprised that the account of Paul's stay in Corinth does not mention the fact that he wrote 1 and 2 Thessalonians during this time. It is clear that he did: 1 Thessalonians in AD 50 and 2 Thessalonians some months later in 50 or 51. These are the earliest of Paul's canonical letters (unless Galatians was written earlier; see reference to this possibility earlier in this chapter and in the introduction to Galatians in chap. 6).

Introductions to the Thessalonian letters are included at the end of this chapter.

Charges before Gallio. This probably marks the end of the period just referred to, during which unbelieving Jews had apparently been frustrated in their opposition to Paul. Finally they decided to charge him before Lucius Junius Gallio; the point may be that Gallio[56] had just come into office, and they hoped he would take their charges seriously, as perhaps his predecessor had not. Gallio was the Roman proconsul for the whole province, and thus he was more powerful than mere civic magistrates. If the Jews could obtain his ruling against Paul, it would be a heavy blow.

There is some uncertainty about the exact nature of the Jews' charges. The accusation may have meant that Paul was preaching a religion not allowed by Roman law (a *religio illicita*); thus they set Christianity off from Judaism (a *religio licita* in the empire) and also charged Paul with being a violator of law.[57] Or it is possible that "contrary to the law" (v. 13) means the Jews' law and that the accusers were attempting to get the secular authority to uphold the purity of the Jewish religion as officially tolerated in the empire.[58] Gallio chose to take it this latter way (v. 15).

The reference to "words and names" (v. 15) suggests that at least part of the charge was similar to those at Philippi and Thessalonica. Gallio was unimpressed. Not even waiting for Paul's defense, he dismissed the case. He recognized that the technicalities were little more than subtle wordplay and chased the litigants from the courtroom.

Verse 17 is ambiguous. Probably these are unbelieving Greeks who took advantage of the occasion to indulge a little anti-Semitic prejudice. They may have taken umbrage at the Jews' persecution of Paul, inasmuch as Paul would have been identified as a friend of Gentiles. We assume Sosthenes had replaced the converted Crispus and was leader of the opposition to Paul.[59] A. N. Sherwin-White suggests the beating was administered by the Jews as synagogue discipline against Sosthenes as a Christian sympathizer.[60] Gallio's time as proconsul in Corinth almost certainly began on July 1 of the year AD 51.[61] The eighteen-month stay of Paul, therefore, ran either from early 50 to mid 51 (if the "many days longer" of v. 18 is added) or from mid 50 to late 51 (if v. 18 is included).

Departure from Cenchrea. After Gallio's favorable ruling, Paul remained in Corinth "many days longer," probably several more months that we can either add to or regard as part of the eighteen months of verse 11. When the time for departure came, it was because Paul wished to visit Syria again.

No doubt he was planning to be in Jerusalem for Passover; he had also observed a Nazirite vow, perhaps as a special consecration following the Lord's appearance to him (vv. 9–10).[62] On completion of the period of the vow, he had his hair cut short, for it could not be cut at all during the period of special consecration under the vow. And he would need to offer the appropriate sacrifice in Jerusalem marking the fulfillment of the vow.

A question might be raised about the appropriateness of Paul's taking part in such a Jewish practice as the Nazirite vow. As we have seen, Paul's rule was that believing Jews still lived as Jews, whereas believing Gentiles should not do so.[63]

When Paul departed Corinth, he had passage by ship from the city's eastern port of Cenchrea.

Ephesus

Ephesus (18:19–21), across the Aegean, was in the Roman province of Asia.[64] Paul may have originally thought to go to Ephesus in the early stages of this second journey, crossing Galatia and heading westward by land. But the Holy Spirit had forbidden him at that point to go there (16:6). Now, however, Paul had certainly got liberty from the Lord to make Ephesus a target for evangelism and the planting of a church.

He planned to go back to Syria first. Therefore he brought Priscilla and Aquila along from Corinth to leave at Ephesus. They would get the work started in his absence, and he would return as soon as possible. With that in mind, Paul visited and spoke in the synagogue, arousing interest. Urged to stay longer, he indicated that he must first visit Jerusalem for Passover and would return before long, God willing. Then together with Silas and Timothy apparently, he sailed from Ephesus.

Caesarea

Caesarea (18:22) was the Palestinian port where Paul disembarked, the usual one for traffic to and from the capital of Judea. Built by Herod the Great, the city had a noteworthy harbor.[65]

Jerusalem

Jerusalem (18:22) is the place meant for greeting "the church." No doubt Paul and his companions observed Passover as planned.

Antioch

Antioch (18:22) in Syria was Paul's home base. His return there with Timothy (and Silas)[66] marked the end of the second journey. The next (third) missionary journey begins in the following verse, so we are given no information relative to this period in Antioch.

Before continuing with the historical record, we turn our attention to the letters that Paul wrote during the second journey.

THE ESCHATOLOGICAL EPISTLES

First Thessalonians

As noted earlier in this chapter, there is general agreement that Paul wrote his two letters to the church in Thessalonica during his lengthy ministry in Corinth on the second missionary journey. With the possible exception of Galatians, the epistle of James may well be the only portion of our New Testament older than 1 Thessalonians. Therefore this letter provides one of the first glimpses we have into the life of the early church.

The events that led to the writing of 1 Thessalonians. The historical incidents that occasioned this letter can be discerned by analyzing 1 Thessalonians 2:17–3:8 and putting that together with Acts 17:1–18:5.

Paul's first visit to Thessalonica, with Silas and Timothy, was during the second missionary journey (review the discussion of Acts 17:1–9 earlier in this chapter).

That visit was relatively brief. The missionaries were forced to leave before they had time to establish fully the new converts. Paul felt strongly about being taken from them (2:17) and desired to finish in them the spiritual work only begun (3:7–10).

Leaving Thessalonica, Paul and his coworkers moved on to Berea and Athens (Acts 17:10–16). During this time, Paul sought opportunity to return to Thessalonica (2:17–18), but on at least two occasions ("more than once," 2:18) specific plans to do that were hindered by circumstances that he understood to be satanic in arrangement.

Those plans falling through, Paul sent Timothy to the Thessalonians from Athens. Timothy would therefore learn how the young Christians were faring and also minister to them.

Timothy returned with his report to Paul, who had moved on from Athens to nearby Corinth (Acts 18:1–5). The report greatly encouraged Paul (3:6–7), and he proceeded almost immediately to write of his joy and to instruct on matters Timothy mentioned.[67]

The date and place where Paul composed 1 Thessalonians. Corinth is the place beyond reasonable doubt. According to Acts 17, Paul left Berea unexpectedly and alone for Athens. He sent word to Silas and Timothy to meet him there quickly, and he waited for them in that city. However, in Acts 18 we read that they came to him in Corinth. As we have seen, though, Luke never tries to tell us every detail. First Thessalonians 3:1–2 supplies some missing information. There it is clear that Paul sent Timothy to the Thessalonians from Athens, so evidently Silas and Timothy did join Paul in Athens as they were instructed. Afterwards the two were sent to revisit the newly established churches—Timothy to Thessalonica, Silas elsewhere (possibly to Philippi), and Paul moved on to Corinth. He was in Corinth when they returned to him as reported by Luke (Acts 18:11).

The Acts record seems clear that Paul's stay in Athens was brief, whereas his ministry in Corinth was for at least a year and a half (18:11). Placing the writing of 1 Thessalonians in Corinth, then, allows the time needed both for Timothy's mission and for the composition of the letter.

Once Corinth is seen to have been the place of writing, the date is not difficult to establish. As he writes, Paul is conscious that he has recently been in Thessalonica. In chapter 1 the memories are fresh in Paul's mind, especially of the Thessalonians' conversion (vv. 5–6, 9). In chapter 2 Paul reviews the fruitful entrance he had into the city (v. 1).

There is no doubt at all, then, that the epistle was written within a few months of Paul's original ministry in Thessalonica. We know Paul stayed in Corinth at least eighteen months. We also know Timothy's return to him there was early in that stay (Acts 18:5, 11).

Therefore we can confidently place the writing of 1 Thessalonians during the early months of that ministry.

That enables us to get close to a specific year on the calendar. For during Paul's stay in Corinth, he was arraigned before Gallio, the Roman proconsul of the province (Acts 18:12). It appears that this took place soon after Gallio came into office, perhaps implying that Paul's accusers had tried before and failed and hoped that the new man would be different.

It is reasonably clear that Gallio became proconsul of the province of Achaia in July of the year 51.[68] Apparently the eighteen months of Acts 18:11 preceded that event. That would mean that Paul's ministry in Corinth began early in the year 50, and so 1 Thessalonians was written in that year.

The destination of 1 Thessalonians. Like Tarsus, Thessalonica was an old and important city. Originally called Therma (Greek for "warmth") because of its hot springs, the name was changed by the Macedonian king Cassender (315 BC) in honor of his wife Thessalonica, stepsister of Alexander the Great. The area was conquered by the Romans in 168 BC. When the district was made into a province and named Macedonia in 146 BC, Thessalonica was made capital and later made *libera civitas*. It, too, was a natural harbor and a trading center as well as being located on the famous Egnatian Highway that crossed the land (now Greece) from the Adriatic Sea to the Hellespont. Because Cassender settled the area with various peoples, its population was heterogeneous. The city is still called Saloniki and more nearly resembles what it was in Paul's day than almost any other city Paul visited.

The church in Thessalonica was founded when Paul, Silas, and Timothy evangelized the city. The story is recorded briefly in Acts 17:1–9 in two stages. First was the customary ministry in the synagogue, tolerated only for three weeks (v. 2). There were several converts, both Jews and Greeks, including some women of influence.

It appears that Paul made Jason's house his teaching place after the synagogue was closed to him, and that explains the assault on his house. This led to the requirement that Jason[69] and others post a bond guaranteeing the peace, and so Paul and his companions had to leave. The implication is that this stage of Paul's ministry was also relatively brief. Paul realized that the work was not well established (1 Thess. 3:5–10).

In 1 Thessalonians 1:9 Paul says his Thessalonian readers "turned to God from idols" during his ministry there. Because that would not be precisely true of Jews or of full-fledged proselytes, we can assume that the majority of the church was made up of converts from heathenism. No doubt the converted proselytes opened doors to reach out to heathen Greeks in the city. That one of Paul's major teachings in 1 Thessalonians is about sexual morality (4:3–8) may also suggest heathen converts, who would have been more likely to need such teaching than Jewish converts. "In addition to possessing all the temptations of a great seaport, Thessalonica was notorious in antiquity as one of the seats of the Cabiri . . . mysterious deities, whose worship was attended with grossly immoral rites."[70]

The purposes of Paul in 1 Thessalonians. This letter is not primarily doctrinal, although many important doctrines of the Christian faith are reflected or mentioned in passing. (That is significant in light of its early date: 1 Thessalonians raises powerful objections to any view that Christian doctrine was formed by a slow, evolutionary process.)

The letter is very personal and practical. In the first three chapters, where most of the verbs are in the past tense, Paul reviews the history of the church and his dealings with them in an intensely personal way. In the last two chapters Paul turns to practical instruction and exhortation. Even the doctrine of the second coming, as important as it is in the letter, is dealt with for practical reasons.

These two major sections suggest two major purposes. First, Paul wrote to express his personal concern and feelings for the Thessalonian Christians. These feelings included a sense of joy and appreciation, especially at hearing Timothy's report (3:1–9; cf. 1:2–10). They also included a grateful review of the fruitful ministry he had there (2:1–13). Many interpreters believe this defense implies there had been some attacks on Paul's character at Thessalonica following his departure.

Second, Paul also wrote to give instruction needed for the further perfection (3:10) of their faith, reflecting such needs as Timothy had reported to Paul. We can discern what they were only by the contents of the letter itself. Included in the problems needing attention were sexual impurity (4:3–8), disorder created by some not working (4:11–12), possible division, reflecting disrespect for leaders (5:12–13), and most important, misunderstanding about the practical implications of the teaching of the second coming, especially as related to believers who die before Christ's return (4:13–5:11).

Other subjects are treated in the letter, but these are the ones that are dealt with in such a way as to suggest problems.[71] Of these, instruction on the practical implications of the second coming gets the most space. It was the most pressing problem.

The theme of 1 Thessalonians. Sometimes it is helpful to state a theme for a book of the Bible; sometimes it is not. One of the dangers is that emphasizing a single theme may blind us to other subjects that do not fit. Because of the variety of subjects treated in this short letter and because of its very personal and practical nature, no single theme relates to all of it. Still, one of the important themes in 1 Thessalonians is *the practical effects of the impending return of Jesus Christ in the lives of believers.*

The letters have often been characterized as Paul's most eschatological ones (from the Greek *eschatos,* "last," and so the doctrine of last things, of the future). Both of them have important sections on things that relate to Christ's return. It is worth remembering, then, that this is one of the key themes of 1 Thessalonians. And though 4:13–5:11 is the major section, every chapter makes some reference to the second coming (1:10; 2:19; 3:13; 4:13–18; 5:1–11, 23).

The Outline of 1 Thessalonians

Formal opening, 1:1

I. A historical review: Paul and the Thessalonians from the beginning until now, 1:2–3:13

A. Paul's appreciation for the church, 1:2–10

1. Prayerful thanksgiving on the Thessalonians' behalf (vv. 2–5)

2. Commendation of the Thessalonians (vv. 6–10)

B. Paul's ministry at Thessalonica, 2:1–6

1. A fruitful ministry: Paul's preaching (vv. 1–12)

2. A fruitful ministry: the Thessalonians' response (vv. 13–16)

C. Paul's continued efforts for them, 2:17–3:13

1. Paul's attempt to return to Thessalonica (2:17–20)

2. The sending of Timothy (3:1–5)

3. Timothy's return and report (3:6–10)

4. Paul's continuing prayer for the Thessalonians (3:11–13)

II. Practical instruction: exhortation and teaching for the Thessalonians, 4:1–5:22

A. Exhortations about the Christians' walk, 4:1–12

1. The nature of Paul's instruction (vv. 1–2)

2. Exhortation to sexual purity (vv. 3–8)

3. Exhortation to brotherly love (vv. 9–10)

4. Exhortation to honest labor (vv. 11–12)

B. The second coming and the Christian dead, 4:13–18

1. The hope that reassures (vv. 13–14)

2. The manner of the saints' resurrection (vv. 15–17)

3. The use of these words for encouragement (v. 18)

C. Watchfulness for the Lord's return, 5:1–11

1. The uncertainty of the time (vv. 1–3)

2. The possibility of readiness (vv. 4–8)

3. The assurance that sustains (vv. 9–11)

D. General instructions for the life of the church, 5:12–22

1. Respect for church leaders (vv. 12–13)

2. Obligations within the fellowship (vv. 14–15)

3. Constant Christian attitudes (vv. 16–18)

4. Response to spiritual manifestations (vv. 19–22)

Conclusion, 5:23–28

Second Thessalonians

Second Thessalonians is a continuation of Paul's correspondence with the Christians in Thessalonica. Apparently there was not a very long time between the two letters.

The date and place for the writing of 2 Thessalonians. There are two main reasons for placing the composition of 2 Thessalonians fairly soon after 1 Thessalonians while Paul was still at Corinth. First is the fact that Silas and Timothy were still with Paul when 2 Thessalonians was written (1 Thess. 1:1; 2 Thess. 1:1–2). The second journey was the only one that included Silas. Furthermore, when Paul left Corinth, the second journey was as good as over; he stopped only briefly at Ephesus and hurried home by way of Jerusalem (Acts 18:18–22). About the only flexibility this allows is the span of time— at least a year and a half—that Paul was in Corinth. If Paul wrote 1 Thessalonians during the early part of that eighteen months, then 2 Thessalonians might have been written up to a year later.

The second reason for this dating is the fact that the main problems behind the second letter are similar to those discussed in 1 Thessalonians: (1) the eschatological emphasis is similar; (2) there is still persecution, probably intensified (1 Thess. 3:3–4; 2 Thess. 1:4–5); (3) there is still misunderstanding related to the doctrine of the second coming, although the specific question is a different one (2 Thess. 2:1–12); and (4) there is still the problem of those not working and taking advantage of their brethren (1 Thess. 4:11–12; 2 Thess. 3:6–15). The likely conclusion, then, is that 2 Thessalonians was written within a year of 1 Thessalonians while Paul was still at Corinth, in 50 or 51.

Some of the more critical interpreters have suggested other possibilities, either that 2 Thessalonians was actually written first or that it was not written by Paul at all and was a later composition in imitation of 1 Thessalonians. Although the inspired text does not indicate which one is first, the two epistles' discussions of similar problems make more sense if Second Thessalonians looks at a later stage of the problems. 2 Thessalonians 2:15 seems best understood as referring to 1 Thessalonians. Furthermore, Paul's references to his original ministry at Thessalonica and to the Thessalonians' conversion are not nearly so many or as fresh to mind in 2 Thessalonians. Indeed, 1 Thessalonians 2:17–3:6 would be impossible to understand if 2 Thessalonians had preceded it.[72]

It is not within the scope of this text to discuss the second suggestion, which would require that we view 2 Thessalonians as a forgery. Donald Guthrie has an excellent discussion of this issue (and of the order of the two letters).[73] Those who hold this view seem to think 2 Thessalonians is too bland and repetitious to have been genuinely Pauline and sent to the same church, but most of 2 Thessalonians develops specific teachings in helpful detail.[74] I. Howard Marshall analyzes all the objections to Pauline authorship and concludes:

> When we examine all the arguments, then, it emerges that neither singly nor cumulatively do they suffice to disprove Pauline authorship. That 2 Th. contains some unusual features in style and theology is not to be denied, but that these features point to pseudonymous authorship is quite another matter. Moreover, the early church had no doubts about the Pauline authorship of 2 Th. The later we set the date of the letter, the more difficult it becomes to explain its unopposed acceptance into the Pauline corpus; indeed, it is hard to envisage how an alleged Pauline letter addressed to a particular church could have escaped detection as a forgery.[75]

The events that led to the writing of 2 Thessalonians. Unlike 1 Thessalonians, the second letter does not make reference to specific circumstances in the background. The following seem obvious.

Someone had taken the first letter to Thessalonica. We are not told who. (Guthrie thinks Timothy would not be both bearer of and included in the opening of the letter,[76] but that reasoning seems weak.)

That messenger would have returned, reporting about developments at Thessalonica and the need for further instruction.

Paul, still unable to go in person, decided to write again.

The purposes of Paul in 2 Thessalonians. Each of the three chapters of this letter appears to deal with a specific problem that had been reported to Paul. These suggest three main purposes.

First, Paul wrote to encourage them in their persecutions. A comparison between the earlier, brief references to this (1 Thess. 1:6; 2:14; 3:3–4) and the second letter's lengthy treatment (1:4–10) suggests that persecution had become more severe in the interval.

Second, Paul wrote to give specific instruction relative to the Lord's coming, as seen in chapter 2. Apparently a false teaching (or at least a misunderstanding) had arisen—that the day of the Lord had already come—and Paul felt compelled to correct that error. Some think that 2:2 means someone had used a letter that was falsely attributed to Paul and taught this frightening distortion of the truth. (This could even be the reason Paul concluded 2 Thessalonians with an authenticating signature in 3:17.)

Third, Paul wrote to exhort the idle and to instruct the church how to discipline them (3:6–15). Apparently the idleness had grown worse and was creating disorder, and more than the mild admonishing of the first letter (1 Thess. 4:11–12) was called for. Paul especially needed to teach the church to discipline the disorderly.

The theme of 2 Thessalonians. As with 1 Thessalonians, there is no one theme that includes everything in this letter, but the eschatological emphasis is still one of the most important themes (1:7–10; 2:1–12; perhaps 3:5).

The Outline of 2 Thessalonians

Formal opening, 1:1–2

I. Personal words: appreciation and encouragement, 1:3–12

    A. Thanksgiving for growth, 1:3–4

    B. Consolation in persecution, 1:5–10

        1. The honor of suffering for Christ (v. 5)

        2. The promise of God's retribution (vv. 6–7a)

        3. The revelation of Jesus as the time for retribution (vv. 7b–10)

    C. Prayer for the Thessalonians, 1:11–12

        1. For the fulfillment of God's calling in their lives (v. 11)

2. For the glorification of Jesus' name (v. 12)

II. Doctrinal correction: the second coming and steadfastness, 2:1–17

    A. Details about the day of the Lord, 2:1–12

        1. Introduction: no need for distress (vv. 1–2)

        2. Two things that must first happen (vv. 3–4)

        3. The present restraining of Antichrist (vv. 5–7)

        4. The character and end of Antichrist (vv. 8–10)

        5. Delusion as judgment (vv. 11–12)

    B. Exhortation to steadfastness, 2:13–17

        1. Grateful assurance (vv. 13–14)

        2. Exhortation (v. 15)

        3. Prayer (vv. 16–17)

III. Practical instruction: confidence and discipline, 3:1–15

    A. Paul's need and confidence, 3:1–5

        1. Request for prayer (vv. 1–2)

        2. Expression of confidence (vv. 3–5)

    B. Discipline for the disorderly, 3:6–15

        1. Withdrawal from the idle commanded (v. 6)

        2. Paul's example commended (vv. 7–9)

        3. The principle to be practiced (v. 10)

        4. The disorderly exhorted (vv. 11–12)

        5. The church instructed (vv. 13 15)

Conclusion, 3:16–18

THE THIRD MISSIONARY JOURNEY

ACTS 18:23–21:17

Luke's transition from Paul's second journey to his third is quite abrupt (18:22–23). Nothing in between is noted except that he spent "some time" in Antioch, probably not a lengthy period.

At the end of the second journey Paul had stopped in Ephesus long enough to leave Aquila and Priscilla there and to promise that he would personally return soon. That promise was heavy on Paul's mind as he began the third journey from Syrian Antioch in about AD 53 or 54.

PAUL'S CHRISTIAN LIFE AND MINISTRY, PART III

AD 53/54–57/58 the third missionary journey, Acts 18:23 21:17

Once again, as we follow the journey, it will be helpful to consult a map (see page 186) as well as to follow the biblical text. As before, the following discussion will indicate the places visited and the events at each place.

Galatia and Phrygia

Galatia and Phrygia (18:23) had been visited on both the previous journeys. This verse serves to indicate only that Paul revisited the churches there on his way to Ephesus. (See chap. 5 for the question

of whether this included northern Galatia; see also the introduction
to Galatians later in this chapter.)

Ephesus

Ephesus (18:24–20:1) was the greatest city of the Roman province of Asia, and Paul spent the major portion of the third journey
there. The point of verse 1 is that he took "the higher-lying and more
direct route, not the regular trade route on the lower level down the
Lycus and Maeander valleys."[1]

Verses 24–28 describe something that had happened at Ephesus
during the interval between Paul's leaving Aquila and Pricilla there
and his return on the third journey. Thus we are introduced to
Apollos. He was a Jew of Alexandria, an able, fervent, and scriptur-
ally knowledgeable speaker, being formally instructed[2] in the Christian
way. However, he lacked some understanding of Christian baptism,
"knowing only the baptism of John." "He combined great biblical
learning and accurate knowledge of the story of Jesus with spiritual
enthusiasm, and proved himself specially gifted in demonstrating from
the Old Testament prophecies that Jesus was the Messiah."[3]

We could wish we knew exactly what he did and did not know.
The only thing clear is that he baptized according to John the Baptist's
form. If we use Acts 1:5 as a key, Apollos apparently baptized only
with water and did not teach about the reception of the Holy Spirit.
But 19:3–4 (discussed below) appears to indicate more than this.

Whatever the defect, Aquila and Priscilla remedied it (v. 26).
They would also have told him about the marvelous work that had
been begun in Corinth, and Apollos's interest was strongly aroused.
Obtaining written recommendation from believers in Ephesus
(Aquila and Priscilla too?), he proceeded to Corinth and became involved in a very effective ministry there. Ultimately, he also became
involved in problems at Corinth as 1 Corinthians 1:12 shows.

Paul's encounter with twelve of Apollos's converts. When Paul arrived
in Ephesus, Apollos had already gone to Corinth. But Apollos had left
behind some who had become believers in Jesus under his preaching
before Aquila and Priscilla had corrected his defective understanding

of baptism; that is apparently the point of verses 1–7.[4]

These men had not experienced "the gift of the Holy Spirit" (Acts 2:38). Apollos had presented baptism as John had, as indicating repentance in preparation for the coming of the messianic kingdom (v. 4), "a baptism of expectation rather than one of fulfillment."[5] But the eschatological messianic kingdom had already come—in one sense at least—and the gift of the Holy Spirit to all believers was evidence of that.

These Ephesian disciples had heard nothing of this (v. 2),[6] welcomed the news, and submitted to Christian baptism, receiving dramatic confirmation of the Spirit's presence. "Even if they had only been baptized with John's baptism, they conceivably knew that John had spoken of a coming baptism with the Holy Spirit; they did not know, however, that this expected baptism was now an accomplished fact."[7]

Three months in the synagogue. As far as the record is concerned, this is the longest time Paul was ever tolerated in the synagogue in any of the cities he evangelized. Paul is still following the pattern we have seen all along.

Two years in Tyrannus's lecture hall. As always, the majority of the Jews finally closed the synagogue to Paul. Verse 9 means that from this point on the Christians—Jews and Gentiles—were no longer part of synagogue life but had their own congregation (a "Christian synagogue," an assembly, a church). This happened in every place.

We know nothing more of Tyrannus.[8] Paul apparently arranged to use his lecture hall during the middle of each day: "Public activity ceased in the cities of Ionia for several hours at 11 a.m. . . . But Paul, after spending the early hours of the day at his tent-making, devoted the hours of burden and heat to his more important . . . business."[9]

The gospel spread throughout Roman Asia during this two-year period. Not that Paul personally traveled (he may have), but his converts (and companions, vv. 22, 29) and others traveling to and fro did the evangelizing. No doubt the churches in Colosse, Hierapolis, and Laodicea were founded during this period and probably all the seven churches of Asia addressed in Revelation 2–3.

A triumphant ministry. Verses 11–20 meld together three examples of the supernatural effectiveness of the gospel in Ephesus, making the point that God's word prevailed over the powers of darkness (vv. 17, 20).

First were "extraordinary miracles" (vv. 11–12). The sweatcloths ("handkerchiefs") and aprons were used by Paul in his leather work (Acts 19:12)—following his usual pattern (Acts 18:3; 1 Thess. 2:9).[10]

Second was the incident involving the seven sons of Sceva. As Jews, these brothers were not supposed to be involved in the black arts. They thought Paul's words, used in casting out demons, were a magic incantation.[11] But the candidate for their exorcism, who certainly recognized Jesus and Paul, did not acknowledge them at all. The picture, though serious, is quite humorous.

Third was the burning of books associated with witchcraft (vv. 18–19).[12]

"Confessing and disclosing their practices" (v. 18) may mean exposing their secret curses and charms, thereby rendering them no longer effective. The passage "tallies admirably with the reputation Ephesus had in antiquity as a centre of magical practice."[13]

A further period in Ephesus, including important communications with the Corinthians. This time (v. 22) may have been in addition to the twenty-seven months already mentioned (cf. 20:31). It followed the laying of plans to revisit Macedonia and Achaia before going to Jerusalem and the sending of coworkers Timothy and Erastus[14] into Macedonia ahead of him.

Although Luke does not tell us, the Corinthian letters make clear that Paul's stay in Ephesus included extensive involvements with the Corinthian church during this period. According to 1 Corinthians 5:9, Paul wrote a letter to Corinth that has not been preserved. Then a delegation of Corinthians came to him at Ephesus with a letter from the church (1 Cor. 7:1; 16:17), and Paul wrote 1 Corinthians in response. Not long after, Paul evidently paid the Corinthians a short visit (going directly across the Aegean) and returned to Ephesus to write a very severe letter (referred to in 2 Cor. 2:4; 7:8).

The introductions to 1 and 2 Corinthians later in this chapter will provide detailed reasons for believing that these troubled dealings with the Corinthians took place while Paul was in Ephesus.

The uprising of the silversmiths. Ephesus was famous for its temple to "Diana of the Ephesians," actually the Greek goddess Artemis, identified with the Roman Diana.[15] (See the insert on page 109.) The temple was one of the seven wonders of the ancient world, four times as large as the Parthenon in Athens. Legend was that the image, perhaps a meteorite that resembled a many breasted female, had fallen from heaven (v. 35). The silversmiths made their living fashioning small replicas of the shrine to sell.

These craftsmen (trade guilds existed) had reason to be upset: Paul's preaching of monotheism and the vanity of idolatry (cf. Acts 14:15–17; 17:22–31) had caused many to turn from their worship of Artemis. They decided to arouse the populace and led a great number of people into the city's amphitheater.[16] The civic assembly met here regularly (presumably one regular and two extra meetings each month),[17] but this would not be an official meeting.

There was utter confusion (v. 32). At first Paul thought to enter and speak (v. 30); although he had not been seized, two of his co-workers had (v. 29). But the local believers prevailed on Paul to keep still (v. 30); even some friendly officials[18] sent word to the same effect (v. 31). Finally, things quieted down enough that the clerk of the city ("who published the decrees of the civic assembly")[19] could divert the throng's attention. This he did by implying that the city's devotion to Artemis was beyond undermining (vv. 35–36), by citing the orderly way the matter could be pursued (v. 38: they could go before the provincial authorities or a regular civic assembly), and by emphasizing the disorderly nature of this particular "assembly" (vv. 37, 39–40). Ephesus was a free city,[20] but the Roman overlords looked with strong disapproval on disorder, and the city's freedom might be threatened if order could not be maintained.

The Roman provincial officials held regular terms in several Asian cities, presided over by the proconsul. Liaison between the city and these provincial officials was maintained by the city clerk.[21] Beyond these, the leading Greek cities in Asia formed a confederation, the representatives from each city being known as "Asiarchs" (v. 31).

There were troubles in Ephesus that Luke tells us nothing about (see 20:19; 1 Cor. 15:30–32; 2 Cor. 1:8–10). Some think these included a time of imprisonment for Paul, but details can be filled in only by speculation. (Some interpreters think that some of the prison letters were written at this time. That possibility will be discussed in the introduction to Philippians in chap. 7.)

Macedonia

Macedonia (20:1–2a) was reached via Troas (2 Cor. 2:12–13). Paul had sent Titus to Corinth (reflecting the troubles referred to above) from Ephesus and met him in Macedonia on this occasion, whereupon he wrote 2 Corinthians during this time in Macedonia and sent it ahead of him to Corinth. See the introduction to 2 Corinthians later in this chapter.

Although Luke does not name cities, Paul no doubt revisited all the places evangelized on the previous journey. This may have been the occasion of a visit to (at least to the border of) Illyricum (Rom. 15:19), inasmuch as the Macedonia itinerary of the second journey did not take him that far.[22]

It is possible that Paul wrote Galatians during this time in Macedonia. Of all Paul's letters, Galatians is the hardest to tell the time and place of its writing. An introduction to Galatians has been included later in this chapter, and these matters will be discussed there.

Greece

"Greece" (20:2b–3) is Achaia, the southern province in the larger area we now call Greece. Apparently Paul revisited Athens and spent the larger portion of three months in Corinth. He wrote Romans during this stay, and in that letter he indicated his hope to visit Rome (and evangelize Spain) after first returning once more to Jerusalem (Rom. 15:23–29). An introduction to Romans has been provided later in this chapter.

Macedonia

Paul's original plan was to sail from Corinth, but a Jewish plot brought a decision to head back through Macedonia (20:3b–4).[23]

Verse 4 names several who were making the journey with him. The number was partly because Paul was sponsoring a collection to take to poor believers in Jerusalem. Some of these men served to represent their churches in carrying the collection.[24] Even though Luke says essentially nothing about this offering (but see 24:17), it is mentioned in three of Paul's letters written during this journey (1 Cor. 16; 2 Cor. 8–9; Rom. 15:25–26).

Philippi

Philippi (20:5–6a) was on the route back through Macedonia. Luke once again joined Paul's entourage. The "we" starts in verse 5 and continues throughout most of the rest of Acts. (The "we" had stopped at Philippi on the second journey, so the connection is subtly accurate.) "The chronological exactitude" of the following account may mean that Luke "kept a log-book."[25]

Apparently Paul wished to tarry at Philippi; the larger group went on ahead to Troas (v. 5). Waiting out the Jewish "days of Unleavened Bread" (v. 6) may have been the reason for the delay. This period, linked with Passover, was in April (from April 7–14 in the year AD 57, for example). If Paul originally planned to be in Jerusalem for Passover, the events at Corinth had changed his plans. He still wanted to be there for Pentecost (v. 16).

Troas

Troas (20:6b–12) was reached by Luke and Paul in five days, a longer time than the usual one or two days (cf. 16:11). There may have been ship's cargo to be loaded at Samothracia or winds contrary to sailing.

Assembly at Troas. The New Testament contains relatively few references to the meetings of Christians. This one indicates assembly on the first day of the week and the breaking of bread, "probably a fellowship meal [the "Agape"] in the course of which the Eucharist was celebrated."[26] They were meeting in an upper room, apparently in the evening,[27] inasmuch as Paul's speaking continued until midnight, which was unusual, and perhaps because of his deep emotions at the time (cf. vv. 17–38 below at Miletus).

The raising of Eutychus. This young man, sitting in an open window, went to sleep and fell outside to the ground below. When the believers rushed down to him, he was dead. Physician Luke would not have been wrong on that point. Paul, however, reassured them (v. 10) and restored him to life, much in the fashion of Elisha of old (2 Kings 4:32–37). The believers were comforted, and the meeting continued until daybreak.

Assos

Paul went to Assos (20:13–14) from Troas on foot. The others booked passage by ship.

Mitylene, Chios, Samos, and Trogyllium

Mitylene (on the island of Lesbos), Chios (an island), Samos (another island), and Trogyllium (20:14–15) are mentioned as places the ship passed by or docked at. This particular ship ("a coasting vessel, due to put in at the main ports along the coast of Asia Minor")[28] was not scheduled to dock at Ephesus, and that suited Paul, who meant to get to Jerusalem in time for Pentecost (v. 16). There were fifty days between Passover and Pentecost; Jerusalem could still be made in time for the latter.

Miletus

Miletus (20:15b–38) was a port about thirty miles from Ephesus at the mouth of the river Maeander, and the ship was due to dock there long enough to send for the leaders of the church at Ephesus.

The farewell address to the Ephesian elders (vv. 17–35; cf. 14:23) is moving and significant. Paul desired to speak to them lest he never see them again (v. 25). The speech is in two parts. In verses 18–27 Paul speaks of his own ministry at Ephesus (just months before) and his present circumstances, and in verses 28–35 he directly exhorts the elders about their responsibilities.

Verses 22–25 present minor difficulties. Was Paul "bound" in the Holy Spirit or his own spirit? Some think Paul was headstrong in this determination to go to Jerusalem, that he went in the face of actual revelation that the Spirit was directing otherwise. The AV uses a small letter in verse 22 (and in 19:21), yet verse 23 also has bearing on the subject, and 21:4 is crucial. It says the *disciples* urged Paul not to go because of what the Spirit revealed, and 21:10–12 is undoubtedly a fuller example of precisely what happened in 21:4. Therefore, "Spirit" can be capitalized in its more natural way. In other words, "Both compulsion and warning were evidently involved in the Spirit's direction."[29] Paul would never have gone to Jerusalem against Divine directive.

Prophets in various churches were receiving revelations about the difficulties that Paul could expect (v. 23). That had already started, and Paul was aware of it even in Corinth when he wrote Romans (Rom. 15:30–31). The lengthy assembly at Troas probably reflected such awareness; likewise the scenes at Tyre (21:4) and Caesarea (21:11–13).

Elders are responsible to exercise oversight/watchcare[30] and to "shepherd" (better than KJV "feed") the church as the flock of God. They must do this selflessly, as Paul had set example (no doubt holding up "these hands" to view. vv. 33–35) and in accord with Jesus' own teaching (v. 35b). Note that this is one of the Lord's sayings that was preserved, probably by the apostles, outside the written Gospels.

Cos, Rhodes, Patara, Cyprus, Tyre, and Ptolemais

Cos (one of the Dodecanese islands) and Rhodes (another of these islands, with port city by the same name) are mentioned only because they were on the ship's route.

On Patara (21:1–2) passage had to be booked on another ship. Cyprus (21:3a) is mentioned just to observe that the ship bypassed this island on its southern side, the ship's port side. "The ship was probably a large merchant vessel; smaller vessels hugged the coast."[31]

The ship was scheduled to be in Tyre (21:3b–6) one week, there to unload the major portion of her cargo (v. 3). Paul and his companions took advantage of the time to spend it with the Christians there. A scene much like that at Troas and Miletus transpired (vv. 4–6). Ptolemais (21:7) was the ship's next stop, further south (the Old Testament Acco, modern Akka/Acre). One day was spent there.

Caesarea

Caesarea (21:8–14) was the last coastal port before the final sixty-four miles inland to Jerusalem. (It is not absolutely clear that the group went there by ship; a land trip from Ptolemais is possible.)

With Philip the evangelist. Paul and his companions stayed "some days" (v. 10) with Philip, who has not been heard from in Acts since 8:40, when he apparently settled at Caesarea. One of the original seven mentioned in Acts 6:1–6, he had four unmarried daughters who had the gift of prophecy (v. 9), perhaps implying that they, too, prophesied of Paul's future.[32]

The prophecy of Agabus. Once again we meet this prophet (cf. 11:27–30), and again Paul will go to Jerusalem. Using Paul's belt, Agabus bound his own hands and feet to portray Paul's coming arrest in Jerusalem. The believers (including Luke, v. 12) begged Paul to change his plans, but his refusal revealed his commitment (v. 13), and they yielded.

Jerusalem

Jerusalem (21:15–17) marked the end of the third journey. Some from Caesarea accompanied Paul and the others who were with him, including a Cypriot named Mnason[33] who had been a believer from the earliest days and who would provide lodging for the group in Jerusalem (v. 16).

Paul's arrival in Jerusalem did more than bring to a close his third missionary journey. It became a major turning point in his life. As the next chapter will show, Paul was arrested in Jerusalem and spent the next four years as a prisoner, first in Caesarea and then in Rome.

Before we examine those events, we should look more closely at the letters that were written during the third journey.

THE DOCTRINAL EPISTLES

First Corinthians

The second group of Paul's letters includes two to the Corinthians, and Galatians and Romans. These are sometimes referred to as his capital or major letters. Even among the most critical scholars, who question the Pauline authorship of some of the letters, there is general agreement that Paul wrote these four.

The letters to the Corinthians are as much practical as doctrinal. It may be that the Corinthian church caused Paul more heartache than any other of his churches. These two letters, then, are "invaluable for the light they throw, not only on the practical problems of a primitive community but also on the personality of the great apostle."[34]

Here it would be helpful to review Acts 18 and that part of chapter 5 that deals with Paul's ministry in Corinth on the second missionary journey, as well as Acts 19 and the part of this chapter that deals with the Ephesian visit on the third missionary journey. That is the background for 1 Corinthians.

The date and place of the writing of 1 Corinthians. We can be certain that 1 Corinthians was written from Ephesus during the third journey for at least three reasons.

First, the third journey was the one during which Paul sponsored a collection to be taken to Jerusalem. First Corinthians 16:1–4 deals with this collection.

Second, 1 Corinthians 16:19 and 16:8 clearly fix the place: Paul sends greetings from the churches of Asia and indicates that he will remain at Ephesus a while longer. This fits perfectly with the fact that Paul spent up to three years in Ephesus on the third journey, during which time the province of Asia was thoroughly evangelized (Acts 19:10). This was, in fact, the next ministry of any significant length following that at Corinth.

Third, Aquila and Priscilla send greetings to Corinth in 1 Corinthans 16:9. When Paul left Corinth toward the end of the second journey, he took this couple with him and dropped them off in Ephesus to get the work started while he went on to Jerusalem, promising to return soon (Acts 18:18–21).

If Paul was in Ephesus from about AD 54 until 56/57, can we place 1 Corinthians at any specific point during that two-to-three year period? We can probably put it during the latter portion, using references to Timothy as a basis. Apparently Timothy was not with Paul when he wrote 1 Corinthians, for he is not named in the formal opening (1:1) as he is in 2 Corinthians 1:1, and the references in 1 Corinthians 4:17 and 16:10 seem to mean that Timothy had already departed Ephesus and was not yet in Corinth. Acts 19:21–22 shows that Paul did send Timothy into Macedonia while he personally stayed in Ephesus "for a while." That seems to have been after the major portion of the time at Ephesus. Furthermore, in 1 Corinthians 16:5–8 Paul speaks of his intention to visit Corinth in the future, after remaining at Ephesus until Pentecost. That, too, would argue that we should put 1 Corinthians "during the last of the three years at Ephesus."[35]

For these reasons, it seems best to date 1 Corinthians at about 56 (possibly 57), written in Ephesus during the latter part of Paul's lengthy ministry there on the third journey.

The events that led to the writing of 1 Corinthians. Starting with Paul's ministry in Corinth during the second journey, a lengthy series of events transpired.

First, Paul left Corinth, deposited Aquila and Priscilla at Ephesus, and went on back to Antioch via Jerusalem to end the second missionary journey.

Second, without a lengthy delay, he set forth on the third journey and made his way across Asia Minor to Ephesus, as he had promised.

Third, in Ephesus Paul learned about the experience of Aquila and Priscilla with Apollos (Acts 18:24–26) and that Apollos had gone to Corinth to minister (Acts 18:27–19:1).

Fourth, at some point during this period Paul wrote the Corinthians a (brief?) letter referred to in 1 Corinthians 5:9. This letter is sometimes called the lost letter or the previous letter.

Fifth, news of the situation at Corinth got back to Paul through various sources; we know at least two specific ones—the family of Chloe (1:11) and Apollos, apparently returned from Corinth to Ephesus (16:12). These reports indicated problems and needs.

Sixth, Paul sent Timothy and Erastus into Macedonia (Acts 19:22), apparently intending that Timothy, at least, should work his way on down to Corinth (1 Cor. 4:17; 16:10). (This may have occurred before or after some or all of the reports mentioned above.)

Seventh, before Timothy had time to get to Corinth, a delegation from Corinth—Stephanus, Fortunatus, Achaicus—came to Paul (1 Cor. 16:17–18), bearing a letter from the Corinthians that asked several questions (7:1).

Eighth, in response to all these sources—the reports, the delegation, the letter—Paul wrote 1 Corinthians. The need was acute.

The destination of 1 Corinthians. The primary addressees of the letter were those in the church at Corinth (1:2), established by Paul during his second missionary journey. The account of that ministry is in Acts 18:1–17 (see chap. 5).

Corinth was a prosperous, commercial city, the capital of the province of Achaia (the southern portion of what we now call Greece), and a Roman colony. Its population was heterogeneous, including Romans, Greeks, Orientals, and Jews. The original city had been destroyed in 146 BC. New Corinth had been refounded by Julius Caesar a century later, and it had rapidly risen to eminence in the Roman world.

A major reason for Corinth's commercial prosperity lay in her propitious situation on the narrow isthmus that connected Peloponnesian Greece to the mainland, with one seaport (Cenchrea) on the east and one (Lechaeum) on the west. Cargoes and passengers could be transferred from one to the other, and smaller vessels "were hauled over- land . . . utilizing a form of railroad composed of wooden rollers."[36] In such ways the stormy seas to the south could be avoided.

Corinth's reputation for immorality was earned by the old city. The word "Corinthianize" was coined as a synonym for fornication; a "Corinthian girl" was a harlot. The temple of Aphrodite was staffed by a thousand prostitutes. "Immorality, drunkenness, dissipations were the order of the day."[37] How much of this was true of new Corinth is difficult to say, but the city certainly did not go "out of its way to redeem the past."[38] Several portions of 1 Corinthians take on pointed meaning against this backdrop.

Paul's experience at Corinth included his lodging and working with Aquila and Priscilla, a short ministry in the synagogue, an eighteen-month ministry in Justus's house, a vision assuring him of success, and the unsuccessful effort by the Jews to arraign him before Gallio. All this makes clear that there were significant numbers both of Jews and of Gentiles in the church, and the latter group included both former proselytes and those converted from outright paganism. Judging from the letter, this last group was probably in the majority. The church population no doubt reflected the mixture of Corinth itself, and that may help explain the disunity and other problems that existed there.

Paul's purposes in writing 1 Corinthians. From what has been said, one may gather the obvious fact that Paul wrote this letter to deal with the several problems he had learned about from one source or another. These can easily be gleaned from the letter itself: "This is the most business-like of all Paul's Epistles. He has a number of subjects with which he intends to deal and he sets about them in a most orderly manner."[39]

There was *serious division* in the church, and Paul wrote to rebuke the factious spirit and bring the factions together. Chapters 1–4, especially, deal with this concern in several different ways.

There was *a case of incest* in the church, and Paul wrote to require the church to discipline the offender (chap. 5).

Reflecting the divisions, probably, there were *lawsuits* between believers, and Paul wrote to shame those involved, as seen in 6:1–8.

There was *danger of sexual immorality*, reflecting, no doubt, the background discussed above, and Paul wrote to enforce moral uprightness (6:9–20).

There were *questions about marriage and divorce*, which Paul wrote to answer in chapter 7.

There was *disagreement about eating food that had been offered to idols*, and Paul wrote to give instruction about that practice (chaps. 8–10).

There were *questions and/or problems about certain matters of order in worship*, and Paul wrote to give direction about these matters, which include the women's veil (11:2–16), the observance of the Lord's supper (11:17–34), and spiritual gifts (chaps. 12–14).

There was a question, at least, and probably a *denial* (on the part of some) *of the doctrine of bodily resurrection*, and Paul wrote to teach the truth on that subject in chapter 15.

Paul also wrote to provide directions for participating in the collection he was sponsoring (16:1–4).

The theme of 1 Corinthians. As varied as the subject matter of this letter is, it would be presumptuous to attempt to state a formal theme for the whole. Even so, one of its most important themes is unity in the Christian community. This comes about because division was a basic problem in the Corinthian church. If we had more detail, we might find that this strife was at the root of quite a few of the problems just listed. Some of them, at least the lawsuits, the disorderly observance of the Lord's Supper, and the competitive spirit associated with spiritual gifts, very clearly reflected the disunity.

The outline of 1 Corinthians. This letter outlines fairly easily, with the transitions from one subject to another usually clearly marked. The greatest uncertainty is whether the last major subject (resurrection, chap. 15) or even the subjects right before that (the women's veil, 11:2–16; the Lord's Supper, 11:17–34; spiritual gifts, 12–14) were asked about in the Corinthians' letter (7:1) or were things Paul had learned about otherwise. The answer to this question will not affect our understanding of the matters nor will the way we provide for them in the outline that follows.

Introduction, 1:1–9
    A. Formal opening, 1:1–3
    B. Expression of gratitude, 1:4–9
  I. Correcting reported conditions, 1:10–6:20

A. The divisions in the church, 1:10–4:21

    1. Introduction of the subject (1:10–11)

    2. First error: dividing over human leaders (1:12–16)

    3. Second error: exalting worldly wisdom (1:17–2:13)

    4. Third error: the fleshly judgment of spiritual immaturity (3:1–4)

    5. Fourth error: misconceiving the relationship among God's ministers (3:5–4:5)

    6. Fifth error: pride (4:6–21)

B. The toleration of incest, 5:1–13

    1. The problem (vv. 1–2)

    2. Direction for discipline (vv. 3–5)

    3. The need for the purity of the church (vv. 6–8)

    4. Clarification (vv. 9–13)

C. The lawsuits in heathen courts, 6:1–9a

    1. The absurdity of the situation (vv. 1–3)

    2. The church's responsibility (vv. 4–5)

    3. The brotherly relationship that is being violated (vv. 6–9a)

D. The danger of sexual immorality, 6:9b–20

    1. General principles involved (vv. 9b–13a)

    2. The Christian's body (vv. 13b–20)

II. Answering the Corinthians' questions, 7:1–11:1

A. Concerning marriage and divorce, 7:1–40

    1. The provision of marriage (vv. 1–5)

    2. The possibility of celibacy (vv. 6–9)

    3. The prohibition of divorce (vv. 10–16)

    4. Parenthetical: contentment with one's status (vv. 17–24)

    5. Practical advice for the unmarried (vv. 25–40)

B. Concerning the eating of food offered to idols, 8:1–11:1

    1. Knowledge as the basis of liberty (8:1–6)

    2. The necessity of regulating liberty (8:7–13)

    3. Paul's example in limiting liberty for the sake of ministry to others (9:1–27)

4. The subordination of liberty to one's own spiritual welfare (10:1–13)

5. The danger of identification with evil powers (10:14–22)

6. Conclusion: practical considerations in limiting liberty (10:23–11:1)

III. Dealing with problems of order in worship, 11:2–14:40

A. The women's head-covering in public worship, 11:2–16

1. Appeal to the order of creation (vv. 3–12)

2. Appeal to propriety (v. 13)

3. Appeal to nature (vv. 14–15)

4. Appeal to church practice (v. 16)

B. The observance of the Lord's Supper, 11:17–34

1. The disorder at Corinth (vv. 17–22)

2. The meaning of the ordinance (vv. 23–26)

3. The seriousness of unworthy observance (vv. 27–32)

4. Instruction (vv. 33–34)

C. The exercise of spiritual gifts, 12:1–14:40

1. A test for spiritual activity (12:1–3)

2. The unity of the spiritual gifts (12:4–31)

3. Love as the essential ingredient in the functioning of the body (13:1–13)

4. The principle of edification: the superiority of prophecy to tongues (14:1–25)

5. Conclusion: practical directions for order in exercising gifts (14:26–40)

IV. Instructing in the doctrine of the resurrection, 15:1–58

A. The resurrection of Christ as essential to the gospel (15:1–11)

B. The essential connection between "resurrection of the dead" and the resurrection of Christ (15:12–19)

C. The fact of Christ's resurrection as guarantee of resurrection of the dead (15:20–28)

D. Practical arguments for the resurrection (15:29–34)

E. Answers to objections about the resurrection body
(15:35–44)
F. The resurrection of the body as an integral part of final
salvation (15:45–57)
G. A practical exhortation in light of the resurrection (15:58)
Conclusion, 16:1–24

Second Corinthians

As already noted, the Corinthian correspondence testifies to the
fact that the church at Corinth probably caused Paul more heartache
than any other of his churches. What in our Bibles is 2 Corinthians
was probably his fourth letter to the church.

Even so, this letter, forged in the heat of trying circumstances,
has been called the greatest preacher's book ever written. From the
furnace comes gold. Paul was forced to think deeply about his ministry and writes out of the perspective gained from the trials and the
soul-searching. In many ways 2 Corinthians is the most personal of
all his letters; it is sometimes painfully so.

The events that led to the writing of 2 Corinthians. There is more
than one theory about the circumstantial background of this letter.
The most probable one is that there was an extra visit and letter between the writing of 1 and 2 Corinthians that took place while Paul
was in Ephesus.

When Paul wrote 1 Corinthians (16:3–9), he planned to stay
longer at Ephesus, then go through Macedonia to Corinth in Achaia
and perhaps spend the winter there, and finally journey on to
Jerusalem with the collection. After Paul sent 1 Corinthians (presumably by the delegation named in 1 Cor. 16:17–18), however, he must
have got word that the situation there was worse rather than better. He concluded that it needed further attention. (This is assumed
to explain the next point.) Therefore Paul changed his previously
announced plan. He decided to go directly to Corinth, expecting
afterward to visit Macedonia (the reverse of his original plan) and
then return to Corinth, (2 Cor. 1:15–16).

Once in Corinth, however, Paul must have changed his plans

again. Instead of visiting Macedonia as previously intended, he quickly returned to Ephesus. (This visit is therefore sometimes called the short visit.) That this is what happened is indicated by several things: (1) 1:17 implies that Paul was being accused of being wishy-washy, of changing plans; (2) 1:23 explains why he has delayed a return to Corinth, but this is a third visit (as is apparent in 12:14; 13:1), not the second visit of 1:15; (3) Acts makes it clear that when Paul finally departed from Ephesus, he went (via Troas) to Macedonia and then to Corinth; (4) even 2 Corinthians confirms that Paul had visited Troas shortly before writing 2 Corinthians (cf. 1:12–13 and 7:5–6). Obviously, then, Paul did not do what 1:15–16 indicated he planned to do; he scrapped that plan, returned to Ephesus, and reinstated his original plan.

If we ask why, the answer appears to be that he was humiliated in Corinth, altogether unsuccessful in reconciling the church to himself. That is his reason for not following the plan of 1:15–16 and for delaying a third visit (1:23–2:1). It is apparent that some individual, perhaps the leader of the opposition to Paul, had personally caused him sorrow (2:5; 7:12). This rebuff explains why Paul scrapped his new plan and returned to Ephesus. It also explains why many call this the painful visit.

Back in Ephesus and heartbroken, Paul wrote a severe letter (some prefer the expression "sorrowful letter").[40] This letter is referred to in 2:3–4, 9 and 7:8–9. That the reference is not to 1 Corinthians is apparent from 2:3: "This is the very thing I wrote to you" seems to mean that he wrote what 2:1–2 has just said, but nothing like this is in 1 Corinthians. Further, 1:4 does not sound like 1 Corinthians, nor does 7:8.

Paul evidently sent the severe letter by Titus, which may be gathered from Paul's anxiety over Titus's return (1:12; 7:5–7). That this painful visit and severe letter are not mentioned in Acts is not a serious objection; Luke never tried to tell everything, and he never referred to Paul's letters. That this letter has not been preserved is also not a problem: "After reconciliation between Paul and the church, this document may have been disposed of by mutual consent."[41]

Paul left Ephesus hoping to find Titus in Troas, but he did not

(1:12–13). Therefore, even though there was opportunity for the gospel in Troas, Paul hurried on to Macedonia where he found Titus (1:13; 7:5–6). Titus was able to report that the severe letter had been effective. The Corinthians (at least most of them) had repented and were now eager for Paul's return (7:7–11). Further, they had disciplined the one who had wronged Paul, and he, too, had repented (1:5–10; 7:12). Paul was overjoyed (2:14; 7:7–9). He could now visit Corinth again, this time not in sorrow, as he had determined he would not visit them again (2:1).

In Macedonia, with his third visit to Corinth in mind, Paul believed that yet another letter was called for. As will be discussed below, there was still a minority at Corinth resisting Paul and accusing him of various weaknesses as a leader. Paul hoped that another letter would clear up even that opposition and prepare for an even smoother visit (12:14; 13:1).

Although this theory is not unanimously held, it is followed by many interpreters. It appears to explain all the references in 2 Corinthians without contradicting Acts. Some would object to its complexity, but there is no reason that the situation could not have been this complex. Those who would omit a severe letter between 1 and 2 Corinthians are forced to read 2 Corinthians 2:3–9; 7:8–9 as referring to 1 Corinthians, and that does not seem likely. Further, they must read 2:5–10 and 7:12 as referring to the discipline of the incestuous member of 1 Corinthians 5, and that is even more unlikely. The man in 2 Corinthians had certainly sinned against Paul personally.

All things considered, the theory outlined above is the best one. The following list summarizes all of Paul's (known) visits or letters to Corinth:

> —first visit to plant church on second journey
> —the lost/previous letter (1 Cor. 5:9)
> —the Corinthians' letter and delegation (1 Cor. 7:1; 16:17)
> —1 Corinthians
> —the short/painful visit, Paul's second to Corinth (2 Cor. 1:15)
> —the severe/sorrowful letter (2 Cor. 2:3–4; 7:12)

—2 Corinthians
—Paul's third visit to Corinth (2 Cor. 12:14; 13:1; Acts 20:2–3)

The date and place of the writing of 2 Corinthians. Second Corinthians was obviously written somewhere in Macedonia. Putting 2:13 and 7:5–6 together makes this clear. So does the point referred to in 8:1 and 9:2–4: Paul is in Macedonia where the collection has been successful, trying to prepare for an equally successful one in Corinth and Achaia.

As for date, putting 1 and 2 Corinthians together with Acts indicates that 2 Corinthians was probably written less than a year after 1 Corinthians. When Paul wrote 1 Corinthians, he planned to tarry in Ephesus until Pentecost in the spring of 56 (possibly 57). Then, when he left Ephesus (in Acts) after Pentecost, he spent some time in Macedonia and three months (the winter months inconducive to travel) in Achaia/Corinth. He first expected to go to Jerusalem in time for Passover, but adjustments had to be made, which delayed him until Pentecost (fifty days after Passover). Almost certainly, then, this was another Pentecost, a year later than the one in Ephesus that followed the writing of 1 Corinthians. Because 2 Corinthians was written in Macedonia before the three winter months in Corinth that preceded this second spring, Passover-Pentecost, it must have been written by the end of the same year that 1 Corinthians was written. If that is so, then 2 Corinthians was written in Macedonia in late 56 (or 57).

Paul's purposes in writing 2 Corinthians. Most of these grow out of the background described above and have already been touched on. Here, they can simply be listed.

With Titus's welcome news (7:6–7), Paul wrote *to express his great relief and joy* over the repentance of the majority of the Corinthians and their reconciliation to him.

Even so, there were still some who resisted Paul's leadership, and he wrote *to defend himself against their accusations and urge the repentance of this minority* before his arrival in Corinth. Such a defensive posture is seen in 2:17 and especially in chapters 10–13.

If we ask which of the original four parties was still resisting Paul, we will find no certain answer. Some contend that this was the Jesus party, others that it was the party of Peter. There is not much of substance to base an argument on. The most that can be said is that there was probably "a recalcitrant group" and that they were being encouraged by some "false apostles who had arrived on the scene" (11:13), who "alleged that Paul's word was not to be trusted."[42]

Paul wrote to *urge the forgiveness and restoration of the one who had wronged him*. That man had responded to the discipline of the church (2:5–10).

Paul also wrote *to exhort the Corinthians about the collection* he was sponsoring for Jerusalem. Chapters 8 and 9 are devoted entirely to this. "It may be inferred that the readers had not fulfilled their earlier promises"[43] in this regard.

The theme of 2 Corinthians. Like most of Paul's letters, this one is not organized around a single theme. Even so, it is helpful to note that one very important theme is the ministry. Paul's trials with the Corinthians evidently made him think deeply about the nature of the ministry: its victories and defeats, its motives and appeals. Especially does the section from 2:14–6:18 deal with this.

The integrity of 2 Corinthians. The student of this letter will soon learn that some interpreters with more critical leanings have decided that 2 Corinthians is not original as it now stands. Detailed treatment of such views is beyond the scope of this text, but a brief treatment may be helpful. For a more thorough treatment and evaluation, the material in Donald Guthrie's *New Testament Introduction* is recommended.[44]

Some have suggested that the section 6:14–7:1 interrupts the flow of the letter; compare 6:13 and 7:2. Further, they have identified this passage as being a fragment of the lost/previous letter referred to in 1 Corinthians 5:9, because the contents might fit (cf. 1 Cor. 5:9 and 2 Cor. 6:14). This view suffers from having to explain why an ancient editor would have inserted it in the middle of 2 Corinthians, and there is not really a close correspondence with 1 Corinthians 5:9.

More common is the view that chapters 10–13 preserve the

whole (or most) of the severe/sorrowful letter. The main argument is that the tone of these last four chapters is totally different from that of the first nine. Whereas the first portion expresses relief and joy over reconciliation, the last part has "unparalleled invective in self-defense."[45] The truth, however, is that the first portion contains hints of this defensive section to come, as in 1:17–3:1; 5:12–13. The view suggested above, that there was a reconciled majority and a rebelling minority, is a better explanation of the difference in tone, and the reference to the "majority" decision in 2:6 would appear to support this. Further, the reference to Titus in 12:18 makes best sense as linked with 2:12–13; 7:5–6. Finally, though 2:3–9 makes it clear that one thing in the severe letter was a demand that the offender against Paul be punished, chapters 10–13 contain nothing of the sort. (For lesser arguments and a thorough defense of integrity, see Guthrie.)

Recent commentaries by C. K. Barrett, Victor Paul Furnish, and Ralph Martin express the view that chapters 10–13 represent a letter written *after* the first nine chapters. According to this theory, after 2 Corinthians 1–9 had been sent, "Paul learned that Titus had misjudged and misrepresented the situation—unless indeed it had radically altered as soon as he left the city."[46] In this case chapters 10–13 would be Paul's fifth letter, following the lost letter (1 Cor. 5:9), 1 Corinthians, the severe letter, and 2 Corinthians 1–9.

A view much less widely held is that chapters 8 and 9 represent two different letters about the collection, one to Corinth (chap. 8) and the other to Achaia (chap. 9).[47]

These claims against the integrity of 2 Corinthians as it now stands are not attacks against their genuineness as Pauline. Even critical scholars are inclined to accept the genuineness of all of 2 Corinthians. But they do maintain that the letter was originally two (or three) letters. The editorial caprice involved in such theories is very unlikely. Why anyone would insert a fragment of the lost/previous letter between 6:13 and 7:2 or combine two very lengthy letters (2 Cor. 1–9 and 10–13) into one completely escapes us. Even if the ending of one and the beginning of another had in some way been lost, it is more likely that they would have been maintained as fragments. Many such fragments of ancient writings have thus been preserved. In fact, there is absolutely no manuscript evidence to support either of the two views above.

None of this is meant to deny that there are intervals, breaks, or changes of tone in 2 Corinthians or in any of the rest of Paul's letters, for that matter. But such changes are far more likely to be accounted for as reflecting interruption in dictation than by a subjective literary criticism that sees the letters as compilations of fragments (some find as many as three fragments in 1 Corinthians and five or six in 2 Corinthians). Especially for Paul's longer letters we can be almost certain that the writing would not have been at one sitting.[48]

The outline of 2 Corinthians. As personal and emotional as much of this letter is, it is more difficult to outline than the orderly 1 Corinthians. This accounts for the wide variety of outlines one will encounter in various commentaries and introductions, especially within the two longer sections (2:14–7:1; 10–13).

Introduction, 1:1–7
    A. Formal opening, 1:1–2
    B. Thanksgiving, 1:3–7
  I. Explanation of events: clarification of misunderstanding, 1:8–2:13
    A. The trouble in Asia, 1:8–11
    B. Dealings with the Corinthians, 1:12–2:13
      1. Paul's clear conscience about his ministry at Corinth (1:12–13)
      2. Defense of his change of plans (1:15–2:2)
      3. The severe letter (2:3–4)
      4. Paul's anxious search for Titus (2:12–13)
  II. The character of Christian ministry, 2:14–7:1
    A. The glory of the ministry, 2:14–4:6
      1. The triumph of the gospel (2:14–16a)
      2. The living attestation of the minister of the gospel (2:16b–3:5)
      3. The superiority of the new covenant ministry (3:6–18)

4. The confident openness of the gospel ministry (4:1–6)

B. The frailty of the minister, 4:7–5:8

1. The minister as an earthen vessel (4:7)

2. The mingling of death and life in experience (4:8–15)

3. The daily renewal of the inner man (4:16–18)

4. The expectation of a new body (5:1–8)

C. The responsibilities of the minister, 5:9–7:1

1. In light of the judgment seat, to please the Lord (5:9–10)

2. In light of the fear of God, to persuade men (5:11–13)

3. In light of Christ's love, to minister reconciliation (5:14–21)

4. As God's coworker, to plead with the Corinthians (6:1–7:1)

III. Explanation resumed: the joy of reconciliation, 7:2–16

IV. The collection for Jerusalem, 8:1–9:15

A. The example of the Macedonians (8:1–6)

B. Reasons for a generous response (8:7–15)

C. The mission of Titus in this matter (8:16–9:5)

D. More reasons for generous giving (9:6–15)

V. Paul's defense and warning, 10:1–13:10

A. Paul's response to his critics, 10:1–18

1. Concerning his boldness and weakness (vv. 1–11)

2. Concerning a standard for evaluation (vv. 12–18)

B. The question of apostleship, 11:1–12:13

1. Paul versus the false apostles (11:1–21a)

2. Evidences of Paul's apostleship (11:21b–12:13)

C. Admonition in light of Paul's impending visit, 12:14–13:10

1. Paul's self-sacrificing spirit toward the Corinthians (12:14–19)

2. Fears about the visit (12:20–21)

3. A warning about discipline (13:1–6)

4. A prayerful desire (13:7–10)

Conclusion, 13:11–14

Galatians

Galatians has often been called the Magna Carta of Christian liberty. Said to be Martin Luther's favorite book in the Scriptures, it has thus been identified as the foundation of the Protestant Reformation. In the most clear and concise manner, Galatians establishes the truth that is at the heart of the Christian gospel: that justification before God is by faith in the finished work of Christ. The works of the law cannot make a person right with God.

Galatians is often listed in the second group of Paul's letters, written during the third missionary journey. That view, however, is by no means unanimous. Galatians is the most difficult of all Paul's letters to date or place, primarily because there are no references in the letter itself to tie in with what we know of Paul's ministry.

"The Epistle to the Galatians has been placed by different critics both the earliest and the latest of St. Paul's writings, and almost every intermediate position has at one time or the other been assigned to it."[49] Two main views vie for the most influence these days. One has been stated above. The other is that Galatians was the very first of Paul's canonical letters.

But before the thorny question of date and place are dealt with, an even more basic problem must be given attention.

The destination of Galatians. This, too, is subject for debate. The problem is that Galatia (1:2) was a name that could be used either in its administrative, official sense to identify the Roman province, or in its original, ethnic sense for the region (in the northern portion of the province) settled by the Gauls.

In our study of Paul's ministry, we have seen that Paul visited Galatia on all three journeys. On the first journey, he established churches in Pisidian Antioch, Iconium, Lystra, and Derbe—all cities in south (provincial) Galatia. On both the second and third journeys Acts indicates that Paul went through Galatia: "through the Phrygian and Galatian region" (16:6), and "through the Galatian region and Phrygia" (18:23). These two references *could* mean ethnic Galatia.

The *North Galatian theory* is that the letter to the Galatians was sent to churches in ethnic Galatia in the northern part of the Roman province. According to this view, Acts 16:6 and 18:23 mean that Paul visited this Galatia on the second and third missionary journeys and established churches there in such cities as Ancyra, Pessinus, Tavium, and Juliopolis. That Luke did not describe this ministry in Acts is not a fatal objection, for there was much that Luke did not tell, as we have seen. This view dominated scholarship until the late nineteenth century.

That so able a scholar as Bishop J. B. Lightfoot held this view in his 1865 commentary on Galatians has probably added to its credibility. Lightfoot's reasons, in brief, are: (1) people used to the area would more likely use "Galatia" in the original, popular sense; (2) Luke uses other place-names in the same narrative that are ethnic-regional rather than official-provincial, like Pisidia (13:14), Lycaonia (14:6), Mysia (16:7), and Phrygia (16:6; 18:23); (3) the way Galatia and Phrygia are linked in 16:6 and 18:23 argues for using them both in the same ethnic sense; (4) Luke does not use "Galatia" in referring to Antioch, Iconium, Lystra, or Derbe.[50] The only weakness in this is that it testifies to Lukan rather than Pauline usage.

The *South Galatian theory* is that the letter was sent to the churches that were founded during the first missionary journey in the southern part of the Roman province of Galatia. W. M. Ramsay (in the 1890s) did more than anyone to establish this view. It has generally gained the ascendancy, if for no other reason than that we know about those churches from the Acts record. Everyone prefers knowledge to ignorance.

Other arguments for this view are: (1) Paul (regardless of Luke's practice) generally uses the provincial names in his letters; (2) the doctrinal problems in Galatia arose out of a Jewish background, and there is more evidence of strong Jewish populations in the southern cities than in the northern ones; (3) although we know Luke did not try to tell everything, it simply is harder to believe that Galatians was addressed to churches Acts is silent about rather than to churches Acts tells us about; (4) the references in Galatians to Barnabas (2:1, 9, 13) come across best if the readers knew him, but Barnabas was not along on the journeys when Paul might have gone into North

Galatia; (5) to use the provincial name would not have been strange: after all, Galatia had been a province since 25 BC; (6) Ramsay's historico-archaeological research made a strong case for the early spread of the gospel in Asia Minor along lines that did not include ethnic Galatia;[51] even Luke's expression (Acts 16:6; 18:23) may best be explained as Galatian Phrygia, around Iconium and Pisidian Antioch, rather than as including ethnic Galatia.[52]

These reasons fall short of proof but appear stronger overall than arguments for the North Galatian view. Even so, the actual understanding of the truth of the letter will not be affected by deciding to espouse either view or by suspending judgment. My own inclination is toward the South Galatian view.

We do well to review briefly the history of these churches, established on the first journey (Acts 13:14–14:23). Four Galatian cities were evangelized by Paul and Barnabas: Antioch of (ethnic) Pisidia (as it was called, even though it was technically in ethnic Phrygia at Pisidia's border), Iconium (also in Phrygia), and two cities in (ethnic) Lycaonia, Lystra and Derbe. (For this background, see chap. 4 of this text.)

As in nearly every church Paul founded, there were significant contingents of both Jewish and Gentile Christians. Especially in Antioch and Iconium there would have been many Jews. But as a general characteristic, Gentile converts, some from heathenism, some as former Jewish proselytes, were in the majority. Galatians itself tends to confirm this, both with its appeal to Old Testament facts that many (Jewish readers) were expected to understand (3:16; 4:22–30) and with its reference to the desire of the false teachers to circumcise Paul's (obviously Gentile) readers (5:2; 6:12, 13).

The date and place of the writing of Galatians. Some interpreters put Galatians early in Paul's correspondence, usually as the first of his letters; others put it later, usually in some association with the other capital letters, 1 and 2 Corinthians and Romans. (The problem obviously involves the one just discussed. Those who hold the North Galatian theory must put Galatians later; those who hold the South Galatian theory may put it early or later.)

The early view is that Galatians is the first of Paul's canonical letters. F. F. Bruce, for example, thinks that Paul wrote Galatians (to
South Galatia, necessarily) from Syrian Antioch during the interval
between the first and second missionary journeys and just prior to the
Jerusalem Council.[53] This would put the letter at about AD 46/47.

This view depends on identifying the Jerusalem visit of Galatians
2:1–10 not with the Jerusalem Council of Acts 15 but with the
visit for famine relief of Acts 11:27–30. Bruce emphasizes that in
its argument against Judaizers, Galatians makes no reference to the
Apostolic Decrees, the Council's decision that Gentiles need not observe Mosaic ceremony, which is understandable if such a Council
had not transpired yet.[54] Further, this would explain Peter's misguided
action at Antioch (Gal. 2:11–14), which might be hard to conceive if
it came after he so staunchly defended Gentile liberty at the Council
(Acts 15:7–11).

Here is what happened, according to this view. Paul and
Barnabas returned to Antioch after the first missionary journey for
the "long time" of Acts 14:28. During that time, Judaizing believers
from Jerusalem came there and proceeded to correct what to them
was Paul's inadequate teaching about the place of Gentile believers in
the faith (Acts 15:1). They would naturally learn about the mission
churches Paul and Barnabas had established in the South Galatian
cities, and some of them would zealously strike out for those places,
too, intent to correct Pauline teaching everywhere they could. Soon,
by some disturbed Galatian believer perhaps, Paul learned what was
up in the Galatian churches and wrote them this letter. Following
that, the turmoil at Antioch led to the decision (Acts 15:2) to go to
Jerusalem for (what we have come to call) the Council. There is no
obvious reason this outline will not work.

Among varieties of the early view we can consider Herman
Ridderbos, who follows Theodore Zahn. He puts the writing of
Galatians at Corinth on the second missionary journey, probably
just before 1 Thessalonians in 50.[55] Like Bruce, he prefers the South
Galatians destination, but he identifies Galatians 2:1–10 with the

Jerusalem Council of Acts 15. This view, though it still puts Galatians first among Paul's letters, is really a middle view, taking much the same approach as many who hold the later view.

The later view is that Paul wrote Galatians sometime after he had been there early in the third missionary journey and during the same period as the letters to Corinth and Rome. The letter could then have been written as early as Ephesus or as late as Corinth on the third journey, depending on just where it fits into the order of 1 Corinthians, 2 Corinthians, and Romans.

Probably the single most important consideration favoring the later view is the affinity between Galatians and Romans and, to a lesser degree, 2 Corinthians. Lightfoot stressed this heavily, citing such things as their common emphasis on justification by faith, along with the quotation of Habakkuk 2:4 (Gal. 3:11; Rom. 1:17), the appeal to Abraham and Genesis 15:6 (Gal. 3:6; Rom. 4:3), and various other parallels (Gal. 4:5–7; Rom. 8:15–17, for example).[56]

The affinity argument is somewhat precarious. Not that it means nothing. The affinity between Colossians and Ephesians, for example, is such that it almost guarantees they were written back to back; likewise for 1 Timothy and Titus. And there is affinity between Galatians and Romans. Furthermore, if Galatians were written shortly before the Thessalonian epistles, one could compare them and find very little to compare. Even so, there is no reason a man cannot write two works with great affinity at entirely different times: "It is hazardous to plot the development of Paul's thought on the basis of occasional letters each of which dealt with a situation as it arose."[57]

There are a few other considerations that can be used to support the later date. For one, Barnabas is not named with Paul in the salutation of Galatians (1:1), even though according to the early view, he was with Paul in Antioch at the time the letter was written and had been co-founder of the churches there. In comparison with the other letters, that is an unusual omission.

Another consideration is that the construction of events required by Bruce's view above strikes one as somewhat improbable. The Judaizers would have to visit Antioch, learn of the new churches in

South Galatia, and go there against Paul's wishes. News would have to get back to Paul of the danger that their false teaching threatened to supplant the gospel there, then Paul would write the Galatians. Only after all that would the tension over the Judaizers' views at Antioch be critical enough to precipitate the decision to go to Jerusalem about the problem. It is especially difficult to picture the church at Antioch waiting this long after the Judaizers first arrived there.

Such arguments do not constitute proof on either side. We are left without an absolutely certain solution. But uncertainty can be lived with. The inclination here is to say that the South Galatian destination and the later date have the best of the arguments but to say that without dogmatism.

Whether to choose Ephesus, Macedonia, or Corinth—all visited by Paul in the last months of the third journey—as the place of composition is almost a matter of tossing a coin. Inasmuch as 2 Corinthians was written from Macedonia, and Romans in Corinth soon afterward, we can put Galatians between them (if there is affinity advantage in doing so). Otherwise there is nothing to commend one place over the other; there are no hints in the letter itself. In the final analysis, the best thing may be to admit that it is convenient to treat Galatians as written on Paul's third journey between 2 Corinthians and Romans, probably in Macedonia in late 56 (or 57).

The problem in Galatia and Paul's purposes in writing. Reading the letter will confirm that there was one basic problem disturbing the churches in Galatia, the teaching of Judaizers. That problem threatened the peace and spiritual welfare of the Christians in these churches on two fronts: (1) Paul's *gospel of justification by faith* was threatened by teaching that Christians, Gentile or Jew, must keep Moses's law; (2) Paul's *personal authority as an apostle* was attacked, a tactic necessary to support correction of his teaching.

Our study of Acts has prepared us to understand the rise of this Judaizing doctrine, and a review of the background of the Jerusalem Council (chap. 4) will refresh one's memory (whether Gal. 2:1–10 equals Acts 15 or not). In brief, some of the early Jewish Christians thought, understandably, that their messianic faith was merely

Judaism perfected. It followed that any Gentile converts must become Jews, just like the proselytes they already practiced making. That meant they would have to submit to circumcision and keep the law of Moses for right standing with God.

As logical as this was, it was wrong. But the Judaizers were insistent and zealous, true to the Pharisaic background of their outlook (Acts 15:5). They were sure they must go abroad, wherever churches were being established, and convince Gentile believers of their position. As they saw it, theirs must become the practice of the church. Thus did such Judaizing teachers invade Paul's churches in Galatia and evidently with considerable success (Gal. 1:6; 3:1; 4:19–20; 5:7).

It seems hard to think that this would have gone on after the Jerusalem Council had settled the issue and after Paul and Silas on the second journey had delivered to the Galatian churches copies of the results of that Council (Acts 16:4). That is, no doubt, the strongest consideration toward dating Galatians before the Jerusalem Council. But as Ridderbos puts it, "Heresy has never been abruptly and suddenly subjugated by the pronouncements of the church. In his later letters, too, *e.g.*, in the one to the Philippians, Paul has to take up the cudgels against Judaism."[58] Entirely apart from Galatians, it is abundantly clear that the Judaizing position was not put to rest by the Jerusalem Council.

Paul represented the chief obstacle to the success of the Judaizers. As the leader of the mission to the Gentiles, his voice carried great weight. And he was as relentless in opposing the Judaizers (Gal. 2:5) as they were in pushing their teaching. In order to prevail, they would have to destroy his influence. Therefore they attacked him at his Achilles' heel. Because he was not one of the twelve, it was very easy to say that his authority was not apostolic, that whatever he knew he got secondhanded and got it garbled at that. Galatians is clear that the Judaizers said just such things.

This understanding of the problem in Galatia leads directly to a statement of Paul's purposes in the letter.

Paul wrote to defend his place and authority as a genuine apostle of Jesus Christ (chaps. 1, 2 primarily), which included establishing that his commission and gospel came directly from Jesus (1:11–24) and that his gospel had been vindicated before the other apostles (2:1–14).

Paul wrote to correct the error of the Judaizers and prove the truth of the gospel he preached (chaps. 3, 4 primarily). This included demonstrating that justification is by faith and not by the law.

Paul wrote to teach about the Spirit-controlled life that accompanies justification by faith (chaps. 5, 6 primarily). This purpose may reflect that his detractors said his doctrine of grace led to licentiousness (cf. Rom. 3:8; 6:1), but Paul would have been careful to teach the opposite truth anyway.

The theme of Galatians. This letter is one that lends itself to statement of a theme—*justification by faith: the life and liberty of a believer in Christ apart from the yoke of the Mosaic law.* This theme dominates the entire letter, and this statement of it brings together both the positive and the negative, both the initial justification and the ongoing life of a Christian as controlled by faith in the finished work of Jesus Christ.

The outline of Galatians. Galatians is not as easy to outline as some of Paul's letters, which explains why the outlines in various commentaries are so different. Even so, the main ideas are clear. As Bruce says about his own outline: "This analysis . . . may help the reader . . . appreciate the flow of Paul's argument; it is not claimed that it corresponds to Paul's conscious strategy in constructing his argument."[59]

Formal opening, 1:1–5

I. Personal defense: the authority of Paul and the gospel he preached, 1:6–2:21

    A. The exclusiveness of Paul's gospel, 1:6–10

    B. The revelation of the gospel to Paul and his divine commission, 1:11–24

        1. Paul's claim: the source of his gospel (vv. 11–12)

        2. Evidence of Paul's claim: his independence of the other apostles (vv. 13–24)

    C. The vindication of Paul's gospel and apostleship, 2:1–21

1. Conference in Jerusalem (vv. 1–10)

2. Peter's inconsistency in Antioch (vv. 11–14)

3. Transitional: the issue at stake (vv. 15–21)

II. Doctrinal argument: righteousness by faith instead of by the law, 3:1–4:31

   A. The Galatians' experience of faith, 3:1–5

   B. The Abrahamic covenant of faith, 3:6–18

     1. Abraham was justified by faith (v. 6)

     2. Abraham's children are that by faith (v. 7)

     3. The Abrahamic covenant is based on faith (vv. 8–9)

     4. Those under the law are under a curse, not the covenant (vv. 10–12)

     5. The Abrahamic covenant is established by Christ's death (vv. 13–18)

   C. The true purpose of the Mosaic law, 3:19–25

     1. It was given "because of transgressions" (vv. 19–20)

     2. It did not supplant God's promises as a means of life (vv. 21–22)

     3. It served as a tutor to bring us to Christ (vv. 23–25)

   D. The standing of believers, 3:25–4:7

     1. The standing of sons (3:26–29)

     2. The difference in this standing (4:1–7)

   E. Appeal to the Galatians, 4:8–20

     1. What is at risk (vv. 8–11)

     2. The personal relationship Paul has had with them (vv. 12–16)

     3. The misguided zeal of the Judaizers (vv. 17–20)

   F. The allegory of Isaac and Ishmael, 4:21–31

III. Practical application: life and liberty in the Holy Spirit, 5:1–6:10

   A. A call to liberty, 5:1–15

     1. Urgent appeal (v. 1)

     2. Warning about the serious things at stake (vv. 2–6)

     3. Denunciation of the troublemakers (vv. 7–12)

     4. Caution: the abridgement of liberty (vv. 13–15)

B. Walking after the Spirit, 5:16–26

1. Not fulfilling the lusts of the flesh (vv. 16–17)

2. Not under the law (v. 18)

3. Yielding the Spirit's fruit rather than the flesh's works (vv. 19–23)

4. Walking as crucified and risen (vv. 24–26)

C. Relationships with fellow believers, 6:1–10

1. Restoring the brother who sins (v. 1)

2. Bearing one another's burdens (vv. 2–5)

3. Supporting the ministry of teachers (v. 6)

4. Doing good (vv. 7–10)

Conclusion, 6:11–18

Romans

Romans is often said to be the greatest of Paul's letters, if not the greatest book of the Bible. Though it may be inappropriate to speak of one part of God's Word as greater than another, there is no denying the great influence of Romans. W. H. Griffith Thomas reports that Chrysostom had Romans read to him every week, that Luther called it the chief book of the New Testament, that Melanchthon copied it twice by hand just to get more thoroughly acquainted with it, and that Coleridge said it was the most profound book in existence.[60] Frederic Godet said: "O St. Paul, had thy one work been to compose an Epistle to the Romans, that alone should have rendered thee dear to every sound reason."[61]

Of all Paul's letters Romans is more like a formal epistle than any other. In some ways it is like an organized doctrinal essay. Bruce says it "deserves to be called 'The Gospel according to Paul.'"[62] Even so, it is still a very real letter, written on a specific occasion to meet the needs of a particular group of people.

The date and place of the writing of Romans. If we assume the unity of Romans as it now stands (a matter to be discussed below), then 15:25–26 helps pinpoint the time of its composition. Paul was about to go to Jerusalem (v. 25) and planned to take along contributions from believers in Macedonia and Achaia (v. 26). This clearly refers to the famous collection that Paul sponsored during his third journey; it thus dates Romans as having been written at about the time the collection was gathered, just before Paul's departure with it to Jerusalem.

We have noted references to that collection in both letters to the Corinthians. First Corinthians 16:1–4 first urged the Corinthians to give. Then 1 Corinthians 8–9 made a final appeal. Here in Romans 15:26, however, Paul indicates that Achaia (the province where Corinth was) had finished the gathering. Therefore Romans must have been written after 2 Corinthians and after Paul's actual arrival in Corinth on the final portion of the third journey.

Add to this Romans 16:1 (Paul commends to the Romans a woman named Phoebe from Cenchrea, a suburb of Corinth; she was apparently carrying the letter) and there is no good reason to doubt that Romans was written during Paul's final visit to Corinth on the third journey, as he prepared to take the collection to Jerusalem. That would date the letter in about AD 56 (or 57).[63]

There are lesser points of confirmation. In 16:23 Paul mentions Gaius as host to himself and to the church; Paul had baptized a Gaius at Corinth (1 Cor. 1:14). In Acts 20:4 we learn that one Sopater was among those who accompanied Paul from Corinth through Macedonia at this time with the collection; in Romans 16:23 greetings are sent from Sosipater, a longer form of the name. In Romans 15:30–31 Paul was aware that he might have to face difficulty in Jerusalem; in Acts 20:22–23 he said he was compelled to go even though there were revelations in every city that bonds and afflictions awaited him there. Further, Romans 16:23 mentions a city treasurer, Erastus; a marble paving-block discovered in Corinth in 1929 but dating to the first century has that as the name of a city official. But because the office is not the same, we cannot be absolutely sure the men were the same.

Acts 20:3 indicates that Paul spent three months in Greece, probably mostly in Corinth, on this occasion. That would be plenty of time to provide for the dictation (Rom. 16:22) of Romans. The whole attitude matches: Paul felt his work in the eastern provinces was done; now, after a visit to Jerusalem, he proposes to visit Rome and then Spain (Rom. 15:18–32).

The destination of Romans. There is no doubt that the letter was intended for the Christians in Rome; 1:7 makes this clear and 1:13 and 15:23–24 tend to confirm it. There is, in fact, nothing against this destination with the possible exception of the lengthy list of greetings in 16:3–15. Some have argued that Paul would not have known so many at Rome (he had never been there) and that some of those named, at least Aquila and Priscilla (vv. 3–5), would more likely be some place other than Rome. This will be discussed further below, but even most who raise this objection still agree that the body of the letter was sent to Rome.

The question, however, is how the Roman church got started and how Paul could feel at liberty to write them, for he had not been there. In the first place, it is reasonably clear that Peter did not found the church. Peter may well have been in Rome later, and the tradition is that both Paul and Peter were executed there during the later stages of the Neronian persecution sometime after AD 64. But there is no reason to think he had been there by the time Paul wrote Romans. In Romans 15:14–24 Paul discusses his sense of freedom to write the letter; among other things he says he did not build on others' foundation (v. 20). It would have been totally out of order for Paul to write such a letter to one of Peter's churches.

A second point to consider about the origin of Christianity in Rome may be found in Acts 2:10. Among the listeners at Pentecost were visitors in Jerusalem from Rome, Jews and proselytes. It is certainly possible that some of these were converted and returned to Rome as Christian Judaists. Whether they established a church, however, we cannot say for sure; it is just as easy to picture them trying to maintain synagogue fellowship or even, as Barrett considers, having a synagogue of their own.[64] In chapter 5 of this text we have taken note that Aquila and Priscilla (with whom Paul made tents in Corinth) were among Jews expelled from Rome by Claudius in AD 49. The historian Suetonius said the reason was rioting among the Jews instigated by (or over) one "Chrestus." If this is a reference to

Christ, that would indicate that belief in Him was creating problems among Jews by that time; we cannot be sure. Even so, there is at least the possibility that Aquila and Priscilla were already believers in Rome before they moved to Corinth.

The third consideration is probably the most important one. In view of the lengthy list of greetings in Romans 16, it is clear that Paul personally knew many people there. It is apparent that a significant part of the church in Rome was made up of converts and acquaintances of Paul who had relocated there. Even Aquila and Priscilla are mentioned (vv. 3–5); they had evidently returned to Rome and a church was meeting in their house. Considering how closely this couple identified themselves with Paul, they may have returned there, at least in part, to help with the work of the church there.

The conclusion that all this suggests is that Paul's own converts and coworkers had played a large role in the Christian community at Rome. That fact would explain fully the freedom he felt to write them as though they were part of his responsibility. Nor is any of this at all unlikely. The world of Paul's time was mobile, and the capital city attracted many. Besides, some may have gone at Paul's encouragement, looking ahead to his own planned visit.

Beyond this there is not much that can be said. It is possible that Romans 16:14–15 refers to house churches other than the one that met with Aquila and Priscilla, but we cannot be sure. Some commentators debate whether the congregation was primarily Jewish or Gentile. However, in view of the identifications in chapter 16 and of the contents of the letter, we should say that there were both. Romans 1:5–6, 13; 6:19; 11:13; 15:15–16, and other statements make clear that there was significant Gentile participation in the church. The space devoted to Jewish concerns (especially chaps. 2 and 9–11) also seems to show that there were Jewish believers involved. C. E. B. Cranfield is confident that "both . . . elements were considerable."[65] If one group or the other was in the majority, it is more likely that the Gentile group was (15:15–16), but one cannot be dogmatic. The Roman church may not have fit the pattern of most of Paul's churches.

Paul's purposes in writing Romans. In view of the unique background of this letter, we do not need a separate discussion of events that led up to its writing. There was no special history of happenings, so far as we know, that occasioned Romans.

What we do know is that Paul, in Corinth on the third journey, felt that he had accomplished what he had set out to do in that part of the empire (15:19, 23). Now, at last, he could lay plans to reach further west, to Rome, where he had wanted to go for a long time, and even to Spain (15:22–24; cf. 1:13). First, however, he must go to Jerusalem with the collection (15:25–32).

Paul wrote *to prepare the way for his planned visit.* The sections 1:10–13 and 15:20–32 make this clear. Paul wanted the Roman Christians to know about his plans. This probably included a purpose "to create interest in his Spanish mission"[66] (15:24). That he was unknown to many of the believers in Rome might have played a small role in the character of the letter; Paul would want the church there to have a good grasp of his teachings about salvation. Ernst Kasemann may take this too far, however, in suggesting that Paul feared "the mistrust and the suspicions of both his person and his work . . . circulating in Rome."[67]

Paul wrote *to meet the needs of the Roman church for a thorough grounding in the basic doctrines of the faith.* This statement of purpose reflects what Romans is. Some interpreters see this as unrelated to any needs in Rome, but that conclusion is exaggerated. The beginning and the ending are as personal and situational as the rest of Paul's writings; Romans was a letter, too.

It is not difficult to conceive that the Christian community in Rome needed the very teaching that Romans gives. As suggested above, there were different lines of influence that had brought Christ to Rome. They had been without apostolic presence. Because Romans spends so much time dealing with Judaistic perspectives, we gather that there was especially a need to set the principle of righteousness by faith for Jew or Gentile over against a narrow Jewish outlook.

Paul wrote *to commend Phoebe to the Roman believers* (16:1–2). This Christian woman was probably going to Rome on business. She may also have carried the letter.

The theme of Romans. Most interpreters, although they may use different words, will agree about the emphasis of Romans. Many select some phrase from the letter itself, like "the gospel" (1:1,9, 16, etc.) or "the righteousness of God" (1:17; 3:5, 21–22).

There is no doubt that *righteous(ness)* and related words play a significant role in Romans. *Justification* and *justify* are the same root. A quick reading of Romans will show how often these words appear. There is an ongoing contrast between the righteousness gained by faith and that which is attempted by works, between the narrow Jewish understanding of God's provision of righteousness and the gospel that He has provided for all. We may say, then, that the theme of Romans is *the righteousness that God provides and recognizes: it is for all by faith and not by works or for the Jews alone.*

In all of this the similarity with Galatians will not be missed. "The arguments which are pressed on the churches of Galatia in an urgent and *ad hoc* fashion are expounded more systematically in Romans, Galatians being related to Romans 'as the rough model to the finished statue.'"[68]

The textual integrity of Romans. As Barrett says, "That . . . Romans was written by the apostle Paul is a proposition which is unnecessary to discuss because it is not in dispute."[69] Still, the serious student of Romans will soon encounter the critical view that parts of Romans, especially chapter 16, were not originally in the letter.

The purpose of this book does not include detailed treatment of views that question the integrity or authenticity of any part of the Scriptures. Even so, a brief explanation of the problem is in order. For a more thorough treatment, Guthrie's discussion is recommended.[70]

The reasons questions are raised relate almost entirely to chapter 16 and the ending of the letter.

Some think it very unlikely that Paul would have known so many people in Rome, where he had never been, as are greeted in 16:3–15. Further, Aquila and Priscilla are included, but they were at Ephesus (not Rome) the last we knew (Acts 18:18, 19, 26), shortly before Romans was written; and they were at Ephesus again later, when Paul wrote Timothy at Ephesus (2 Tim. 4:19).

The suggestion has been made, therefore, that chapter 16 (at least most of it) may have originally been sent to Ephesus, perhaps as a whole letter of introduction of Phoebe or even as part of a longer letter (our Ephesians?), and later got mistakenly attached to the end of Romans. Romans 15:33 could be the conclusion of original Romans.

In fact, there is nothing unlikely about Paul's knowing so many people at Rome.[71] Indeed, the long list of names could turn out to argue that Paul had not been there, inasmuch as he never greeted such a list in writing to churches were he *had* been. "But in a church like Rome, where he was not personally known, it would serve as a useful commendation that so many of the Christians there were his former acquaintances."[72] Further, of the twenty-two persons named in verses 6–15, not one can be shown to have been at Ephesus; while (1) Urbanus, Rufus, Ampliatus, Julia, and Junia are specifically Roman names, and (2) besides the first four of these names, ten others, Stachys, Apelles, Tryphosa, Hermes, Hermas, Patrobas (or Patrobius), Philologus, Julia, Nereus are found in the sepulchral inscriptions on the Appian Way as the names of persons connected with "Caesar's household" (Phil. 4:22), and contemporary with Paul.[73]

As for Aquila and Priscilla, there is nothing against their having returned to Rome, for that is where they had lived earlier. In addition to their business and the changing situation in Rome, there is also the fact that they made themselves helpers of Paul in establishing churches. The picture we have is simply that in AD 49 they were expelled with all Jews from Rome and relocated in Corinth; in about 51 they relocated in Ephesus, helping Paul; by about 56, when Romans was written, they were back in Rome hosting a church there (Claudius died in 54, and his edict would have lapsed at least by then); then in about 66, when 2 Timothy was written during the Neronian persecution they were again in Ephesus in Asia. (Aquila was born in Pontus in Asia Minor; Acts 18:2).

The other reason questions are raised about the ending of Romans is a textual one. There are some manuscript variations relating to the concluding doxology (16:25–27) and the repeated benediction (16:20b, 24). Although the weightier manuscripts have the doxology at the end of chapter 16, the actual majority have it at the end of chapter 14; a few have it both places, and one has it after chapter 15. The benediction appears in some at the end of verse 20, in others, as verse 24, and in some at both places. Beyond this, there is some reason to think that a short version of Romans (without chapters 15–16) did circulate at one time in early Christian history, which might explain how so many manuscripts came to have the doxology at the end of chapter 14.

These details need not occupy us any further here. All sorts of theories have been proposed to explain these phenomena. After all things are considered, there is finally no persuasive reason for abandoning the view that Romans was written as it now stands. And there are good reasons for maintaining this view: (1) the introductory section (1:8–13) fits perfectly with 15:14–32; (2) 14:1–23 is not complete without 15:1–7; (3) there are no existing manuscripts to represent the so-called shorter recension; and (4) there is nothing improbable, as noted above, about the contents of chapter 16.

The outline of Romans. Considering the nature of the letter, we are a little more justified in using a doctrinal outline. Regardless of the wording used, there is fairly wide agreement among many interpreters about the major subject division of Romans.

Introduction, 1:1–15
    A. Formal opening, 1:1–7
    B. Paul's interest in Rome, 1:8–15
    C. The theme: the righteousness of God, 1:16–17
  I. The need of mankind for righteousness before God, 1:18–3:20
    A. The need of the world in general, especially the Gentiles, 1:18–32
      1. Mankind under the wrath of God (v. 18a)
      2. Man's inexcusable blameworthiness (vv. 18b–23)
      3. The evidence of God's judgment (vv. 24–32)
    B. The fact that the Jews are not exceptions, 2:1–3:8
      1. The impartial judgment of God (2:1–16)

    2. The failure of the Jews under the law (2:17–29)

    3. Answering Jewish objections (3:1–8)

  C. Conclusion: the sinfulness and guilt of all, 3:9–20

    1. A universal charge (v. 9)

    2. Scriptural proof (vv. 10–18)

    3. The clinching proof (vv. 19–20)

II. The provision of God for man's righteousness, 3:21–4:25

  A. The divine method of justification, 3:21–31

  B. Illustration: the case of Abraham, 4:1–25

    1. Abraham was not justified by works (vv. 1–8)

    2. Abraham was justified before he was circumcised (vv. 9–12)

    3. The Abrahamic promises were not based on the law but on faith (vv. 13–22)

    4. The application of the illustration to us (vv. 23–25)

III. The Christian experience of righteousness with God, 5:1–8:39

  A. The immediate results of justification, 5:1–21

    1. The present effects of God's justification of us (vv. 1–11)

    2. Contrast between these effects and those of Adam's fall (vv. 12–21)

  B. The believer's new relationship to sin, 6:1–23

    1. Dead to sin: the meaning of baptism (vv. 1–11)

    2. Free from the dominion of sin: the analogy of servitude (vv. 12–23)

  C. The believer's new relationship to the law, 7:1–25

    1. Dead to it: the analogy of the marriage bond (vv. 1–6)

    2. Appreciating the ministry of the law (vv. 7–25)

  D. The believer's new life in the Holy Spirit, 8:1–39

    1. The effects of the indwelling Spirit (vv. 1–27)

    2. Our assurance in the purpose of God (vv. 28–39)

IV. The righteousness of God and the standing of the Jews, 9:1–11:36

  A. Israel's rejection and the righteousness of God, 9:1–33

    1. Opening lament for Israel's condition (vv. 1–5)

2. The consideration that election was never by fleshly descent (vv. 6–13)

3. The consideration that election is a sovereign act of God (vv. 14–24)

4. The consideration that God had warned Israel by the prophets (vv. 25–29)

5. The consideration that Israel rejected righteousness by faith (vv. 30–33)

B. Israel's rejection as her failure to heed the gospel, 10:1–21

1. Israel's misguided zeal (vv. 1–5)

2. The nearness of the salvation Israel has missed (vv. 6–13)

3. The worldwide gospel that Israel has rejected (vv. 14–21)

C. Israel's rejection and the purposes and promises of God, 11:1–36

1. The consideration that not all Israelites are rejected (vv. 1–10)

2. The consideration that God purposed to provide for Gentile salvation (vv. 11–24)

3. The consideration that all Israel will yet be saved (vv. 25–32)

V. The practice of righteousness in the believer's life, 12:1–15:13

A. The Christian's service, 12:1–21

1. A call for consecration (vv. 1, 2)

2. A basis for service (vv. 3–8)

3. Responsibilities toward others (vv. 9–21)

B. The Christian's obligations, 13:1–14

1. Obligation to civil authorities (vv. 1–7)

2. The debt of love (vv. 8–10)

3. Responsibility to live as sons of light (vv. 11–14)

C. The limitations of liberty, 14:1–15:13

Conclusion, 15:14–16:27

A. Paul's motives and plans, 15:14–33

B. Messages and greetings, 16:1–24

C. Doxology, 16:25–27

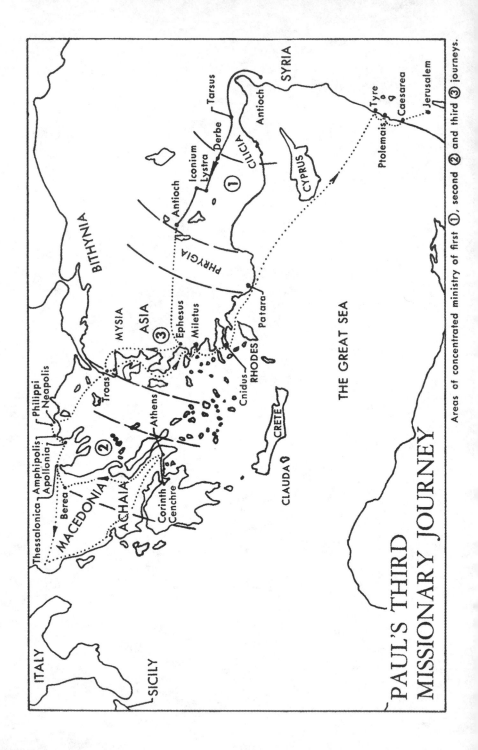

PAUL'S THIRD
MISSIONARY JOURNEY

Areas of concentrated ministry of first ①, second ② and third ③ journeys.

7

Paul the Prisoner

Acts 21:18–28:31

When Paul arrived in Jerusalem at the end of the third journey (Acts 21:17) near Pentecost in about AD 57, he did so with some apprehension, expressed in Romans 15:30–31. He also desired that the offering he was bringing (called a "service" both in Rom. 15:31 and in 2 Cor. 8–9) would be acceptable to the Jewish believers there, hoping perhaps that it would serve to bring closer together the Gentile and Jewish wings of the church. He may even have thought of this visit as one more attempt to reach his own nation. (See Rom. 9·1–3 and 10:1, written only weeks before.) As the rest of Acts shows, this visit to Jerusalem would be Paul's last, and his worst fears would be realized.

PAUL'S CHRISTIAN LIFE AND MINISTRY, PART IV

1. AD 57/58 final visit and arrest in Jerusalem, Acts 21:18–23:11
2. 57/58–59/60 imprisonment in Caesarea, Acts 23:12–26:32
3. 60 journey (as a prisoner) to Rome, Acts 27:1–28:16
4. 61–62/63 witness (as a prisoner) in Rome, Acts 28:17–31

As before, the Scripture text should be read carefully as each of these is examined.

JERUSALEM AT THE TIME
OF PAUL'S ARREST (C. AD 58)

The story of Paul interacts with the situation of the Jews in Jerusalem after the middle of the first century. Therefore, a survey of some of the main factors that have bearing on Paul's experiences should be helpful in understanding Acts 21:18–23:11.

POLITICAL POWER IN JUDEA

At the time of Paul's last visit to Jerusalem, Judea was under Roman procurators, administered as an imperial province (see chap. 2). The procurator was Felix, to be followed by Festus. Both of them sat in judgment on Paul at Caesarea, the official seat of government. "On particular occasions, especially during the main Jewish festivals . . . the Roman governor went up to the city and resided in Herod's former palace."[1]

The Jews, however, had an internal government that the Roman authorities gave as much latitude as possible (as in other areas of the empire). Although the procurator exercised supreme judicial authority, "the ordinary administration of the law, both in criminal and civil matters, was left to the native and local courts."[2] In the case of Judea this means local sanhedrins in various communities and, especially, the Great Sanhedrin in Jerusalem, "the forum for every judicial decision and every administrative measure which could either not be dealt with by the lesser local courts or was reserved to the Roman governor himself."[3]

Still, "the Roman authorities could at any time take the initiative themselves and proceed independently,"[4] especially when political disorder threatened. That explains why Lysias tried first to get the Sanhedrin to handle the case of Paul; failing that, he sent him to procurator Felix in Caesarea.

That Paul was a Roman citizen contributed; Romans were considered answerable to the *Roman* law rather than to local courts.

TROOPS IN JERUSALEM

Though there were regular legions in Syria, there were only auxiliary troops in Judea, as in other provinces administered by procurators (see chap. 1). Such troops were generally recruited in the provinces; in Judea that meant non-Jews, inasmuch as Jews were exempt "to avoid conflict with their observation of Jewish festivals and the sabbath regulations."[5]

The troops served under the command of the procurator. In Judea at the time, there were apparently five cohorts of infantry plus a unit of cavalry. Most of these were garrisoned in Caesarea, with small contingents in other cities and towns. A full cohort was maintained in Jerusalem, quartered in the fortress/citadel of Antonia, which lay just north of the Temple with easy access to the outer court of the Temple by two flights of steps. "The direct connection between citadel and Temple court was of importance, for the latter had to be under constant surveillance. At the high festivals, guards were posted in the arcades surrounding the Temple-courts."[6] These were the troops under Claudius Lysias.

RELIGION AND THE TEMPLE

In Palestine, as generally throughout the empire, the Romans were tolerant of the Jewish religion, usually respecting Jewish scruples. During the period AD 6–41, the procurators (prefects) controlled the appointment of the high priest, but from AD 44–66 this was done by the Herods (see chap. 2). In most cases Jewish objection to anything even suggesting human or animal veneration was observed, so that the "Roman troops dispensed with their standards, which bore the emperor's image, when entering Jerusalem,"[7] and the copper coins minted in Palestine carried no human image (even though the circulation in Judea of the Roman coins minted elsewhere that did carry Caesar's image could not be avoided). The Romans generally left the Temple and its ceremony alone and did not require emperor worship, apparently, "satisfied with a sacrifice offered by the Jews twice daily in the Temple 'for Caesar and the Roman nation.'"[8]

There were occasional exceptions. Caligula made a foolish and finally aborted effort to have an image of himself erected in the Temple. On another occasion Pilate had the troops enter Jerusalem with their standards but had to back down.

The Temple that Paul was seized in, Herod's Temple, was begun in 20/19 BC and not fully completed until a half-dozen years after Paul's arrest. On the Temple mount, it was beautiful and lavish. A series of paved courts led to the sanctuary proper. First was the outer Court of the Gentiles (with access from the citadel, as noted above), a terrace separated from the rest by stone latticework with tablets that warned Gentiles to proceed no further on pain of death—a prohibition the Romans upheld. Then came the Court of the Women, the Court of the Israelites, the Court of the Priests (including the altar of burnt offering), the Porch leading to the Sanctuary (the Holy Place), and finally the Holy of Holies (empty in New Testament times).[9] The scene in Acts 21 involves Paul first in the place of sacrifice where he was seized and dragged out to the Court of the Gentiles; there he was rescued and arrested by Lysias.

THE POLITICAL CLIMATE AT THE TIME

The tense climate in Jerusalem at the time may have contributed to Paul's predicament, whether at the hands of the Jews or of the procurators. During the last procurators (AD 44–66) the relationship between the Romans and the Jews deteriorated. Under Cumanus (48–52) there was a

series of outbreaks, beginning with an insulting indecency
done by a soldier on guard at the Temple during Passover.
In the riot that followed, the troops routed the crowd, and
some 20,000 lost their lives in the stampede.[10] Another
incident involved a band of Jews, led by two Zealots, who
invaded Samaria on a mission of revenge. The matter culminated in the deaths of the rebels but also in Cumanus's exile
by emperor Claudius.

Cumanus was followed in office by Felix (AD 52–60)
before whom Paul appeared. "Under Felix rebellion became
permanent."[11] In private life and in public life, "He believed
he could commit all kinds of enormities with impunity."[12]
Hostility toward Rome increased in Judea. The Zealots increased in favor with the people. As part of the Zealots' pro-
motion of rebellion against Rome, the *sicarii* (from the Latin
sicae, "short daggers") arose as political assassins. One of their
victims was the High Priest Jonathan. (The Egyptian mentioned in Acts 21:38 was a fanatical Zealot.)

Patriotism rose in Jewish Palestine. The taxation, though
not really the problem, was an oppressive sign of subjection.
Taxation in the provinces was controlled by census, involving two kinds of direct taxes: one on agricultural produce,
the other a poll-tax that included a property assessment as
well as a per capita head tax. There were also various kinds
of customs/duties, especially those imposed on the movement of goods in trade. These latter were collected by the
publicans (tax-farmers) to whom were leased the revenues of
a particular district for a fixed sum. Excess collections went
into their pockets, but short-fall came from there too. The
collection of the taxes proper was the direct responsibility
of the procurator, who apparently made use of the Jewish
authorities for this purpose.[13]

Oppressive taxation or not, the policies of Felix succeeded in "alienating a great part of the nation; from this

time on, the preaching of resistance against Rome continued incessantly and the agitation to take up arms never stopped until that objective was reached."[14] That finally culminated in the revolt that was ended by the crushing of the Jews in AD 70.

Jerusalem and Judea were in ferment, then, when Paul arrived in about AD 58. On the one hand, the tide of Jewish patriotism made his Gentile associations (Acts 21:28; 22:21) all the more sensitive. On Lysias's part, even the very hints of disorder were dealt with quickly (Acts 21:31–32) and the possibility that Paul was a Zealot was investigated thoroughly (Acts 21:37–38). As for Felix, he was already object of enough hatred of the Jews; fearing recall (as eventually happened in AD 60), he wished to do whatever he could to please the Jews (Acts 24:27). None of this worked for Paul's benefit.

FINAL VISIT AND ARREST IN JERUSALEM
(ACTS 21:18–23:11)

James's Suggestion

Verses 18–26 are hard to understand only if what has been said earlier about Acts 15 and 16:3 is not taken into account. Paul's practice was that Jewish Christians should still live as Jews, lest they offend them and be unable to reach them. Gentile Christians, however, must not be expected to adopt Jewish practices. Paul's response to the suggestion of James and the elders in Jerusalem fits right into that. (For comments on James, review the account of the Jerusalem Council in chap. 5.)

James and the Christian Jewish elders[15] in Jerusalem indicated to Paul the fact that many who were "zealous for the Law" (v. 20) understood him to be anti-law, teaching not only the Gentiles to be free of Mosaic ritual but also the Jews. They understood what Paul's practice really was, and they were in agreement. But we can readily understand how easily the reports about Paul got confused. So James suggested a way Paul could publicly dramatize his own careful regard of Jewish ways (v. 24); James himself was happy to recall that such things did not apply to Gentiles, as the results of the Jerusalem Council clearly had testified (v. 25).

There were four of the Christian Jews who were temporarily under a Nazirite vow (vv. 23–27). "Apparently they had contracted some ceremonial defilement and had to undergo a purificatory rite in the temple."[16] Seven days would be required, with the head shaved on the last day and the required offerings the day following. Paul agreed to join with them and bear the expenses of the offerings,[17] thus demonstrating his zeal for the Jewish ways (cf. Acts 18:18, chap. 5).

Paul's Arrest

Some unbelieving Jews from Asia recognized Paul in the Temple. (There would be many visiting Jews in Jerusalem during the Passover-Pentecost season.) They raised an outcry against him, as an enemy of all things Jewish. They said he had defiled the Temple by bringing a Gentile inside. They had seen a fellow Asian (Trophimus of Ephesus; cf. 20:4) with him earlier and jumped to this conclusion.

That accusation brought an outburst of passion. It was a capital crime to defile the Temple. Gentiles, permitted in the outer courtyard, could by no means enter the inner precincts.[18] So Paul was dragged into the outer court and assaulted. Although historians have not yet settled whether the Sanhedrin could put to death without approval by the Roman-appointed official, many think they could in cases of Temple violation. It is apparent that the Jews considered Paul guilty of this very crime.[19]

Word of the uproar came quickly to the captain of the Roman garrison in Jerusalem, a military tribune, Claudius Lysias by name (23:26).[20] He and his troops (probably 160 men, for "centurions" is plural) came and took Paul from the mob into their own custody. The soldiers were stationed in the fortress of Antonia, connected with the Temple's outer court by two flights of steps. This fortress had been reconstructed by Herod the Great. It was given its name in honor of Antonius (Mark Anthony).[21]

The situation was explosive. On an earlier occasion Archelaus had sent a detachment of soldiers to put down a riot in the Temple only to see his soldiers stoned and fleeing. "It was not until Archelaus called out his whole force that he was able, amid great bloodshed, to suppress the rebellion."[22] Closer to Paul's time, a similar situation had cost 20,000 lives.

There was such confusion that Lysias could not discern the problem; he proceeded to make his way, with the prisoner, back to the fortress. Mounting the steps and speaking Greek, Paul asked to speak to Lysias. The tribune was surprised. He had wondered if Paul was the fugitive Egyptian who had fomented an earlier rebellion. Seeing that he was not, Lysias gave Paul the liberty he sought to address the crowd from the stairs.

Speech to the Jerusalem Mob

When Paul turned to address the crowd, he gestured for silence and spoke in Aramaic (21:40). The mob quieted as Paul gave testimony.

This address has been touched on earlier (chaps. 2 and 3). The crowd listened until Paul spoke of his calling to evangelize Gentiles, and when that hated word was said, they listened no longer. After all, bringing a Gentile into the Temple was what this uproar was about in the first place. They reacted violently, calling for Paul's immediate execution.

Aborted Scourging

Lysias, no nearer to understanding the problem, decided on an examination that seldom failed. He planned to have Paul whipped to discover the truth (v. 24). The whip, or scourge, used had multiple leather thongs with bits of bone or metal attached; death often resulted. Paul informed the centurion who was left in charge by Captain Lysias that he was a Roman citizen, for whom such a beating would be unlawful. Lysias was summoned, and Paul convinced him that it was true.[23] The scourging was canceled.

Before the Sanhedrin

Lysias, still frustrated, sent word the next day that the Sanhedrin should assemble, and he would bring Paul for a hearing (22:30). The council chamber was "situated on the western slope of the temple hill."[24]

First, Paul offended the Council, especially the priests' side (the Sadducees). His claim to have lived his life "with a perfectly good conscience before God" was regarded as blasphemous, and he was struck on the mouth. His angry outburst (23:1–3) was a double affront. Reproached, Paul apologized (vv. 4–5).[25]

Second, Paul divided the Council. Recognizing (as he knew well) that some were Pharisees and others Sadducees, he claimed that the resurrection was the underlying issue behind his arrest, referring obliquely to the resurrection of Jesus. That set off the old doctrinal argument; the Sadducees denied resurrection and the Pharisees affirmed it (v. 8). Under the circumstances the Pharisees found themselves defending Paul (v. 9), and the Council was in such disorder that Lysias had to send soldiers to rescue Paul.

The Lord's Appearance

That night, in a vision, perhaps, the Lord Jesus personally appeared to Paul, who was confined in the fortress, and assured him that he would yet bear witness of Him in Rome. From this point on the movement in Acts is away from Jerusalem and (eventually) to Rome.

IMPRISONMENT IN CAESAREA (ACTS 23:12–26:32)

The Plot to Ambush Paul

More than forty men bound themselves under a curse not to eat or drink before they killed Paul.[26] They planned to have Paul summoned once again to the Sanhedrin and to kill him on the way there.

Somehow Paul's nephew learned of the plot and informed Paul and then Lysias of it. This is the only reference in the Bible to Paul's family. "It appears that the mother of this young man retained some sisterly affection for her brother, and something of that affection had been passed on to her son."[27]

Move to Caesarea

Lysias recognized that Jerusalem was too dangerous for Paul. The Roman procurator resided at Caesarea, and he was the one who should handle the case. The Jews obviously wanted Paul executed, and capital cases normally required the personal judgment of the Roman governor.[28] Guarded by a contingent of troops (v. 23), Paul was sent to Caesarea at night.

As was customary in such cases, Lysias prepared a letter to the Roman governor Felix to explain why he was sending him. The precise contents are apparently quoted in verses 26–30; it is probable that Luke was later permitted to copy the letter when he was preparing Acts (much of which might well have been prepared while Paul was in Caesarea).

On Paul's arrival Felix learned that Paul was from Cilicia. Had Paul "come from one of the client kingdoms [nearby], it would have been proper to consult the ruler of the state in question."[29] He arranged for Paul to be kept confined in the *praetorium*[30] to await a formal hearing.

Before Felix

Marcus Antonius Felix was the Roman procurator of Judea from AD 52 to 59. He was a ruthless ruler, risen from emancipation from slavery through political influences. The historian Tacitus said of him, "He exercised the power of a king with the mind of a slave."[31]

The hearing took place five days after Paul's arrival in Caesarea. The Sanhedrin was represented by Tertullus, the counsel for the prosecution (v. 1), a practice that apparently was a matter of choice.[32] Tertullus presented charges in his opening speech, which began with the customary compliments to the judge (vv. 2–4). The three accusations were very general:[33] Paul was a troublemaker, a leader of the heretical Nazarenes,[34] and he had attempted (note the modification) to profane the Temple (vv. 55–56).

Paul's defense (vv. 10–21) also begins with (more temperate) compliments to Felix. He explained that only twelve days had passed since his arrival in Jerusalem (probably six in Jerusalem, one in transit and five in Caesarea); that the charges could not be proved (v. 13); and that he had come to Jerusalem to bring alms (v. 17). He pointed out that the Asian Jews who had seized him ought to be present to testify against him (v. 19). In summary, he said: "I never never did anything against the law of the Jews or the temple or Caesar." (This threefold summary by A. N. Sherwin-White[35] probably reflects the threefold thrust of the charges.)

Felix deferred judgment on claim of needing Lysias's testimony (vv. 22–23): Lysias was "the only independent witness as to the fact of any civil disturbance."[36] Paul was confined and under the guard of a centurion but given quarters where visitors could freely come.

No doubt Felix's self-seeking character was involved in the action taken. He could ill afford to offend the Sanhedrin, for he did not now enjoy the same political leverage in Rome he once had. With the change of emperors from Claudius to Nero, Felix's brother Pallas had less influence.[37] (See also the background insert on page 205 for other factors that might have affected Felix's judgment.)

Two Years in Confinement

Following Paul's formal hearing, Felix and his Jewish wife, Drusilla, arranged to hear Paul. Drusilla was Felix's third wife. Formerly the wife of a king of Emesa, she was persuaded by Felix to desert her husband and marry him. Her Jewishness was Idumaean, for she was the daughter of Herod Agrippa I. (She had violated Jewish law by marrying a pagan.) Paul's message was direct. He spoke of righteousness, self-discipline, and judgment. Felix became agitated and put him off (vv. 24–25). Afterward, Felix often spoke with Paul, partly in hope of a bribe (v. 26).

When Felix vacated his office, he left Paul bound over for his successor, which may not have been unusual.[38] He certainly had other things on his mind, being recalled to Rome under a cloud. (Even while Paul was in prison, there had been street fighting in Caesarea between the Jewish and Syrian inhabitants, and Felix had been unable to settle the issue.)[39]

Before Festus, Appeal to Caesar

Porcius Festus succeeded Felix as procurator of Judea in AD 59. His brief administration (until his death in AD 61) was "not accompanied by such excesses as marked that of his predecessor or of his successors," but he was "inexperienced."[40]

On Festus's first official call on Jerusalem, the Jewish leaders informed him about the pending case of Paul, hoping that the new procurator would order Paul's return to Jerusalem (vv. 1–3). Festus, however, required the Jews to go to Caesarea for a hearing (vv. 4–6).

Festus was inclined to schedule a full trial in Jerusalem (v. 9). Paul realized he would not live to stand trial there, so he exercised yet one more of the Roman citizen's privileges: He appealed to Caesar (vv. 10–11). Roman law at the time forbade any governor "to kill, scourge, chain or torture a Roman citizen, or even to sentence him in the face of an appeal or prevent him from going to Rome to lodge his appeal there within a fixed time."[41] "By the time of Nero . . . the emperor rarely heard a case himself but delegated the task to others."[42] (But notice the implication of Acts 27:23.)

Festus accepted the appeal—he probably had no choice—thus getting the thorny case off his hands (v. 12).[43] The "council" (Latin, *consilium*) referred to was a group of advisers chosen by the procurator. Festus could not delegate his responsibility in a capital case, or in one dealing with a Roman citizen, to the native Sanhedrin, but "nothing prevented him from using the Sanhedrin . . . as his own *consilium*."[44]

Before Herod Agrippa

Herod Agrippa II was king (with Roman approval, of course) over parts of Galilee and Perea as well as other districts in northeastern Palestine. (See the insert in chap. 2). He and his consort Bernice, who was also his sister,[45] came to Caesarea for a protocol visit, welcoming the new procurator to his post. After several days, Festus mentioned to him the case of Paul (v. 14) and filled him in on the background (vv. 15–21).

Agrippa responded by expressing a desire to hear Paul himself; Festus was happy to oblige (v. 22). The next day a number of local dignitaries joined Festus and his royal guests in the judgment hall to hear the famous prisoner (v. 23). Festus reviewed the case and indicated that he desired help in framing the report to Nero that would accompany Paul to Rome (vv. 24–27). Probably the group functioned as the consilium referred to above (25:12). It consisted "partly of high-ranking Roman military officers and partly of civilians from the local population ('the principal men of the city')."[46]

Paul's speech was similar to a formal defense, including the introductory courtesies (vv. 2–3).

Festus interrupted his excited presentation (v. 24), but Paul pressed home his point, especially to Agrippa (vv. 25–27). The Herods, as Idumaeans (Edomites), were regarded as Jewish proselytes and were not ignorant of Jewish ways. Furthermore, Paul always regarded even his formal defenses as occasion to give witness to the gospel.

Agrippa's response (v. 28) is subject to debate. Some think it means he was near persuasion; others, that he was incredulous or sarcastic: "Would you try to persuade me with such a little speech?" Paul's rejoinder (v. 29) may indicate that he at least chose to take it the former way.[47]

The conversation (vv. 29–32) indicates opinion only. Agrippa probably advised Festus about what to write when sending Paul to Rome.

JOURNEY AS A PRISONER TO ROME
(ACTS 27:1–28:16)

This trip can best be examined in the same way as the three missionary journeys, listing places and events and following closely the biblical text and a map (see page 263).

Caesarea

Caesarea (27:1–2) was the starting point. Both Luke ("we") and Aristarchus of Thessalonica (19:29; 20:4) were along. Perhaps they were permitted to book passage on the ship in order to accompany Paul, or they may have assumed the position of servants of Paul. Luke could have signed on as ship's doctor.

The ship on which Julius, the centurion in charge, arranged transport was a merchant/passenger vessel from Adramyttium, a port city of Mysia in northwestern Asia Minor. The ship's captain planned a course that would take them as far as Asia. The destination of this ship was up the Asian coast (v. 2).

Sidon

Sidon (27:3) was another port city seventy miles up the coast from Caesarea. Julius allowed Paul (with a guard, of course) to go to his local friends to receive care.

Cyprus

Cyprus (27:4) is mentioned only to note that the ship sailed "under the shelter," or lee, of the island, that is, between it and the coast of Asia Minor where there was better protection from strong winds. They sailed near Cilicia and Pamphylia (v. 5a).

Myra

Myra (27:5–6), on the southern coast of Asia Minor in the district of Lycia, was one of the main ports for the grain trade between Egypt and Rome. There passage on a large merchant vessel of Alexandria headed for Rome was arranged (v. 6). (Alexandria had one of the largest fleets of Mediterranean trading vessels.) The 276 people aboard (v. 37) included crew, passengers, soldiers, and prisoners.

Cnidus

Cnidus (27:7) was an Asian port further west. Probably the ship was scheduled to dock there, but as they approached, the winds were wrong (from the northwest), and they headed southwest for the island of Crete. (F. F. Bruce, however, thinks they were choosing between stopping at Cnidus and going on.)[48]

Salmone

Salmone (27:7–8) was a port city on the eastern end of Crete; they sailed by it in a barely successful effort to get on the sheltered side of Crete for protection from the winds out of the north.

Fair Havens

Fair Havens, near Lasea (27:8–12), was a sheltered port on the southern side of Crete, and the ship anchored there safely. Days went by as they waited for better winds. "The fast" (v. 9) was the Jewish Day of Atonement, observed on Tishri 10. It is mentioned here to indicate that they were in the time of year when sailing on the open Mediterranean was dangerous. They would have to find a place to dock for the worst winter period. "The dangerous season for sailing began about September 14 . . . ; after [November 11] all navigation on the open sea came to an end until winter was over,"[49] and inactivity continued at least until early February. (In the year 59, for example, Tishri 10 was on October 5.)

Paul spoke with the centurion. He advised that they stay in Fair Havens (v. 10).[50] But this port was not particularly spacious, and the ship's owner hoped to be able to get on around to Phoenix, modern Phineka, on the western end of Crete where there was a better port (v. 12). Finally, a south wind blew. With just enough sail out to make their way, and hugging the coastline, they headed for their destination (v. 13).

Open Sea off Clauda

Off Clauda (27:14–29) the ship was caught by a storm. Forced out to sea, they were helpless to do anything more than "be driven along," or scud before the wind (vv. 14–15) for the next fourteen days (v. 27). The sailors called such a wind "Euraquilo," meaning northeast wind (in some manuscripts, "Euroclydon," a southeast wind raising mighty waves).

As they ran on the sheltered side of the island of Clauda, they barely managed to take the dinghy that was tied to the ship on board. (It was used in the harbor to get back and forth from the ship's anchorage to shore.)[51] They also undergirded the ship, which was accomplished by lowering cables beneath the vessel and tying them tightly. That would serve to help hold the ship together in the rough seas.

The seamen feared they would be driven into "the shallows of Syrtis" (called the Syrtis Sands) off the coast of Africa (v. 17). "The ship was laid to on a starboard tack (with her right side to the wind), with storm sails set, and so she drifted slowly, at a mean rate of one and a half miles per hour, in a direction about eight degrees north of west."[52]

The next day they put most of the cargo (wheat, v. 38) overboard (except what was needed for ballast) and on the following day much of the ship's tackle (vv. 18–19), perhaps the "mainyard," a spar as long as the ship. The storm continued without abating. There was little hope (v. 20). The ship was probably leaking, and land could not be found.

Then Paul had another revelation (vv. 21–26), this time that the lives of them all would be spared (v. 24), even though there was to be shipwreck on an (unnamed) island.

Sure enough, they soon realized they were approaching land (v. 27). Their "soundings" (actually they used hand lines) indicated increasing shallowness; first twenty, then fifteen fathoms (a fathom is six feet, originally the length of line that matches the height of a man, arms raised). They dropped anchor (four, from the stern) and "wished for daybreak" (vv. 28–29); obviously, the storm had lessened. Investigators conclude that they were passing Koura on Malta's east coast, about 475 miles from Clauda. (The "Adriatic Sea" here refers to the Mediterranean Sea east of Sicily.)

Malta

Off the coast of Malta (KJV, "Melita"; Acts 27:30–28:10) the ship's crew let down the dinghy "on the pretense of intending to lay out anchors from the bow" (v. 30). Paul understood that they were secretly planning to abandon ship, and he informed Julius. Soldiers were sent to cut the lowering ropes and let the dinghy fall away (vv. 31–32).

As day approached, Paul encouraged all to take food, setting the example himself (vv. 33–36). The fasting reported in verse 33 may not have been altogether religious. Rough seas do strange things to people's stomachs, and most of the 276 people on board (v. 37)[53] were not seasoned sailors. The remaining cargo was jettisoned so the ship would sit high in the water (v. 38).

When it was light, they could see a break in the shoreline and hoped to sail in there (v. 39). They cut away the anchors, freed the rudders (which had been lashed to, as they ran before the wind), raised the foresail, and headed in (v. 40). But they could not see the underwater mud reef, and the prow of the ship got stuck on that. Such a ship is helpless, and the waves soon began to break up the stern (v. 41).

It was necessary to abandon ship. The soldiers in charge of the prisoners were concerned about their possible escape. The guards could be held accountable, to the point of forfeiting their lives.[54] Their first thought was to kill the prisoners (v. 42), but Julius directed otherwise (v. 43). Thus all 276 persons made their way safely to land (vv. 43–44). The place now identified as St. Paul's Bay is probably the correct one.[55]

Once on land they learned from its non Greek speaking (KJV, "barbarous")[56] people where they were (28:1). The people were kind and built a bonfire for the derelicts, who were cold and wet (v. 2). Helping gather wood, Paul was bitten by a snake (v. 3). Immediately the island's superstitious people concluded that the gods were using this method to get justice on one who might otherwise escape (v. 4). But Paul shook off the snake without harm (Mark 16:18: he was not purposely "handling snakes"), so the people quickly changed their minds, concluding instead that Paul must be a god (v. 6). (There are no poisonous snakes on Malta today: the local legend is that Paul banished them from the island on the occasion.)[57]

The island's governor was named Publius; he arranged quarters for the unexpected visitors (v. 7). His father was suffering from fever and dysentery, and Paul healed the man (v. 8). The word spread. Others who were sick were brought to Paul, and he healed them too (v. 9). As a result, the Maltese treated the entire group with great kindness and provided supplies when they finally left the island, three months later, on another Alexandrian grain ship that had beaten the storm to Malta and was wintering there. On its figurehead was a carving of "the Twins," Castor and Pollux. "Their constellation, Gemini, was considered a sign of good fortune in a storm."[58]

Syracuse, Rhegium, and Puteoli

Syracuse (28:11–12), on the eastern coast of Sicily, was the ship's first stop. Three days were spent there, perhaps to unload some cargo or because the winds were not yet stable.

Rhegium (28:13), the ship's next stop, was on the western tip of the toe of the Italian boot-shaped peninsula. They "sailed around" (KJV, "fetched a compass"), tacking because of the winds.

Puteoli (28:13–14), up the Italian coast, was the ship's farthest docking port, the main stop for the Alexandrian grain ships. From here, the remaining journey to Rome was by land. There were Christians at Puteoli, and Julius readily acceded to the request that they stay a week with these fellow believers. Perhaps he had business there that made this convenient.

The Market of Appius and Three Inns

The Market of Appius (28:15), about forty to forty-five miles from Rome, and Three Inns (28:15), ten miles nearer, were places on the Appian Way. Some of the Roman Christians had come out as far as these two places to meet Paul and his companions and accompany them into the city. (Word would have reached Rome during the seven days in Puteoli.)

ROME WHEN PAUL ARRIVED THERE

Often called *The Eternal City*, Rome was founded in 735 BC on its famous seven hills, bluffs on the east bank of the Tiber guarding a strategic spot where the river was easy to cross.

When Paul arrived there in about AD 60, Rome was "in the full flush of her growth."[59] The walls measured some thirteen miles around, encompassing about six square miles. The camp of the imperial, or praetorian, guards where Paul was taken was at the northeastern corner of the wall.

Under Augustus the city had been divided into four-teen districts. Major roads led from the heart of the city in various directions; these included the Appian Way (to the south) on which Paul entered the city and the Ostian Way (to the port of Ostia on the southwest) where, according to tradition, Paul was beheaded. Augustus bragged that he had found Rome a city of brick and left it a city of marble, but there is considerable exaggeration in that.

Centers of public life were forums, open market places. The most important one, at the city's heart, was the Roman Forum, the center of government. The area included the Senate House, an assembly hall, and temples for Mars and Saturn. Here also was the golden milepost, from which all distances on the Roman roads were measured.

Surrounding the Forum were four of the seven hills, each displaying magnificent buildings. On the Capitoline Hill were temples, including one for Jupiter, the head of the pantheon. On the Palatine Hill were the palaces of the emperors and of other noblemen. On the Caelian Hill was a temple to the deified Claudius. On the Quirinal Hill were the newer forums constructed by Julius and Augustus.

This does not begin to describe the splendor of the public buildings of Rome. Everywhere the city was marked by temples, triumphal arches, basilicas, fountains, palaces, mausoleums, and the like. In AD 28 alone, Augustus received senatorial approval to rebuild or restore eighty-two temples in need of repair. "The houses of the rich, usually on the various hills of the city, were sumptuous."[60] Rome enjoyed the profits of three continents.

In stark contrast were the tenements where the great majority of the Romans (variously estimated at from half to a million)—the lower and middle classes—lived. These were block-long constructions, several stories high (Augustus limited them to six stories), containing oneroom flats. The higher the apartment, the lower the (still exorbitant) rent. The buildings were often flimsy, subject to collapse and in constant danger from fires. Even so, the poor were provided with free wheat and water, and wine was cheap. Still, "Rome was essentially a great slum."[61] There was such congestion that vehicular traffic was forbidden in the daytime. By night the side streets were jungles of crime.

Also dating back to Augustus, a police force and a fire-fighting force had been organized. Three cohorts of policemen kept order; seven cohorts of *vigile* (each responsible for two districts) fought fires.

Most of Rome's inhabitants "worked hard for meager incomes. The needs of the urban population were served by thousands of small shopkeepers. . . . Less reputable were street vendors, ragpickers, and the street-walkers who loitered near the Circus Maximus."[62] (Prostitution was under government control.) The grain fleets of Africa and Egypt, bringing wheat as tribute, kept Rome supplied with the bread for its basic diet of bread, olive oil, and wine. There were few vegetables, and meat was almost never on the table of any except the rich.

There had been a large influx of foreigners into Rome by New Testament times, affecting and being affected by the life of the city. Ethnic groups tended to settle in certain areas. There were concentrations of Jews, for example, in four of the western districts where there were at least thirteen synagogues. We may assume that the first Christians were in the same area.

Among the interesting features of life in first-century Rome were the aqueducts, the public baths, and the circuses. The aqueducts were cement-lined pipes, supported on giant arches, that brought water for great distances, supplying Rome with some 200 to 300 million gallons each day.[63]

Only the villas of the wealthy had private baths. But there were many free, public baths—170 in Augustus's time, perhaps 1,000 by the end of the first century. Although the city was dirty, the people were among the cleanest in the ancient world. The more elaborate baths included specialty rooms (like one for a hot bath, one for a cold bath, a steam room) and might have an exercise room, a library, or even a brothel, in conjunction. Men and women bathed together.

The circuses were places for races and other athletic events. The Circus Maximus below the Palatine Hill was the greatest of these, accommodating 150,000 spectators. Events were free to the public. Chariot racing was the most popular sport and offered the same kind of dangers that modern automobile racing affords. Gambling on the outcome was popular, and riots were not uncommon. There were also gladiatorial games, involving man against man or beast in mortal combat. Bloodthirsty crowds (as at modern bullfights) could signal for the death or for the sparing of the life of the defeated combatant. By the time of Claudius there were 159 holidays per year, with 93 of them devoted to the games.

Rome

In Rome (28:16), Paul (along with the other prisoners) was delivered to "the soldier who was guarding him" for confinement. The Praetorian Guard was a corps of elite troops of the imperial Roman army. They had to be native Italians. Stationed for the most part in Rome, they served various state functions, including the guarding of the emperor[64] and prisoners sent from the provinces. (The precise office of the soldier who received Paul from Julius is debated. Some think he was the prefect of the Praetorian Guard; more likely he was a subordinate officer.)[65]

Because of Julius's good word, no doubt, Paul was assigned to private quarters, either in the imperial compound or in civilian quarters nearby. Under the watch of one guard, to whom he would probably be chained by the wrist,[66] he could have as many visitors as desired (v. 30).

WITNESS AS A PRISONER IN ROME (ACTS 28:17–31)

Paul's prison stay in Rome is regarded as his witness/ministry there (23:11).

Witnessing to the Jews

Even as a prisoner, Paul maintained his pattern of contacting first the Jews. After three days he invited leading Jews to his quarters (vv. 17–20). They disavowed any communication from Jerusalem about him (v. 21) and expressed interest in learning more about this "sect" (v. 22). A later day was set, and a considerable number of Jews came to hear Paul. The exchange lasted all day (v. 23).

The outcome was exactly the same as in other places: some believed, others—the majority—did not (v. 24). Paul concluded the session in precisely the same way as he had concluded dealings with Jews in city after city (cf. 13:46–47 and the comments in chap. 4). The Jews departed, ultimately to divide, as in every other place (v. 29).

Two Years in Rome

The final two verses of Acts summarize the two years Paul spent in confinement in Rome. For his case to come to trial, accusers would have to come from Jerusalem. If not, two years may have been a legal limit, during which specific judgment must be made against him or he must be released. However, there is serious uncertainty about this. Sherwin-White discusses the evidence carefully. He concludes that there probably was not such a rule.[67] The Roman system put strong pressure on accusers: "The reluctance of the judicial administration to permit the abandonment of charges except in most extreme circumstances is apparent."[68] But because of the difficulties of travel from the provinces, ample time was allowed. Add to this that the court docket was sometimes congested and that the young Nero was notably disinterested in judicial efficiency, and the two-year period is not at all surprising. The Jews of Jerusalem probably delayed their coming as long as they dared.

During the two years, Paul continued to enjoy the relative liberty of being under guard in rented quarters. No doubt he made significant contribution to the progress of the gospel and of the Roman church while in these circumstances, fulfilling the intentions expressed in Romans 1:10–16.

It is also likely that Paul wrote the four prison epistles— Colossians, Ephesians, Philemon, and Philippians—during this two-year imprisonment in Rome. There is some difference of opinion about this. Some interpreters place one or more of these at Ephesus on the third journey. Some put the writing of some or all of them at Caesarea during the two-year detention there. But the traditional view is still probably the best one, and for that reason we turn our attention now to the introduction to these four letters.

PRISON EPISTLES

The prison epistles are also sometimes characterized as Christological. There is a greater emphasis on the doctrine of Christ's person and work than is common in the other letters. That is more a result of the teachings needed, however, than of any changing emphasis of Paul's.

Colossians

The date and place for the writing of Colossians, Philemon, and Ephesians. These three letters are linked together in a special way, and therefore we treat this particular question for all of them at once. (Philippians will be discussed independently later in this chapter.)

First, internal comparison makes it clear that they were all written at the same time and place and sent by the same messengers to the same area, the Roman province of Asia.

Colossians and Philemon are linked in several ways. The letter to Philemon accompanies the return of his runaway slave, Onesimus (Philem. 10–16); and Onesimus was with Tychichus in delivering Colossians (Col. 4:7–9). This last reference (Col. 4:9) identifies Onesimus as "one of" the Colossians. Colossians 4:17 and Philemon 2 both have a word for Archippus at the letters' destination. No doubt, then, Philemon lived in Colosse. Further, the greetings in the two letters are from essentially the same persons (Col. 4:10–14; Philem. 23–24).

Colossians and Ephesians are also linked, especially by the parallel contents: the old man–new man contrast (Eph. 4:22–24; Col. 3:9–10), the treatment of wives-husbands, children-parents, and slaves-masters (Eph. 5:21–6:9; Col. 3:8–4:1); the lesson on music (Eph. 5:19–20; Col. 3:16–17); Paul's concept of his ministry (Eph. 3:2–9; Col. 1:23–29)—these are some of the more obvious examples. Furthermore, the mission of Tychichus in bearing the letter, as in his own personal role, is precisely the same in Colossians 4:7–8 and Ephesians 6:21–22. It is true that Ephesians does not share the personal greetings that Colossians and Philemon share, but that is easily explained by the impersonal nature of Ephesians, a point to be discussed below.

Second, granted this close connection, where and when did Paul write them? Three main answers have been given: Rome, Caesarea, and Ephesus. All of these proposals have in common one obvious thing, that Paul was in prison when he wrote. That is clear from Colossians 4:3, 10, 18; Philemon 1, 9, 13, 23; and Ephesians 3:1; 4:1; 6:20. But there are no references to specifics that might point to a certain place of imprisonment.

Rome is the traditional location, going all the way back to Eusebius (AD 325). In favor of this identification, the other two claims have certain weaknesses (see below) and the Roman imprisonment described in Acts has a better fit. For example, Rome is a likely haven for a runaway slave. It would have been easy to get lost in the crowd of the capital city. Also, we know from Acts that Luke and Aristarchus accompanied Paul to Rome (Acts 27:2), and both of them were with Paul when the letters were written (Col. 4:10; Philem. 24).

Perhaps the most important consideration is that the circumstances of the Roman imprisonment seem to fit those of the writing of the letters. In particular, as described in Acts 28:30–31, Paul's relatively free situation fits well the picture of a prisoner who can write letters (using a scribe), have coworkers at his side (like those named in Col. 4:7–14), and be concerned about carrying on a proclamation of his own (Col. 4:3–4; Philem. 10; Eph. 6:19–20).

Caesarea is another possibility, not especially popular in recent studies. Paul was there for two years (as in Rome), and that certainly would provide the time needed. According to Acts 24:23, there was relative freedom in that period, too, and it is possible that a considerable number of friends, including Luke and Aristarchus, who had accompanied Paul to Jerusalem out of Macedonia (Acts 20:4), stayed close by after he was arrested and transferred to Caesarea.

The weaknesses of this view are that Caesarea would be an extremely unlikely place for Onesimus to go; that Paul in Caesarea would not likely be planning, on release, to visit Philemon in Colosse (Philem. 22) in view of his current determination to go to Rome (Acts 19:21; 23:11; Rom. 15:23–25); and that a witnessing ministry for Paul as prisoner in Caesarea is much less likely than in Rome.

Ephesus has been an increasingly popular option among younger scholars, even though it suffers from the serious weakness of the silence of Acts about an Ephesian imprisonment. To remedy this, advocates of this view point out that Paul did encounter serious troubles in Ephesus (2 Cor. 1:8–10). It is admitted that Acts does not tell of all Paul's imprisonments (as 2 Cor. 11:23–26 shows).

212   PAUL THE APOSTLE

Furthermore, there is a tradition that Paul was a prisoner in Ephesus,
even if "the value of these traditions is very limited."[69] And there may
be good reason for Luke's silence about this (theoretical) episode in
Ephesus. Some think it was connected with Asian proconsul Junius
Silanus, poisoned in AD 54 by Nero's mother, and the period of an-
archy that followed. If so, it would have been impolitic for Luke to
refer to this in an account he expected to be read in Rome.[70]

An imprisonment in Ephesus is plausible, and these prison epistles might have been written there. The advantages of such a view
are that the distances and likelihood of the travels of Onesimus and
Epaphras from Colosse to Paul at Ephesus (100 miles) are more re-
alistic than to Rome (1200 miles); that Paul's hope to visit Philemon
soon (Philem. 22) is more probable; and that the impression that the
Colossian church had *recently* been established (1:4–9, 21–23; 2:1,
2, 5–7; 3:7–10) would thus be sustained.[71]

The weaknesses of this view, in addition to the fact that the imprisonment itself must remain a supposition, are that if the Ephesian
imprisonment was as desperate as to be life-threatening (2 Cor.
1:8–10), there is no reason to believe that the relaxed outlook of
these three prison epistles, with associates and ministry, would fit
there; that Luke, so far as we can tell from Acts, was not with Paul
in Ephesus; and that, as C. H. Dodd expressed it, "If we are to *surmise*, then it is as likely that the fugitive slave, his pockets lined at
his master's expense, made for Rome, because it was distant, as that
he went to Ephesus *because* it was near."[72] We may add that those
who hold this view are inclined to place the writing of Philippians
there too. But though there is plenty of time in the Roman imprisonment to account for the altogether different outlook of Ephesians,
Colossians, and Philemon as compared to Philippians, there is no
reason to think that the (theoretical) Ephesian imprisonment was a
very long one.

All in all, at least until surer support of an Ephesian imprisonment arises, the traditional view has the greater probability. The
question remains, when during that period (AD 60–62) was the letter written? For reasons that will be discussed in the introduction to

Philippians below, it seems more likely that these three were written first and Philippians later. Even so, there must have been time for Epaphras (Col. 1:7; 4:12–13), as well as the other co-laborers who did not go as Paul went (4:7–14)—excluding Luke and Aristarchus, at least—and for Onesimus to go to Rome after Paul was transferred there. The letters were therefore probably written in about AD 61.

The destination of Colossians. The question is when was the Colossian church founded and by whom? Quite clearly, Paul regarded it as within his bailiwick. He would not have been so presumptuous to write such a letter otherwise (cf. Rom. 15:20). But Acts makes no mention of a visit to Colosse. We might overlook that except that the letter reads as though written to people Paul has "heard of" (1:4) and who have not "personally seen" his "face" (2:1).

Probably, then, Paul did not personally evangelize Colosse. Perhaps Epaphras did. Colossians 1:5–7 seems clearly to mean that they learned the gospel from him, and 4:12–13 testifies to his zeal for them and for those in the nearby cities of Laodicea and Hierapolis. We do know that "all who lived in Asia" were evangelized during the three-year stay of Paul in Ephesus on the third journey (Acts 19:10). Although that might have included some movements of Paul not described in Acts, it might just as well mean that Paul's coworkers and converts moved about in different parts of the province, preaching. There would be traffic in and out of the commercial hub of Ephesus anyway, and Paul could easily have had contact with some of the Colossians in that manner. He certainly appears to know Philemon, his wife, and Archippus (Philem. 1–2; Col. 4:17), as well as Nymphas, who may have lived at Laodicea (Col. 4:15). Epaphras himself may have been a native Colossian converted at Ephesus during the period (Col. 4:12).

Whether by converts visiting Ephesus, then, or by a coworker, Epaphras, dispatched to Colosse, or both, Paul would regard the church as part of his Gentile mission. And not only the church at Colosse, but those at Hierapolis and Laodicea as well (Col. 4:13, 16).

Colosse was a relatively small town in the Lycus river valley, in the Phrygian region of Asia.[73] Its population was mostly native Phrygian, but with a number of Greek and Jewish inhabitants. Its principal commerce involved the wool of sheep that grazed on the slopes of the valley. A special color of dyed wool made there was called *colos sinus.* The religious atmosphere was a mixture of local, Greek, and possibly even Iranian, Egyptian, and Jewish influences.[74] This may help us understand the church's susceptibility to the "fancy" religious heresy that invaded them (below).

The events that led to the writing of Colossians. The main development is that Epaphras had come to Paul and brought the word that occasioned the letter. As we have noted, Epaphras was a native Colossian, perhaps a convert of Paul's during the Ephesian ministry of the third journey, who had returned to evangelize Colosse and begin a church there. He may have been pastor of the church. Apparently he went to Paul to minister to him. Clearly he is not about to return to Colosse (Col. 4:12–13; Philem. 23). Even so, one of his main motivations for going may have been a sense of need for Paul's help in dealing with heretical teaching at Colosse. He certainly reported to Paul both the good (1:4, 8) and the bad.

The secondary thing is that Onesimus, also, had come to Rome. Apparently he came as a runaway slave who in some way got in contact with Paul, was converted, and was now about to return to his master Philemon at Colosse. (See the introduction to Philemon below.) Paul took the occasion to write the three letters, sending them by Tychichus (Col. 4:7; Eph. 6:21) and Onesimus (Col. 4:9; Philem. 10–13) to Asia. (He may have sent yet another letter, to the Laodiceans; see Colossians 4:16. This will be discussed in the introduction to Ephesians.)

The purposes of Paul in writing Colossians. That there was heresy in the Lycus Valley all interpreters are ready to admit. But the nature of that false teaching is exceedingly hard to define. The problem is that we have nothing to go on except for what we read in the letter itself, and it is not always easy to diagnose an illness by the medication administered, especially in theological matters.

For the purposes of this text, the surest way may be to follow Donald Guthrie, who is content not to give the heretical teaching a name, but to draw from the letter itself the elements of error that Paul apparently deals with.[75]

To begin, there was a Christological problem. From 1:15–19; 2:9, and throughout, it is reasonably clear that the heresy involved an incorrect understanding of the fullness of Christ's deity and pre-eminence as Lord of the universe. It is apparent that the false teachers grouped Christ with other powerful entities in the supernatural realms rather than above all other beings (1:16–17).

Also, there was a "philosophical" side to the false teaching, as we gather from 2:8. "Philosophy" is literally "love of wisdom," and "wisdom" comes up frequently in the letter (1:9, 28; 2:3, 23; 3:16; 4:5). The heretics apparently claimed some greater wisdom or knowledge than ordinary believers possessed.

That there was a Judaistic element involved as well may be seen from references to circumcision (2:11; 3:11) and to concerns about food, holy days, new moons, and sabbaths (2:16–17). However, Paul's response is not the same as in Galatians (or Philippians) where "original" Judaizers were the target.

In addition, there was an ascetic emphasis on self-denial. This was manifested in such "decrees" that commanded the things Paul quotes and discounts in 2:21–23.

There was apparently a worship of angelic beings of some sort; 2:18 is the key verse here, but it has been interpreted in many different ways. This may tie in with the first point mentioned above.

Finally, in some way the word translated "elementary principles" (KJV, "rudiments") in 2:8, 20 indicates an aspect of the problem. The Greek word (*stoicheia*) may mean elementary teachings (like our "the ABCs" of something), or it may refer to the basic elements of the universe (2 Pet. 3:10, 12). In this latter sense the word might possibly be used to refer to elemental spirits, good and bad, that inhabit the atmosphere—cosmic powers that affect men's affairs and must be reverenced or placated.[76] But in saying this we are already beyond what can be drawn from Colossians without help from other sources.

If all this sounds like a Duke's mixture, that may be exactly what it was. Various attempts have been made to relate this to known religious or philosophical outlooks in the world of Paul with uncertain results. J. B. Lightfoot tried to match this in large part with the teachings of the Essenes, primarily because of the Jewish and ascetic elements involved.[77] Ralph P. Martin sees a "strange theosophical cult," a "first century Scientology" that combined Jewish, Christian, and "gnosticizing" elements, with Iranian and Pythagorean ideas thrown in for good measure.[78]

What most interpreters seem willing to agree on is that the heresy was a Judaizing Christian gnosticism,[79] but only a pre-Gnosticism or incipient Gnosticism, not the full-fledged Gnosticism of the second century. *Gnosis* is the Greek word for knowledge, and a gnosticizing view is one that claims for its adherents special knowledge and power that the uninitiated do not have.

This probably included Greek philosophical notions; the Greek view that matter is evil may have been the source of the asceticism. This philosophical "secret" may have included the idea that

> God's fullness is distributed throughout a series of emanations from the divine, stretching from heaven to earth. The "aeons" or offshoots of deity must be venerated and homage paid to them as "elemental spirits" or angels or gods inhabiting the stars. They rule men's destiny and control human life, and hold the entrance into the divine realm in their keeping. Christ is one of them, but only one among many.[80]

If it is thought incredible that this could be mixed with Judaistic tenets, one has only to think of Philo of Alexandria, whose syncretism of Hebrew theology and Greek philosophy was like this in many ways.

To summarize, here are the major errors involved in the heresy at Colosse:

1. Christ was regarded as a deity less than fully God.
2. Other "angelic" beings were reverenced.

3. Jewish ceremonialism was practiced.

4. Stringent ascetic self-denial was taught.

Of these points we can be reasonably sure.

Paul's first purpose, then, was to give teaching that would correct these errors. This purpose occupies him in the first two chapters. His second purpose, in the light of the wrongly based practice of the heresy, was to give the true Christian basis of ethical practice. This occupies him in the last two chapters.

The theme of Colossians. Probably no letter of Paul's was consciously organized around a single theme. Even so, we may follow a host of interpreters who see *the preeminence of Christ* as a theme that tends to dominate Colossians. What we have already seen about the heresy there is the background for this. Paul finds a solution for the doctrinal aberration in putting Jesus Christ in His proper place, especially in the first two chapters.

This begins in 1:13–22, where we have a presentation of the truth about both the person and the redemptive work of Christ: He is head of "all things" (vv. 16–17) and has provided reconciliation for "all things" (v. 20). Then, in chapter 2, Christ is the One in whom are all the treasures of wisdom and knowledge (v. 3), the One in whom all the fullness of the Godhead dwells (v. 9), the reality of which the ceremonies were shadow (v. 17), the "head" of the Body (v. 19). Even the practical section presents Christian living as being risen with Christ and seeking a life that is "hidden with Christ" where He sits at God's right hand (3:1–4).

There is no question that giving Christ "first place in everything" (1:18) is the secret to sound doctrine and straight living. When He is at the center, everything falls into its proper place around Him.

This emphasis on Christ may be the reason that the Holy Spirit is essentially unmentioned in Colossians (in obvious contrast with Ephesians), 1:8 being the only exception.

The outline of Colossians. For the most part, the letter consists of two main sections, with typical personal matters preceding and following.

Formal opening, 1:1–2

   I. Thanksgiving and prayer for the Colossians, 1:3–14

   II. The doctrinal section: the preeminence of Christ, 1:15–2:23

      A. The person and work of Christ, 1:15–23

         1. The preeminence of Christ's person (vv. 15–19)

         2. The reconciling work of Christ (vv. 20–23)

      B. Paul's role in the ministry, 1:24–29

         1. Paul as sufferer for the church (v. 24)

         2. Paul as minister/servant of the church (v. 25a)

         3. Paul as revealer of a mystery (vv. 26–27)

         4. Paul as preaching to present saints perfect to God (vv. 28–29)

      C. Correction of errors in teaching, 2:1–23

         1. Warning against persuasive words that do not find in Christ the treasures of wisdom (vv. 1–7)

         2. Warning against human traditions that appear wise but seek perfection outside Christ (vv. 8–17)

         3. Warning against an angelology that does not hold to Christ as the one head (vv. 18–19)

         4. Warning against ascetic self-denial not in accord with having died with Christ (vv. 20–23)

   III. The practical section: Christ is our life, 3:1–4:6

      A. The basis of Christian practice: buried and raised with Christ, 3:1–4

      B. Putting on the new man, 3:5–17

         1. Putting off the "old self" (vv. 5–9)

         2. Putting on the "new self" (vv. 10–17)

      C. Christian family life, 3:18–4:1

         1. Wives and husbands (vv. 18–19)

         2. Children and parents (vv. 20–21)

         3. Slaves and masters (3:22–4:1

      D. Living before the world, 4:2–6

         1. Praying about Paul's witness (vv. 2–4)

         2. Giving their own witness (vv. 5, 6)

IV. Personal: messages and coworkers, 4:7–17

Conclusion, 4:18

Ephesians

Within the ranks of conservative scholarship, Ephesians is commonly regarded as "one of the loftiest products of inspiration," fitly termed by Dr. Pierson "the Switzerland of the New Testament."[81] Even those critical scholars who regard the work as a later composition by a disciple of Paul's are often ready to acknowledge that the letter expresses the very sum and substance of Paulinism in a sublime fashion, "a brilliant and comprehensive summary of Paul's main theological emphasis."[82]

The authenticity of Ephesians. Except for the pastorals, the authorship of most of Paul's letters has not been seriously questioned except by the more extremely critical scholars like F. C. Baur and the Tubingen school, who taught that only the four capital epistles were really Pauline. The student of Paul will soon learn, however, that Ephesians is questioned in some circles even by some who want to be known as evangelical. Some awareness of the debate is therefore helpful, even though It Is beyond the scope of this text to explore the matter in detail.

One of the problems lies in the rather unique nature of Ephesians. It has no personal greetings or references to current circumstances, and it seems to represent the readers as not personally known to Paul (1:15; 3:2). All of this is strange in a letter to a church where Paul had spent such a long time: three years during the third missionary journey.

The main objection to Pauline authorship lies in its literary relationship to the other letters, especially Colossians. As critics put it, Ephesians and Colossians are too much alike for dependence to be denied, but they are too different for both to have been produced by the same author in similar circumstances; the one uses words and phrases used by the other but with different meanings and applications. The best explanation of this, they think, is that Ephesians was written long after Paul's death (say, in AD 90) by one who was especially familiar with Colossians (and to some degree with his other letters) but who did not have a copy of Colossians in hand to consult when he wrote. Some suggest that this pseudonymous writer wrote Ephesians to serve as a summary of Pauline teaching and an introduction to Paul's letters, perhaps at a time (late in the first century) when they were being collected in early trends toward canonization. This view is sometimes known as E. J. Goodspeed's. That scholar even suggested that Onesimus was the post-Pauline author.[83]

Conservative scholars prefer the explanation that Paul wrote both letters. That would account for the interdependence between them. The differences may be traced to the apostle's different purposes. In other words, he wrote each without actually consulting the other yet within a short period of time.

The argument, of course, is much more complex than that. The interested student will do well to read the thorough treatment of Guthrie,[84] who presents fairly and answers clearly the variety of objections. One of the key issues involved is that of pseudonymous authorship. Those who claim to be evangelical and yet doubt Pauline authorship are inclined to believe that it was an acceptable practice in early Christianity to write under the name of an apostle, that this would not have been regarded as dishonest at all. Such claims rest on shaky ground, as Guthrie shows in an excellent appendix.[85]

Regardless, there are two facts not in doubt. First, the letter claims to be by Paul not only in 1:1 but in a typically biographical section, beginning at 3:1. Second, the historical evidence for the acceptance of Ephesians as genuine by the church is very early and very strong. The very first canon, for example, was that of Marcion in about AD 140; it included Ephesians, and Marcion accepted only the letters of Paul as having authority. The chain of such external attestation from AD 95, when Clement of Rome used it, is unbroken. It seems clear that 1 Peter reflects knowledge of Ephesians; if Ephesians was later than Paul, then 1 Peter was likewise later than Peter.[86]

There is at least one other important point that comes from the letter itself. The reference to Tychichus's mission in 6:21–22 does not fit if Ephesians was written by someone other than Paul.[87]

The date and place for the writing of Ephesians. This matter has already been treated, inasmuch as Colossians, Philemon, and Ephesians were beyond any reasonable doubt written at the same time and place. (Review especially the discussion of the link between Colossians and Ephesians.) As with Colossians, then, we date Ephesians in about AD 61, written from Rome during Paul's two-year imprisonment there.

It would be next to impossible to prove which of these three prison letters was written first. Arguments based on literary interdependence are always rather tenuous. Some interpreters think Paul wrote Ephesians first; most believe that Colossians was first. For one reason, the Colossian situation was the thing that caused the letters to be written, with Ephesians written to take advantage of the need to send a letter to Colosse. For another thing, it seems natural that the longer letter followed the shorter one, giving further development in a second treatment. But that is not a decisive argument by any means.

Regardless of which was written first, these considerations favor dealing with Colossians first and then with Ephesians.

The destination of Ephesians. For no letters except Galatians and Ephesians is there any real debate about where the letters were sent. For Ephesians the question is whether the letter was meant specifically for Ephesus. Here are the reasons this question exists.

First, there are no personal greetings or references to current circumstances in the letter even though Paul had spent three years in Ephesus. True, some of Paul's other letters do not contain much in the way of greetings, either: 1 or 2 Thessalonians, Philippians, Galatians especially. But the silence of Ephesians is more obvious because it stands beside Colossians and Philemon. In both of those, detailed greetings are sent from a list of names (Col. 4:10–14; Philem. 23–24).

Second, Ephesians stands almost in a vacuum of circumstances. No one is associated with Paul in the opening; no reference is made to any event or prior contact. The only exceptions are the references to Paul's bonds (3:1; 4:1; 6:20) and to Tychichus's mission (6:21–22). (The theory of some, that the last chapter of Romans belongs on

Ephesians, has already been mentioned and rejected in the introduction to that letter.)

Third, Paul appears to regard his readers as people not personally acquainted with him. He had heard of their faith (1:15; cf. Col. 1:4–8). They may have heard of the stewardship of God's grace given to him (3:2). The tone of this is much like that of Colossians, and we are reasonably assured (as noted above) that Paul had not been to Colosse.

Finally, these facts might have been explained in some other way, but their tendency is underscored by the fact that the words "at Ephesus" are missing in some of the Greek manuscripts: three, in fact.[88] By far the great majority of the manuscripts have the words. Still, these are three of the oldest manuscripts in existence, and many scholars regard them highly.

This is not the place to discuss the science of textual criticism, as the comparison of manuscripts is called. Even on the basis of currently accepted principles, the absence of "at Ephesus" from such a few ancient copies is not enough to produce confident judgment. The most that can safely be said is that the possibility is raised that Ephesians 1:1 did not originally have "at Ephesus," a possibility that might get very little attention if it were not for the other reasons.

In all this, we are on highly speculative ground. If the original letter did not have "at Ephesus" but read, "to those who are saints and faithful in Christ Jesus," then how do we explain the letter? Who was it for? How did the great majority of manuscripts come to have the words? The answer that has been suggested is that Ephesians was originally a general letter sent not to one specific church but intended for any church, especially those in Asia, as a sort of encyclical. This would explain all the points above.

This might also explain how some copies came to have the words "at Ephesus." If the original did not have such words, perhaps it ultimately came to reside at Ephesus and was commonly called Ephesians. Then some scribe, making a copy in later generations, thought there was an omission and inserted the words. Or there may have first been a marginal note identifying where the original was, and a later scribe misunderstood and put the words in the text. It is possible that there were several original copies, of course; if so, when the letters were collected in early canons, the Ephesian copy was the one collected. Some have even speculated that one original had "at Ephesus" and another did not.

One more point may be mentioned. Colossians 4:16 refers to a letter sent to Laodicea. Could that be our Ephesians? The view of Ephesians just discussed would open the door to that possibility; even so, that is far from certain. Whether Ephesians was a circular letter or not, Paul may have written a letter specifically to the Laodiceans, one we do not possess. (The so-called epistle to the Laodiceans among the Christian pseudepigrapha is certainly not it, and the fact that Marcion identified Ephesians as Laodiceans proves nothing.)[89]

In summary, it seems very clear that Ephesians was intended, at least, to include Ephesus. Whether the letter was also intended for a wider circle of churches, especially in Asia, thus explaining its impersonal nature, is a possibility that should not be ruled out.

All this means that the Acts account of Paul's ministry in Ephesus (review 18:18–20:38) does provide us with the background of the believers who first received Ephesians. Paul had three contacts: (1) stopping in Ephesus in the late stages of the second journey; (2) the three-year ministry in Ephesus on the third journey; and (3) a farewell address to the Ephesian elders in Miletus later on the third journey. The middle one of these is the most important one. It was the period when "all who lived in Asia heard the word of the Lord, both Jews and Greeks" (Acts 19:10), that is, the time when the first readers of Ephesians were evangelized, whether we think of all the churches in Asia or of the Ephesian church only. The third contact just mentioned has significance, too, because even those who doubt that Paul wrote Ephesians acknowledge that "there is an unusual degree of correspondence between Ephesians and the speech of Paul in Ac. 20 to the Ephesian elders."[90]

The purposes of Paul in writing Ephesians. The Colossians' need for correction and Onesimus's return to his master produced the letters to the Colossians and Philemon. Tychichus and Onesimus delivered those letters. Apparently Paul decided to write Ephesians to be delivered at the same time, to the same general area.

These assumptions provide us with a general purpose for Ephesians. Paul wrote to expound further some of the themes touched on in Colossians. Not that the heresy at Colosse was equally threatening at the other churches in Asia. In that case he would have sent Colossians to them all. But Paul knew that falsehood has a way of spreading, and so he wanted to share some of the same truths, albeit in a less polemical way, with other churches in the area. Some have compared Colossians to the "pound of cure," and Ephesians to the "ounce of prevention."

Beyond this we can tell about Paul's purposes only by what he wrote. Obviously he wanted to give teaching on the standing of believers in Christ (chaps. 1–3), on a Spirit-controlled walk that is worthy of that standing (chaps. 4–6), and on the need for a strong stand in the battle against the forces of evil (6:10–20). Some have called this the wealth, walk, and warfare of the believers, a popular summary that is better than many such oversimplifications.

The themes of Ephesians. There are certain emphases that characterize Ephesians, and brief mention of these will help prepare for closer study of the contents of the letter.

In comparison with Colossians, there is a similar emphasis on the preeminence of Christ, on His headship over all things and over the church, on His exalted place as Lord over all creation—1:10, 20–23 provide good examples. Even so, the thrust is different. Where Colossians emphasizes Christ's preeminent place, Ephesians develops a truth only barely touched on in Colossians, namely, that believers, being in Christ, have an exalted standing with Him. If, for example, Christ has been exalted to God's right hand "in the heavenly places" (1:20), then it is also true that we sit together "in the heavenly places" in Christ (2:6). In one sense, the entire first three chapters of Ephesians describe that position we have as believers in Him.

Many have used this phrase "in the heavenly places" or one like it as a thematic statement for the letter. That may be an exaggeration, but there is no denying the significance of the phrase, occurring in 1:3; 1:20; 2:6; 3:10; and 6:12.

There is also an emphasis placed on the Holy Spirit. As noted above, Colossians 1:8 is the only reference to the Spirit in that letter. Ephesians stands in obvious contrast, with the Holy Spirit mentioned in 1:13, 17; 2:18; 3:5, 16; 4:3–4, 30; 5:9, 18; and 6:17–18. Among other things, the possession of the Spirit within is seen as part of the believer's spiritual treasure in Christ in chapters 1–3. As such, He is both "seal" (1:13; 4:30) and "pledge" (1:14). Most important, in chapters 4–6 the believers' relationship to the Spirit is seen as the secret of victorious living. Being filled with the Spirit (5:18) at least includes experiencing a full measure of the unity that the Spirit creates (4:3–4), not grieving the Spirit (4:30), and yielding the fruit of the Spirit (5:9). It also manifests itself in a special way in the believers' community life (5:18–21).

Finally, we should mention that one of the emphases of Ephesians is certainly the church as the body of Christ, meaning especially the church in general rather than in its local manifestation. When most of Paul's letters use the word *church*, particular local churches are meant. Colossians and Ephesians, however, turn our attention to the so-called invisible church. Ephesians develops this theme in detail. Thus 1:22–23 begins the treatment; 2:19–22 presents the church not only as God's household but as a house—a temple—being built for Him to inhabit. And 4:4–16 (especially vv. 11–16) is as helpful a picture of the functioning of the church as can be found (perhaps just as applicable to a local church as to the universal church). Finally, the section 5:25–33 is unique, comparing the church to Christ's bride.

The outline of Ephesians. As many have noted, Ephesians does not have either the pattern of Romans, with its logical progression, or of 1 Corinthians, with its succession of subjects. Even so, there is a general similarity in that the early chapters are "mainly affirming Christian truths of belief or experience," whereas the later chapters "consist largely of exhortations to conduct."[91]

Formal opening, 1:1–2

I. A doxology of doctrine: the position of believers in the exalted Christ, 1:3–3:21

    A. The eternal purpose of God for His people, 1:3–14

        1. Preamble: the God of all blessings (v. 3)

        2. God's eternal plan to bless us (vv. 4–6)

        3. The realization of these blessings in time (vv. 7–14)

    B. Prayer for the believer's understanding, 1:15–23

        1. For a spirit of wisdom and revelation (v. 17)

        2. For inner enlightenment (vv. 18–19)

        3. For a grasp of the power displayed in Christ (vv. 20–23)

    C. Our present salvation: contrast with the past, 2:1–22

        1. From death to life (vv. 1–10)

        2. From alien status to citizenship (vv. 11–22)

    D. Paul's ministry in preaching and prayer, 3:1–21

        1. Paul's stewardship in the gospel (vv. 1–13)

        2. Prayer for the readers (vv. 14–21)

II. Practical instruction: a walk worthy of our standing, 4:1–6:20

    A. The functioning of the body of Christ, 4:1–16

        1. The unity of the Spirit (vv. 1–6)

        2. A diversity of gifts (vv. 7–11)

        3. Functioning together toward maturity (vv. 12–16)

    B. The walk of the new man, 4:17–5:21

        1. The condition of unbelievers (4:17–19)

        2. Conversion to a new way of life (4:20–24)

        3. Putting on "the new man" (4:25–31)

        4. Living as children of God (5:1–7)

        5. The difference between light and darkness (5:8–17)

        6. Being filled with the Spirit (5:18–21)

    C. Christian family life, 5:22–6:9

        1. Wives and husbands (5:22–33)

        2. Children and parents (6:1–4)

        3. Slaves and masters (6:5–9)

D. A call to arms, 6:10–20

Conclusion, 6:21–24

SLAVERY IN THE TIME OF PAUL

Slavery in the New Testament must not be interpreted in the light of the enslavement of blacks in pre–Civil War America. In general the system was not nearly so reprehensible, nor was it particularly racial. In Paul's day there were millions of slaves and former slaves (freedmen). In many areas slaves greatly outnumbered free persons. The will of one wealthy Roman listed more than 4,000 slaves as property.[92] Most slave families came to be such as prisoners-of-war or by piracy.

There are two sides to the picture of the general condition of slaves. On the dark side (usually emphasized by the earlier commentators) is the fact that a slave was his owner's chattel, with almost no rights under Roman law, absolutely at the master's disposal. Only cohabitation, not marriage, was allowed, with companions sometimes assigned by lot. Many masters were cruel and punishments severe. An offender might be scourged, mutilated, or crucified—perhaps for a minor offense. J. B. Lightfoot cites an incident when according to law, all four hundred slaves of one man were executed when one of their number had slain his master.[93] (The incident, which provoked considerable public tension, took place in AD 61, thus very close to the time Paul wrote Philemon.) Often, then, slaves tended to learn to be mean, conniving, and treacherous.

On the other hand (as tends to be emphasized by more recent writers),[94] the lot of the slave was often better than unattached poor laborers who worked for hire, begged, or stole. Some writers, in fact, make a case for the essentially worthwhile character of slaves during this period. Slaves were as

well or better dressed, fed, and paid than their free counterparts in the laboring class. A slave who was industrious and
frugal could expect freedom within seven years. In general,
slavery was a means whereby a captive in war could be educated and trained in Roman ways before becoming a Roman
citizen. Many hundreds of thousands of freedmen were in the
empire in Paul's day, having either been given their freedom
or purchased it with their savings. Perhaps it was the *tendency*
of slavery to lead toward freedom, with owners often helping to establish their freedmen in trades or businesses. Many
slaves were intelligent and cultured, having positions of great
trust and responsibility, involving—as well as field hands and
household drudges—architects, sculptors, painters, poets,
musicians, librarians, physicians, and the like.

Laws Regarding Fugitive Slaves

One legal privilege of a fugitive slave was to have an in-
tercessor (Latin, *precator*) on his behalf. Paul, although in
prison, assumes something of this position in writing to
Philemon. (Lightfoot prints an exceedingly interesting letter
from the younger Pliny, pleading with a friend on behalf of a
runaway slave who had sought his intercession.)[95]

There were ways a fugitive slave might seek help. One of
those was to seek refuge in the home of a friend at the family
altar. This provision, originating in Athenian law, was apparently widespread in the empire and raises the possibility that
a fearful and/or guilt-stricken Onesimus had taken the initiative in seeking out Paul's hired house (Acts 28:30) in Rome.

On the face of it, to harbor a fugitive slave was a violation of Roman law, and that fact would probably have
been at least part of the reason Paul was determined to send
Onesimus back to Philemon.

Even more interesting, the person who gave refuge to
a runaway slave was liable to the slave's owner for the value

of any work lost. An early papyrus (c. 150 BC) offers reward for the recovery of two runaway slaves. If the finder can fix the slaves with someone harboring them, the reward will be even higher, apparently because of the possibility of recovering such damages.[96] In this light Paul's guarantee of whatever Philemon reckoned Onesimus owed him is intriguing. Though Paul surely could not be held legally liable, Philemon 18 may be an assurance that he will exercise the role of the slave's harborer anyway. Even in rabbinic law, a runaway slave had to make good the time of his absence; this may be Onesimus's debt that Paul offered to pay.

Philemon

This shortest of all Paul's letters is more like a letter between friends. Even so, it has been warmly regarded by the church since the earliest collections of Paul's letters were made. As Lightfoot puts it. "The letter . . . does not once touch upon any question of public interest. It is addressed apparently to a layman. It is wholly occupied with an incident of domestic life. The occasion which called it forth was altogether common place. . . . Yet to ourselves this fragment . . . is infinitely precious."[97]

The variety of its teaching may not be wide, but it gives us an important insight into Paul's manner of dealing with at least one aspect of the problem of slavery.

The date and place for the writing of Philemon. What has been said above in the introduction to Colossians about the time and place of its writing will apply equally to Philemon, inasmuch as they were composed by Paul at the same time and place and sent together to Colosse. A comparison of Colossians 4:9–14 with Philemon 10, 23–24 makes this clear. Add to this that Archippus is mentioned in both (Col. 4:17; Philem. 2).

It really does not matter which of the letters was written first.

When Paul wrote Colossians, it had already been decided that Onesimus, the runaway slave, would return to Philemon (Col. 4:9), so that this note to Philemon might have been written before or after Colossians or Ephesians, for that matter.

Therefore Philemon may be dated in about AD 61, written from Rome during Paul's two-year imprisonment there.

The destination of Philemon. Like the pastoral letters, Philemon was sent to an individual. Inasmuch as he is the first one addressed (v. 1), he is the primary target of the letter. Once the opening is past, nearly everything said is directed to him. Paul uses the singular pronoun and addresses him as "brother" (vv. 7, 20).

There is no good reason to question the traditional view that Philemon lived in Colosse. Colossians 4:9 identifies Onesimus as one of the Colossians, and both Colossians 4:17 and Philemon 2 speak of Archippus. It is true that some interpreters have made a case for Laodicea as Philemon's hometown. About the only reason for doing so is that Archippus is mentioned in Colossians right after a reference to Laodicea (4:15–17). But that is hardly significant. The closing, miscellaneous items in Paul's letters often stand alone and have little or no relationship to one another (see Rom. 16 or 2 Tim. 4:10–21 for good examples). If Philemon were to be placed at Laodicea, Colossians 4:9 would have to mean that Onesimus was "one of you in the region" rather than "one of you at Colosse"; the latter seems more likely.

If Philemon lived in Colosse or Laodicea, for that matter, and if Paul had not personally visited that area (see the introduction to Colossians above), then how had Paul and Philemon become personally acquainted? Indeed, Philemon is identified as "beloved" to and "fellow worker" of Paul and Timothy (v. 1). Further, verse 19 says, "You owe to me even your own self," apparently implying that Philemon had been converted to Christ by Paul. All we can do is assume that Philemon had been where Paul was at some time. In that case Ephesus, during the third-journey three-year stay there, is the probable place. As a slave owner, Philemon was a man of some means; that he would travel even frequently from Colosse to the metropolis of his province would be likely. He might easily have come under Paul's personal influence in Ephesus, been converted, and worked with Paul and Timothy there. Indeed, he might well have been partly responsible for the spread of the gospel to Colosse (along with Epaphras, Col. 1:7; 4:12–13).

Only brief mention needs to be made of an alternative theory about the letter. J. Knox has suggested that Archippus was the owner of Onesimus, that Paul did not know him personally, and so included Philemon in the address as someone he did know who could be counted on to help influence Archippus to heed the letter and release Onesimus. This view presents too many problems and has not gained much following. Guthrie has a good treatment of the pros and cons.[98]

The events that led to the writing of Philemon. In addition to the connection with Colossians, Philemon has its own specific background of events, to be discerned from the letter itself: (1) Onesimus, a slave of Philemon's, had run away from his master, which was not uncommon. Apparently he had stolen things at the time of his departure (v. 18). That, too, was common (cf. Tit. 2:9–10). In one sense, anything taken with him was his master's, for he himself was his master's property. The runaway had sought to get lost in the city of Rome (as discussed earlier). "He seems to have done just what the representative slave in the Roman comedy threatens to do, when he gets into trouble. He had 'packed up some goods and taken to his heels.' Rome was the natural cesspool for these offscourings of humanity."[99] (2) In some way unknown to us Onesimus had come in contact with Paul—who was in detention in rented quarters in Rome—and had been converted (v. 10). One can only speculate how that came to pass. Epaphras, for example, might have come across him by accident and brought him to Paul for advice. For one reason or another, Onesimus might have sought out Paul. The result is what counts, regardless of how it came about. (3) Paul, who was sending Tychichus (Col. 4:7–8; Eph. 6:21–22) and letters to Onesimus's home territory, believed it was right that Onesimus should return to his master. He therefore included this personal letter to influence Philemon's reception of the converted runaway.

The purpose of Paul in writing Philemon. The events just noted have made Paul's one purpose clear: he wrote to restore Onesimus to Philemon. The only question is how much was involved in that restoration. Certainly Paul wanted Philemon to receive Onesimus with love and forgiveness without punishment for any theft involved. Verses 12, 15–18 make that much clear. That, alone, was crucial, for in the Roman world there were almost no limits on what a master could inflict on a slave.

It is also possible that Paul wanted more. Although he does not ask directly, he seems to hope that Philemon will send Onesimus back to Rome to minister to Paul, as possibly Onesimus had been doing in the time following his conversion. This seems to be the point of verses 13–14 and possibly 21. Such an action might even involve the freeing of Onesimus from slavery, although Paul does not directly ask for that.

The outline of Philemon. As a one-point letter, Philemon needs no outline. The student who has observed the method used thus far in this text will automatically think of the following:

Formal opening, 1–3
    A. Thankful prayers for Philemon, 4–7
    B. Request for Onesimus, 8–21
        1. The attitude of Paul's request (vv. 8–9)
        2. The subject of the request (vv. 10–12)
        3. A desire Paul had quenched (vv. 13–14)
        4. The way Philemon should receive Onesimus (vv. 15–19)
        5. Paul's appeal and confidence (vv. 20–21)
Conclusion, 22–25

Philippians

Philippians is one of the most relaxed letters of Paul. It is apparent that there were few problems in the church and nothing to disrupt the warm relationship Paul enjoyed with them. Paul's obvious joy in spite of prison circumstances makes the letter all that much more a source of joy for us.

Philippians is the fourth of the prison epistles but not linked with the other three as they are linked with each other. The destination is entirely different, inasmuch as Philippi was in Macedonia and the other three went to Asia. And Paul's outlook, expressing expectations of freedom soon or at least of a decision in his case (2:24), is different.

The date and place of the writing of Philippians. The chart in chapter 4 represents the traditional view that Philippians was written during Paul's two-year Roman imprisonment (Acts 28:30–31) of AD 61–62/63, probably after the other three prison epistles. This view cannot be taken for granted. Several matters must be considered.

The letter itself indicates various facts about Paul's situation at the time of writing: Timothy was with him (1:1); he was in chains (1:7, 13–14, 16); a palace guard was observing him (1:13); although death was a real possibility, he expected to live on and minister longer (1:20–25; 2:24); he expected a decision on his situation (2:23); he sent greetings from "those of Caesar's household" (4:22). Further, a lengthy chain of communication back and forth between Paul and the Philippians had taken place (2:25–28; 4:18).

It is obvious that Paul is in prison, but where? The references in 1:13 and 4:22 are important. The palace guard mentioned in 1:13 is literally "the whole *praetorium.*" As we have seen earlier in this chapter (see the discussion of Caesarea), that could refer to the residence of any Roman governor, including that of Caesar in Rome. Or it could refer to the Praetorian Guard in Rome.

"Caesar's household" (4:22) certainly means the imperial household, and that would strongly favor Rome. One's family included his servants. That some of the vast array of soldiers and domestics involved in the service of Nero and the palace had become Christians is not surprising at all. In fact, the long list in Romans 16 contains a number of names that "occur in the *Corpus* of Latin Inscriptions as members of the Imperial household, which seems to have been one of the chief centres of the Christian community at Rome."[100]

All this tends to support the traditional view, dating Philippians during the Roman imprisonment described in Acts 28. Whether it should be dated early or late in that two-year period (AD 61–62/63) is harder to say. The tone of 1:25 and 2:24 is hopeful, and 2:23 sounds like Paul expects a decision soon. Many interpreters are therefore inclined to put Philippians after the other three prison epistles, nearer to the end of the two years, say in 62. It would be possible, however, to put it before them as Lightfoot does.[101]

To be considered is the fact that a rather lengthy chain of events between Philippi and Paul led to the writing of the letter (see below). This would seem to mean Philippians could not have come soon after his arrival in Rome. Furthermore, greetings are not sent from Luke in 4:22 (in contrast with Col. 4:14; Philem. 24), an omission that would be extremely strange (in view of Luke's ministry at Philippi) if Luke were with Paul when he wrote; Luke was with Paul in Rome when he arrived there.

There are other views. There is some support for Caesarea, as has been discussed in reference to the other three prison epistles and need not be discussed again here. There is another view, however, which has gained in favor with some interpreters in recent years[102]— that Philippians was written from an Ephesian imprisonment that occurred during the third missionary journey. Some of the points made in presenting this view are as follows.

There were difficulties at Ephesus that might have included a prison experience. Second Corinthians 1:8–10 refers to a time of affliction in Asia that so threatened death that Paul despaired of life. That Acts does not relate such an imprisonment is no objection in light of 2 Corinthians 11:23–26. There is a tradition that Paul was imprisoned at Ephesus.

The Philippian awareness that death was a real possibility (1:20) fits well with this.

The lengthy chain of communications between Paul and Philippi is more likely to have transpired between Philippi and Ephesus, a journey of eight days or so, than between Philippi and Rome, a journey of six weeks or longer.

Some things in Philippians sound as if the writing is much closer in time to the founding of the church than the dozen years that

would have elapsed before the Roman imprisonment. See 1:30 and
4:15–16 as well as 1:26; 2:12, 22. Such references create an impression that "It is unlikely that Paul had seen the church in the interval
since its foundation."[103]

Placing Philippians at Ephesus on the third journey would
make Philippians 2:19–23, with the plan to send Timothy shortly,
fit neatly with Acts 19:22, where Timothy and Erastus were sent
from Ephesus to Macedonia. Further, Paul's own hope to revisit the
Philippians (Phil. 2:24) would then fit precisely with the purpose
of Acts 19:21 and with the fact that Paul subsequently did revisit
Philippi on the last leg of the third journey.

There was a crisis in Ephesus in AD 54 (which would match
Paul's stay there) precipitated by the assassination of the Asian procurator Junius Silanus. Paul's trouble might have been connected, although if so we know not how.[104] On that premise, Luke's silence
about the matter could be explained, for there were political implications; Silanus's poisoning had come at the instigation of Nero's
mother, and reference to the upheaval might have been very unwise
for Luke's purpose.

Of course there would be a *praetorium* in Ephesus, and "Caesar's
household" might be broad enough to include members of the imperial staff who resided at Ephesus on the emperor's business.

Such are the considerations offered for an Ephesian composition of Philippians. Without belaboring the point, we may observe
that the arguments show little more than the possibility there was
an Ephesian imprisonment and that, if so, Philippians might have
been written there. The traditional view still has the greater probability. Bruce admits "Of all the possible meanings of *praetorian guard,*
the most appropriate in this context is 'praetorian guard.'"[105] Martin
concludes his discussion by acknowledging that "all possible identifications can present arguments that have strengths and weaknesses"
and by citing Martin Dibelius's admission that "a definite solution
of this problem can hardly be reached."[106] As Guthrie puts it, "If the
Roman hypothesis were proved untenable the Ephesian would probably be unchallenged."[107]

The events that led to the writing of Philippians. The letter reveals that a series of events transpired before Philippians was written. News of Paul's prison situation reached Philippi, as implied by the following: (1) the Philippians sent Paul a gift, by Epaphroditus (1:7; 4:14, 18), (2) Epaphroditus had become critically ill after arrival there (2:26–27), (3) news of his serious illness had got back to Philippi (2:26), (4) the fact that they had heard of his illness, and were concerned about it, had got back to Epaphroditus (2:26), and (5) Epaphroditus had recovered (2:27).

It would be impossible to say exactly how long all this took. Given the means of travel in those days, by land and sea, the letter at least could not have been written very soon after Paul's arrival in Rome (or very soon after any other incarceration, for that matter, even though travel from Philippi to Ephesus would not have taken nearly so long as to Rome). Assuming Rome, there would have been a distance of some 730 land miles, plus a sea voyage of a day or two across the Adriatic. Two months might have easily been required,[108] even if urgency could have made it faster. If we assume that the Philippians had got word of Paul's transfer to Rome by the time he himself arrived there, then all the events given above could have transpired within a year but probably not a lot less.

The immediate occasion of Philippians, then, is clear. Epaphroditus had recovered and was preparing to return to Philippi, partly to reassure the Philippians (2:25, 28). Paul took the opportunity to write.

The destination of Philippians. We know precisely when the Philippian church was founded, on Paul's second missionary journey, the story being told in Acts 16:9–40 (see chap. 5). Contact with women at the Jewish "place of prayer" (probably not a regular synagogue) led to the conversion of Lydia, a businesswoman and proselyte. Later, the casting out of a demon from a slave girl led to the beating and overnight jailing of Paul and Silas, which produced the conversion of the jailer. There were, therefore, at least two families to provide a nucleus for a church, Lydia's and the jailer's (Acts 16:15, 33). The account does not sound like it describes a very lengthy stay. Regardless, it is apparent that Luke stayed in Philippi to continue with the work when Paul and the others moved on to Thessalonica. Philippi may have been Luke's hometown.

Paul revisited Philippi twice on the third journey. If the Ephesian origin of Philippians as opposed to the Roman is correct, then Philippians was written before these brief third-journey contacts. Regardless, they add nothing to our knowledge of the Philippian church.

Philippi was a Roman colony in Paul's time (Acts 16:12). First established and given his name by Philip of Macedon (father of Alexander the Great), it was the site of Octavian's (Augustus) defeat of Brutus and Cassius and of their suicides in 42 BC. Augustus then made it a colony, which primarily means that he settled there a number of retired soldiers and their families.

Such colonies were considered as parts of Italy transplanted to other places. Consequently, among other things, they were not subject to the provincial government but self-governing and also exempt from the poll and property taxes. The veterans would all be Roman citizens and would possess the power, even though many others might settle and live there. Pisidian Antioch, Lystra, and Corinth (also colonies), according to the Acts record, "have as many Hellenes and Jews in their streets as Romans";[109] but that does not seem to be true of Philippi.

Philippi is also called "a leading city of the district of Macedonia" (Acts 16:12). Macedonia, untypically, was subdivided into four regions; the phrase, then, may simply mean that Philippi was in the first part.[110] Regardless, "The Roman colonies were well aware of their superiority to any provincial Greek city, however large."[111] "Roman patriotism was strongly influential at Philippi," then, and "many verses in [Philippians] presuppose exactly that pride and obligation which marked out Roman colonists"[112] (1:27; 2:15; 3:20).

All this leads to the implication that there was not a large Jewish population in Philippi and fewer Jews in the church than in most of Paul's churches. Everything about the Acts record tends to confirm this. There would have been some Jewish influence, of course. That Lydia was a proselyte indicates that. There was at least enough possibility of Jewish influence that Paul gives brief warning against Judaizers in 3:2–7. Even so, the great majority of the congregation was obviously of pagan background.

Some interpreters suggest that the fact that nearly all were of similar Gentile background may help account for the lack of serious problems at Philippi. Whether or not that is the case, the Philippians were one of Paul's closest and most supportive churches. The letter is almost wholly without tension, warm and personal. Even problems within the church are relatively minor.

The integrity of Philippians. The serious student will soon encounter views that Philippians is not one but two or more original documents later combined and edited. (The most extremely critical view, that Philippians is not authentically Pauline at all, is not held by many interpreters, even among non-evangelical scholars.)

The main reasons for doubting the integrity of Philippians are the abrupt transition in 3:1 and the assumption that the thanks for the gift in 4:10–20 would have been the very first thing said. One of the most radical results of this kind of internal, literary criticism is the suggestion that there are really three letters: letter A, a note of thanks (4:10–20); letter B, from prison (1:1–3:1a) and letter C, a letter of warning (3:16–4:3; 4:8–9)—written in this chronological order.

It is beyond the scope (and assumptions) of this text to interact with such views. The student who is interested may want to read R. P. Martin's thorough discussion. He treats the objections to integrity more sympathetically than most conservatives would; even so, he concludes: "These settings are very speculative. . . . It is possible to set the various parts of the letter into a set of circumstances that does not require the postulating of different epochs in Paul's missionary life."[113]

The purposes of Paul in writing Philippians. The purposes of Philippians can be stated more simply and directly than for most of Paul's letters. There were no serious conditions that needed lengthy attention.

Paul wrote *to acknowledge the gift the Philippians had sent* (4:10–18), *which includes thanks for their partnership support of him all along* (1:3–7).

He wrote *to reassure them about his own prison circumstances*, as we gather from the section that begins "I want you to know" (1:12–26).

He wrote *to encourage steadfastness in face of opposition* (1:27–30). The city's intolerance of Judaism would no doubt extend to the Christians.

He wrote *to give general exhortation about Christian living* (2:1–18), especially. One cannot read these exhortations without feeling that there was at least a mild spirit of self-assertiveness on the part of some, thus contributing to tension.

He wrote *to give warning against Judaizing influence* (3:1–21). It is possible that more than Judaizers are involved here. It is also arguable whether there was false teaching already at Philippi, or if Paul was simply warning against it should it come.

He wrote *to urge the reconciliation of Euodia and Syntyche*, two leading women in the church (4:2–3).

Themes in Philippians. Philippians is not the kind of work that one wants to state a single, dominant theme for. Even so, there are some themes that reappear throughout the letter and are worthwhile to follow.

A prominent theme is *joy*. The basic root (Greek verb *chairo*, noun *chara*) occurs sixteen times: in 1:4, 18 (twice), 25; 2:2, 17 (twice), 18 (twice), 28, 29; 3:1; 4:1, 4 (twice), 10. A synonym (exulting/boasting) occurs three times: 1:26; 2:16; 3:3.

Another prominent theme not so often noticed is *the Christian's mind*. One's "mind" includes his attitude and outlook, the way he thinks and what he values; and that has everything to do with being a true Christian. The basic Greek verb (*phroneo*) occurs eleven times: 1:7; 2:2 (twice), 5; 3:15 (twice), 16, 19; 4:2, 10 (twice); with a compound (lowlimindedness/humility) in 2:3. Other roots similarly translated are in 1:27; 2:20; 4:7, 8.

It would also be profitable to trace the theme of *fellowship* (Greek *koinonia*) in Philippians. Especially noteworthy are 1:5; 2:1; and 3:10.

The outline of Philippians. As a personal letter, Philippians does not lend itself easily to subject divisions. Few turning points are clearly marked. The following outline is therefore as much for our convenience as to follow natural divisions of thought.

Formal opening, 1:1–2
    I. Thanksgiving and prayer for the Philippians, 1:3–11
    II. Reassurance: Paul's attitude in his bonds, 1:12–26
        A. Paul's joy in the furtherance of the gospel, 1:12–18
        B. Paul's joy in life or death, 1:19–26
    III. The first hortatory section about Christian living, 1:27–2:18
        A. Exhortation to a life worthy of the gospel, 1:27–30
        B. Exhortation to unity and unselfish service, 2:1–11
        C. Exhortation to salvation living, 2:12–18
    IV. Paul's plans and coworkers, 2:19–30
    V. Warning against Judaizers: everything is in Christ, 3:1–4:1
        A. First warning: against confidence in circumcision, 3:1–3
        B. Paul's personal experience as testimony against Judaizers, 3:4–14
        C. Exhortation to share Paul's attitude, 3:15–16
        D. Second warning: against "the enemies of the cross," 3:17–19
        E. Exhortation to citizens of heaven, 3:20–4:1
    VI. The final hortatory section about Christian living, 4:2–9
    VII. Acknowledgment of the Philippians' gifts, 4:10–20
Conclusion, 4:21–23

8

THE LAST
YEARS OF PAUL

Scholars debate whether Paul's life ended immediately after Acts 28:31 or extended beyond. Each of these two possibilities has its supporters. The question is complex, involving tradition, points of interpretation, and the fact that movements suggested in the Pastoral Epistles (1, 2 Timothy and Titus) do not appear to fit it with anything recorded in Acts.

THE TWO SIDES OF THE ISSUE

Paul's Imprisonment Ended in Death

Did Paul die at the end of the two-year imprisonment of Acts 28? The tradition is strong that Paul was beheaded by command of Roman emperor Nero (AD 54–68). Those who think this execution took place right after Acts 28 have various observations to make that support or explain their view. To begin, Luke would not have ended his account if this were not the end of Paul's life and ministry. Again, Luke did not describe Paul's execution for emotional reasons, to spare his readers the pain of what he meant to be obvious. The ending (vv. 30–31) is much more victorious the way it is. Moreover, Luke would never have left Acts 20:25, 38 in his account if Paul had been wrong and had actually lived to visit the Ephesians again. Also, not only Acts 20:25, 38 but the last several chapters of Acts as well have the implied drama of Paul's moving toward his death. Finally, the Pastoral Epistles probably were not written by Paul anyway but pseudonymously by a later Paulinist, and so it does not matter that the movements of Paul referred to therein cannot be fitted into the Acts history. (Most who deny any extension of Paul's life beyond Acts would say this; some would tackle the difficult task of fitting the pastorals in the framework of Acts.)

Paul's Imprisonment Was Followed by Further Ministry

Did Paul live and minister beyond Acts 28? The more traditional view is that Paul was released and carried out further missionary work, going west as far as Spain and back east as far as Asia. Those who hold this view also make various observations on their side.

First, assuming the pastorals are authentically Pauline, it is much easier to account for the movements referred to in them in a post-Acts ministry. These include the following.

1 Timothy 1:3. According to this verse, Paul left Timothy at Ephesus and journeyed on into Macedonia from where he writes. However, only once in Acts did Paul go from Ephesus to Macedonia, on the third journey. But on that occasion Timothy was sent ahead (Acts 19:22).

Titus 1:5; 3:12. These verses indicate that Paul had left Titus in Crete. He was soon to be relieved, however, and was instructed to join Paul in Nicopolis for the winter. In Acts, Paul's only visit to Crete was while he was under arrest, being transferred from Caesarea to Rome. Nicopolis is not mentioned in Acts at all, although a visit there could theoretically be fitted in to the part of the third journey that took Paul into Macedonia and Achaia after the three years at Ephesus. (This assumes that the Nicopolis meant was in the district of Epirus in the province of Achaia.)

2 Timothy 1:16–17; 4:13, 20. Shortly before writing 2 Timothy, Paul had left a cloak and some books at Troas (4:13). He had also left Erastus at Corinth and Trophimus at Miletus (4:20). Such movements seem impossible to fit into Acts, inasmuch as Paul did not arrive in prison in Rome until at least two years after visiting Corinth, Troas, and Miletus on the last leg of the third journey. Furthermore, he did not stop at those ports on his trip to Rome.

These movements would be extremely difficult to place in the book of Acts without unduly stretching Luke's historicity. It is true that Luke never tried to tell everything. And by a bold stretch of imagination one might fit 1 Timothy and Titus into the third journey, assuming that Paul made an unrecorded visit to Crete and that 1 Timothy 1:3 means he sent (rather than left) Timothy to Ephesus from Macedonia. Even then, however, there seems to be no way to make 2 Timothy fit the Roman imprisonment of Acts 28.

Second, Paul planned to visit Rome and then to go on to Spain (Romans 15:24; Acts 19:21). It is attractive to believe that this purpose was Spirit-motivated and finally fulfilled.

Third, there is an early tradition (found in Clement of Rome, the Muratorian Canon, and Eusebius)[1] that Paul was released from the first imprisonment and ministered at some length, including the fulfilling of his desire to evangelize in Spain (Rom. 15:24).

Fourth, that Luke did not tell of Paul's further ministry is no real problem, for his stopping point was determined by his theological purpose: to trace the gospel's movement to Rome as the capital of the Gentile world. There is also a possibility that Luke's ending was determined by another factor. Many think that Acts was partially written so the account could be used in Paul's trial. If so, Luke wrote it (the gospel also) during the four years Paul was in prison in Caesarea and Rome. Therefore, a description of Paul's ministry after the imprisonment was not needed. Furthermore, Luke's writing might easily have ceased when the two years of Acts 28 ended. In that case verses 30–31 could have been added before the work was made available in broader Christian circles. That would explain why 20:25 was left in. For one thing, Luke might not have minded an awareness of Paul's ignorance of his own future movements any more than we do. For another thing, Paul might not have returned to Ephesus before Acts was finished and published.

Fifth, the Jews of Jerusalem would probably not have been able to get judgment against Paul in Rome any more than in Caesarea. They would have chosen to hurt Paul as much as they could, and that would be by delaying as long as possible. Luke's readers, understanding all this, would have understood him to imply a release.

Finally, that Nero would have ordered Paul's execution at this point in time (AD 62) is very improbable. A Neronian execution of Paul is much more likely in 66/67. Nero's persecution did not begin until after the famous fire of AD 64, which destroyed nearly a fourth of the city. According to Tacitus, Nero was suspected of starting that fire, so he blamed the Christians to shift attention from himself. (Officially, then, Christians were prosecuted as "incendiaries" instead of for religious reasons.) Although the vendetta was officially limited to Rome, there is strong tradition that it reached out to take both Paul and Peter: "Within less than half a decade the leadership of the church in Jerusalem, of the Pauline mission, and of the mission to the Jews had been extinguished by martyrdom even though there was no official policy of persecution."[2]

THE YEARS AFTER ACTS

The discussion above leads to an uncertain but probable conclusion, namely, that Paul was released in AD 62 and made further itineraries to Spain and to the Aegean region (Crete, Ephesus, Greece); that he was arrested again at Nero's behest in 65/66; and that he was beheaded in Rome in 66/67.

As already noted, several threads of ancient tradition support this view (although they add little to our meager knowledge of what might have transpired between AD 62 and 66 in Paul's life). Clement of Rome, writing in about AD 96, said Paul "reached the limit of the west,"[3] but one may argue whether he meant Spain. In the Muratorian canon, dated in the latter part of the second century, the statement is made that Luke's Acts fails to tell of "Paul's journey when he set out from Rome for Spain."[4] The apocryphal Acts of Peter, probably written by AD 180, describes Paul's departure from Italy by sea for Spain. In the fourth century, ecclesiastical writers like Eusebius and Jerome indicated that this was the tradition.

Assuming, then, that Paul was released at the end of the two years referred to at the end of Acts, we still cannot trace his movements. We can only say for sure what is contained in the Pastoral Epistles: that Paul went back as far east as Crete, Ephesus, and Greece, and that he wrote 1 Timothy and Titus during that itinerary. The possibilities will be discussed in more detail below. Probably Paul went to Spain. That tradition is strong.[5]

At any rate, once we assume the probability that Paul died in the persecution that followed the great fire, some helpful things can be said. On the night of July 18/19, AD 64, the fire broke out at the northeastern end of the Circus Maximus. It burned for five days, completely destroying three and severely damaging seven more of the city's fourteen divisions. (See the insert on page 205.) Nero was away at the time but hurried back. Rumors spread that he was responsible, seeking opportunity to reshape the city as he wished. In order to divert suspicion from himself, he accused the Christians of the crime and initiated inquisition and outrageous persecution. According to the Roman historian Tacitus,

> those who confessed were arrested; then, on their information, a huge multitude was convicted. . . . Their execution was made a matter of sport: some were sewn up in the skins of wild beasts and savaged to death by dogs; others were fastened to crosses as living torches to serve as lights when daylight failed. Nero made his gardens available for the show and held games in the Circus, mingling with the crowd or standing in his chariot in charioteer's uniform. Hence, although the victims were criminals deserving the severest punishment, pity began to be felt for them because it seemed they were being sacrificed to gratify one man's lust for cruelty rather than the public weal.[6]

By orders of such a madman, Paul was arrested. We do not know the circumstances, but there is nothing improbable about it. Paul would have been regarded as a leading promoter of the Christian faith in the empire. He may have been taken at Nicopolis (Tit. 3:12) and transported from there to Rome, but that is very uncertain. Indeed, he might have gone to Rome of his own accord; he might also have been arrested there. We cannot be sure of the charge: perhaps of propagating an illicit religion, perhaps of fomenting strife throughout the empire, perhaps even of "having instigated the Roman Christians to their supposed act of incendiarism."[7]

This time Paul's prison circumstances would have been very different from the relative freedom described in Acts 28:30–31. Second Timothy 1:16–18 probably implies that Onesiphorus had difficulty finding and visiting him. We cannot be sure, but he may well have spent some time in the dungeons that are traditionally shown as the place he awaited execution.

At some point Paul had a preliminary hearing (2 Tim. 4:16–17). No one stood with him, which is understandable, perhaps, in a time when to be identified as a Christian meant death. Even so, he had not been immediately condemned (v. 17). Still, Paul had no illusions, knowing that he had finished his course and that the time of his departure from this life was at hand (2 Tim. 4:6–7). Under such circumstances his last letter to Timothy was written.

Not long after—we do not know whether Timothy arrived in time (2 Tim. 4:21)—the verdict came and the sentence of death was pronounced. According to the tradition, which fits what we know of the times, early one morning Paul was taken outside the walls of the city on the Ostian Way and beheaded. The Roman executioner would probably have used a broad, double-bladed sword that would have severed the head with one powerful stroke. We are in no doubt that Paul, at last absent from the body, was immediately present with his Lord (2 Cor. 5:8).

THE PASTORAL EPISTLES AS A GROUP

The fourth group of Paul's letters is usually called the Pastoral Epistles. Unlike the rest (Philemon excepted), they were written to individuals rather than to churches. Timothy and Titus were two of Paul's closest associates in the ministry, engaged in building up churches already founded. Consequently, whether their function was exactly like that of a modern pastor or not, their concerns and responsibilities were certainly pastoral.

The student of these three letters soon encounters two special problems. First, when were they written? Do they represent a period of life and ministry that followed the two-year Roman imprisonment of Acts 28, or were they written during the period of history covered by Acts? Second, can we safely assume they are Pauline? Critical scholars have generally answered no. As a result, there is a widespread view that the pastorals are considerably later than Paul. Both of these problems will occupy us in this section. What is to be said about one of the letters will apply for the most part to all three.

The Question of a Post-Acts Ministry

Most who defend the Pauline authorship of the pastoral letters place them in a period following Acts. As noted, one of the problems of the pastorals is that certain incidents and movements referred to in them do not seem to fit the Acts record. Therefore, though a few interpreters have tried to fit the pastorals into Acts,[8] the more probable explanation is that these incidents fit a period of Paul's ministry following Acts. This possibility fits well with other considerations, previously mentioned: (a) the tradition that Paul was released and ministered afterward both in Spain and as far east as Asia Minor; (b) the improbability that the Jews could have prevailed against Paul in Rome, especially in view of their failure in Caesarea before Felix; (c) that Nero would not have had reason to execute Paul in AD 61/62 because his persecution of Christians did not begin until after the fire of 64; (d) the strong, early tradition that Paul (and Peter) were victims of the persecution that followed the fire.

All things considered, the theory of a release and further ministry following the two years of Acts 28:30 seems best. Once we accept a post-Acts ministry, there is no problem with the historical circumstances of the pastorals, even though we have no knowledge of the course of events of that ministry except for the references contained in them. We may assume that Paul fulfilled the implied promises to Philemon (v. 22) and the Philippians (2:24). We may provide space for founding churches in the West, in Spain in particular, although we have only the tradition to support this. If the pastorals were written during such a period, Paul definitely traveled in the Aegean area: Crete, Asia, Macedonia, and Achaia. He also was arrested and reimprisoned in Rome, apparently going directly there from an itinerary that included Miletus, Troas, and Corinth (above). Otherwise, we have no way of putting these movements together, nor do we know how long this period of freedom lasted. The general view, following Eusebius, is that Paul was beheaded in about AD 66/67. If that is so, the period of freedom would have been from about 62–66, or a period of three to five years.

The Authenticity of the Pastorals

It is beyond the scope of this text to deal with arguments against Pauline authorship in detail. The student would do well to read the thorough treatment of the issue by Donald Guthrie.[9] In brief, the main objections to Pauline authorship are as follows.

The historical situation, which has just been answered above.

Differences in literary style. Statistical analysis shows that there is a great deal of unusual vocabulary and usage in these letters, as compared to the other ten letters of Paul. Such an argument tends to overlook the differences that are called for by varied subject matter, differences in audience, changing circumstances, and the way a person might change style of expression over a period of time. An extensive itinerary of two or three years in Spain and points west, for example, would have exerted great cultural and linguistic influence on Paul, completely apart from normal maturing.

Ecclesiastical development. The pastorals seem to represent a very developed structure of church offices, with carefully defined standards for the elders and deacons (1 Tim. 3:1–13; Tit. 1:5–9), with prohibition of ordaining a recent convert (1 Tim. 3:6), with a formal program for widows (1 Tim. 5:3–16), and with Timothy and Titus apparently possessing something like the authority of bishops over a wide territory.

In fact, Paul began ordaining elders as early as his first journey (Acts 14:23), summoned and addressed the Ephesian elders in Miletus (Acts 20:17), spoke of the bishops and deacons in Philippians (1:1), and generally taught respect and support for the ministry of defined leaders (1 Thess. 5:12–13; Gal. 6:6). No doubt organization gradually became more important, with the Philippian and pastoral

letters reflecting that. Surely Paul, growing nearer to his own departure from the scene, would have been interested, with his experience
as background, in laying down guidelines. "He would have been the
most shortsighted of men if he had not done so."[10] Nor is there any
reason to think of Timothy and Titus as exercising any role beyond
that of representatives of Paul himself, a kind of "Vicars Apostolic."[11]

Doctrinal tradition. The pastorals are said to reflect a concern for
fixed doctrinal formulations uncharacteristic of Paul. The regular citation of "faithful sayings" (five times, as compared to none in the
other ten letters) is one example. However, it is reasonably clear that
Paul sometimes quoted early Christian hymns or confessions in the
earlier letters.

Some have also said that the doctrinal errors referred to in the
pastorals represent the full-fledged Gnosticism of the second century,
thus making the letters too late for Paul. But there is little if anything
in the pastorals to differentiate the errors from those at Colosse, for
example. The Gnosticism of the second century was surely preceded
by incipient forms.

Conservatives are convinced that nothing in the pastorals is too
late for Paul and that the stylistic-vocabulary differences are no more
than might be explained by differences in circumstances and personal
development. The reasons for the theory that the pastorals are not
authentically Pauline are weak.

By contrast, the reasons for accepting them as genuine are
strong. Externally, the evidence is strong. Except for Marcion and
his followers, who picked what suited them, there is an unbroken
line of acceptance of the pastorals as genuine all the way from the
Apostolic Fathers (Clement, Ignatius, and Polycarp[12]) to the advent
of nineteenth-century rationalistic criticism. Internally, the evidence
is also clear. All three letters claim to be by Paul and refer to known
coworkers, like Timothy, Titus, Luke, Tychichus, and Priscilla and
Aquila. A pseudonymous writer would have had not only to sign
Paul's name but also to invent the elaborate background of incidents,
movements, and characters involved, including references to Paul's
own life (as in 1 Tim. 1:13; 2 Tim. 1:5–6; 3:11).

Furthermore, it is hard to believe, as some claim, that writing pseudonymously under the name of an apostle was an accepted convention among Christians of the late first and second centuries. Guthrie considers this carefully and concludes: "Not a single comparable parallel from early Christian literary practice can be produced in support."[13] In fact, the evidence is in the opposite vein; one Asian presbyter who composed a Corinthian letter in Paul's name was condemned and deprived of his office.[14] We may be confident that the pastorals would have been flatly rejected had they not been manifestly genuine writings of Paul.

PASTORAL EPISTLES

First Timothy

The date and place of the writing of 1 Timothy. In the chart in chapter 4, 1 Timothy was dated at about AD 64 or 65, written from somewhere in Macedonia. The place seems clear enough (1:3). The date is not so clear, depending on a hypothetical reconstruction of Paul's movements between the two Roman imprisonments.

If we allow time for an extended itinerary into the western empire, including Spain, and if the date of Paul's execution by Nero's agent was 66, then we might place the western tour in 62–64 and an eastern one to the Aegean region in 64–65. As can readily be seen, other possibilities might work as well.[15] In truth, 1 Timothy (and Titus) might have been written at any time after Paul was released, depending on when he went back to Ephesus and Macedonia.

The events that led to the writing of 1 Timothy. Again, we have nothing beyond what has just been said. It is apparent that Paul was moving about among the churches he had ministered to earlier, although not back in Syria or Palestine. The itinerary, if we put Titus and 1 Timothy together, included Crete, Ephesus, Macedonia, and Nicopolis (in Epirus).

Based on 1:3 (and 1:20), it is probable that Paul and Timothy had been traveling together and came to Ephesus. When Paul decided to move on to Macedonia, he asked Timothy to stay in Ephesus to minister. From Macedonia, Paul wrote back to Timothy so that both he and the church would have a written description of what was to be done. Some suggest that developments in Ephesus had caused Timothy to write or otherwise send word to Paul, indicating a need for help, but that remains speculation.

The destination of 1 Timothy. Timothy is a well-known figure both in Acts and in Paul's other letters. It is apparent that he was the one of Paul's coworkers who was most his "son" in the faith and in the work (1 Tim. 1:2; 2 Tim. 1:2), although Titus was also dear and faithful (Tit. 1:4).

We may briefly recount the history of Timothy's involvement with Paul. He seems to have been a native Lystran, converted on Paul's first journey (Acts 16:1–2). His mother was Jewish; his father, Greek (Acts 16:1). (See also 2 Tim. 1:5). He was circumcised and joined Paul's team on the first leg of the second journey (Acts 16:3). His gift of ministry was confirmed by the laying on of Paul's hands (2 Tim. 1:6) and the hands of elders (1 Tim. 4:14). He was with Paul throughout the rest of the second journey, being specifically mentioned at Berea (Acts 17:14–15) and Corinth (Acts 18:5). During this period, he was sent at least once to Thessalonica, from Athens, to work with the church there and bring news to Paul (1 Thess. 3:1–6). He is named with Paul in both letters written on the second journey (1 Thess. 1:1; 2 Thess. 1:1). He was with Paul at Ephesus on the third journey and was sent on ahead into Macedonia (Acts 19:21–22). He was still with Paul on the final leg of the third journey as Paul headed for Jerusalem with the collection (Acts 20:4). Of four letters thought to have been written on the third journey, Timothy is included in the opening of only one, 2 Corinthians, but he is also mentioned in Romans (16:21) and 1 Corinthians (16:10), where he had been sent (4:17). We cannot tell that he accompanied Paul to Rome (Acts 27:2), but he was there when Paul wrote Colossians (1:1) and Philemon (v. 1) as well as Philippians (1:1; 2:19–23).

All this gives us a clear picture. Timothy was a constant companion and trusted coworker. It is apparent that he was either at Paul's side or on a mission sent by Paul from the time he joined Paul until the end of Paul's life. Of the ten earlier letters, Timothy is mentioned in seven, being included as co-writer in six. We cannot be precise about his age. If we assume he was, say, twenty at the time he joined Paul and Silas on the second journey in about AD 48 or 49, then he would be about thirty-six or thirty-seven in the year 65, which would fit the then current concept of "youthfulness" (1 Tim. 4:12).

When Paul wrote this letter, Timothy was at Ephesus. In all probability the letter was meant for the church, too. If so, it is the second letter of Paul's to include the Ephesians in its original readers.

The nature of the errors referred to in 1 Timothy. The background of 1 Timothy involved certain false teachings. In the letter Paul does not spend any particular passage dealing with the errors in any systematic way, not even in refuting them. Regardless of that, one of his reasons for writing Timothy and for leaving him in Ephesus in the first place was for Timothy to spend time instructing "certain men not to teach strange doctrines" (1 Tim. 1:3).

From Paul's passing references to the errorists, we may draw the general conclusion that the teaching was similar to that which had existed at Colosse when Paul wrote that letter sometime earlier. If that is the case, then we may say here, as in the introduction to Colossians, that there was a mixture of Jewish and Christian elements that may have been a forerunner of the full-fledged heresy of Gnosticism of the second century. A survey of the letter itself reveals the following references to error.

The letter mentions *myths, endless genealogies, fruitless discussion* (1:3, 6), *worldly fables* (4:7), *controversial questions and disputes about words* (6:4–5), *worldly and empty chatter* (6:20). Paul is not trying to refute this, but to expose it as useless and argumentative, whatever it is.

The Jewish law was in some way involved (1:7), and so perhaps the Old Testament genealogies were the ones referred to in 1:3.

Ascetic practice included abstention from marriage and certain foods (4:3).

Whether connected or not, there was *a striving to be rich* (6:5–10).

There was *knowledge* (Greek, *gnosis),* falsely so called (6:20).

There was *a denial of a future resurrection* (assuming that the

Hymenaeus of 2 Tim. 2:17–18 is the same as in 1 Tim. 1:19–20).

One is inclined to agree with Martin Dibelius and Hans Conzelmann: "A picture of the opponents can hardly be reconstructed."[16]

The purposes of Paul in writing 1 Timothy. What has been said in the last two sections leads to a statement of purposes.

Paul wrote *to strengthen Timothy's hand in resisting false teaching.* Some interpreters think Timothy may have been timid or discouraged and needed a little spine-stiffening. More likely is the suggestion that the church needed to know what Paul expected of Timothy. The letter may have been written for the sake of both Timothy and the church.

Paul wrote *to provide instruction about administering the affairs of the church.* This included matters of church order (2:8–15), the qualifications of bishops and deacons (3:1–13), the program for widows (5:3–18), and other matters.

Paul wrote *to challenge Timothy personally about how he should conduct himself* in his life and ministry to the church. Chapter 3:15 expresses this well, and other passages develop the purpose (4:7–8, 12–16; 5:1–2, 21–23; 6:11–14).

The outline of 1 Timothy. As semi-personal as the letter is, it is hard to outline, even though some of the changes of subject matter are obvious. The following outline should suggest the main areas of discussion.

Formal opening, 1:1–2
   I Paul's commission to Timothy, 1:3–20
      A. The need to correct false teaching, 1:3–11
      B. Paul's exultation in his own ministry, 1:12–17
      C. A charge to Timothy, 1:18–20
   II. Teaching about order in the church, 2:1–3:16
      A. Prayer in the church, 2:1–8
         1. The nature of prayer (v. 1a)
         2. The scope of prayer (vv. 1b, 2d)
         3. The aims of prayer (vv. 2b–1)
         4. The men who pray (v. 8)

B. Women in the church, 2:9–15
1. The women's adornment (vv. 9–10)
2. The women's submission (vv. 11–15)
C. Leaders in the church, 3:1–13
1. The bishops, or overseers (vv. 1–7)
2. The deacons (vv. 8–13)
D. Concluding word for Timothy, 3:14–16
III. Dangers to the church and Timothy's responsibility, 4:1–16
A. The danger of false teaching, 4:1–5
B. Timothy's response to false teaching, 4:6–10
C. Timothy's personal life and ministry, 4:11–16
IV. Timothy's ministerial work with various groups, 5:1–6:2
A. Relationships with all groups in the church, 5:1–2
B. The Program for Widows, 5:3–16
1. The difference between widows with and without family (vv. 3–8)
2. The difference between those to be enrolled and those not to be (vv. 9–15)
3. A final word (v. 16)
C. Dealings with the elders, 5:17–25
1. The elders' remuneration (vv. 17–18)
2. The correction of elders (vv. 19–20)
3. Timothy and the elders (vv. 21–25)
D. Instructing Christian slaves, 6:1–2
V. Final charge to Timothy, 6:3–19
A. Withdrawal from unsound teachers, 6:3–5
B. Contentment versus covetousness, 6:6–10
C. A call to the man of God, 6:11–16
D. Instructions for wealthy believers, 6:17–19
Conclusion, 6:20–21

Titus

Although Titus is not merely a shorter version of 1 Timothy, it is very much like it. As one of the pastorals, the letter shares the same problems that are raised about 1 Timothy. These questions about the historical background of the pastorals and their authenticity have already been discussed above. Indeed, nearly all the introductory matters can be treated with brevity, recalling the discussions in the introduction to 1 Timothy.

The date and place of the writing of Titus. Because we have no record of the events behind these letters except for the letters themselves, we cannot be dogmatic about how Titus and 1 Timothy are historically related. Even so, there are two kinds of reasons for linking them closely. First, both are tied to places in the same general part of Paul's world, namely, the Aegean region. Second, the contents of the two letters are very similar. Paul's concerns are much the same. It is very probable that the two letters were written at about the same time and place.

This time and place we have said to be somewhere in Macedonia in about AD 64 or 65. That will fit in with the only place reference in the letter. In 3:12 Paul indicates that he has made plans to winter in Nicopolis, using the word "there" (not "here"). Nicopolis (assumed to be the one in the district of Epirus or the northwestern coast of Achaia) was not far from Macedonia.

The events that led to the writing of Titus. According to 1:5, Paul had left Titus in Crete to give direction to what sounds like a relatively young group of churches on that island. The situation is very similar to that of Timothy in Ephesus. Paul had moved on, perhaps visiting Ephesus and leaving Timothy there. Now, sometime later, Paul was in contact with two other preachers, Zenas and Apollos (3:13). They were going to pay Crete a visit on their own itinerary. Paul took advantage of their plans to write this letter and send it to Titus by them.

The purposes of Paul in writing Titus. In general these are the same as for 1 Timothy with some points of difference. The main purposes are these.

Paul wrote *to remind and instruct Titus about administering the church affairs* in Crete. There was more than one congregation on the island (1:5); apparently they or at least some of them were young

churches and needed setting in order, especially the ordaining of elders to lead the churches (1:5–9).

Paul wrote *to exhort Titus about his own personal character and
life*, as an example before the churches (2:7–8, 15).

Paul wrote *to warn Titus about false teachers* and to encourage
him to resist them firmly (1:10–14). This attention does not seem
to permeate the letter as much as 1 Timothy. We may surmise from
that that the threats were not so serious as in Ephesus. Even so, there
was need for Titus to guard against falsehood. It is apparent that the
same kind of error was a possible threat in Crete; at least some of the
same kinds of words (although much more briefly) are used in warning Titus. There are the same "myths" and "commandments of men"
(1:14), the same "foolish controversies and genealogies and strife and
disputes about the Law" (3:9; cf. 1 Tim. 1:4, 7; 6:20). For discussion
of the nature of the errors Titus must resist, then, see the discussion
in the introduction to 1 Timothy.

Paul wrote *to direct Titus to make plans to leave Crete and meet
him,* later, in Nicopolis; Artemas or Tychichus would be sent to relieve him at that time (3:12–13).

As in the case of 1 Timothy, Paul probably intended that the
letter to Titus be read by the churches in the island, thus serving to
exhort them and strengthen Titus's hand.

The destination of Titus. Although the situations and letters are very
similar, we do not know nearly so much about Titus as about Timothy.
To begin with, we have already seen that Titus is never mentioned in
Acts. Although the theory that he was Luke's brother (or other relative)
might explain that silence, it must remain mere theory.

From 1:4 we gather that Titus was, like Timothy, a genuine son
of Paul's in the faith. Even so, and entirely apart from the silence of
Acts, we assume he did not have quite the standing of Timothy. He is
not mentioned in Paul's own letters with anything like the frequency
of Timothy. Whereas Timothy is listed with Paul in the opening of six
of the ten earlier letters, Titus is not named in this way in any of them.

The earliest incident we can connect Titus with is the visit to
Jerusalem described in Galatians 2:1–10. Whether that was the

Jerusalem Council (of Acts 15) or the famine visit (of Acts 14:29–30) has been argued in the introduction to Galatians (chap. 6). Either way, Titus was with Paul at that point before the second journey at least. Further, the incident makes clear he was a Gentile, his uncircumcision being something of a test case.

The next thing we can connect Titus with is the third journey when Paul labored long in Ephesus. He was deeply involved in Paul's painful interactions with the Corinthian church during that period, being mentioned in 2 Corinthians 1:13; 7:5–7; 8:6, 16, 23; 12:18. In reference to the involvement at Corinth, Donald Guthrie notes that it was "a particularly difficult and delicate mission and since the outcome appears to have been a happy one, it is clear that Titus was a man of unusual tact who possessed high qualities of leadership."[17]

Except for these two matters, we cannot link Titus to other activities with Paul except for those involved with the writing of the letter to him and a subsequent reference in 2 Timothy 4:10.

The background of Titus's field of ministry in Crete is also unknown to us beyond what we read in the letter. Crete is not mentioned in Acts except for the stopover of the ship on the way to Rome (Acts 27:7–13). There is no reason to suspect any missionary activity by Paul on that occasion, although the stop there might have kindled his interest. That might explain the visit he and Titus (and Timothy, perhaps) made there after release from the first Roman imprisonment.

Probably the gospel had already reached Crete, mentioned in Acts 1:11. Surely some from Pauline churches in the Aegean area, if nowhere else, had been there. Even so, Titus 1:5 sounds like there were relatively few churches and that they needed to select and ordain officials. Beyond this, we cannot say much about the makeup or circumstances of the churches on Crete.

The Outline of Titus

Formal opening, 1:1–4

    I. Two specific responsibilities of Titus in the churches, 1:5–16

        A. The ordaining of elders, 1:5–9

        B. Resistance to false teaching, 1:10–16

1. The existence and activity of false teachers (vv. 10–11)
2. A witness against them (vv. 12–13a)
3. Rebuke commanded (vv. 13b–16)
II. The teaching that Titus is to give the churches, 2:1–3:11
    A. The behavior of all groups in the church, 2:1–10
      1. The older men (v. 2)
      2. The older women (vv. 3–4a)
      3. The younger women (vv. 4b–5)
      4. The younger men (v. 6)
      5. The example of Titus (vv. 7–8)
      6. The Christian slaves (vv. 9–10)
    B. The obligations of grace, 2:11–15
    C. The Christian's relationship to the world, 3:1–8
      1. The Christian as servant to the world (vv. 1–2)
      2. The Christian's experience of grace (vv. 3–8)
    D. Final instruction about false teaching, 3:9–11
Conclusion, 3:12–15

Second Timothy

Of all Paul's letters, 2 Timothy is the most poignant. It is the great apostle's final letter, showing awareness that he was about to meet face-to-face again the one whom he had met thirty years earlier on the Damascus road and served faithfully the rest of his life.[18] Even so, it is by no means maudlin. Indeed, the prevailing note is victorious. A deathbed letter it may be, but Paul's impending departure (4:6) is not occasion for tears. Instead, it is an occasion, on one hand, for eager anticipation; on the other hand, for the retiring warrior to pass along to his dearest coworker a charge to carry on the fight.

Therefore, although 2 Timothy shares some things in common with the other two pastoral letters, it really stands apart from them and all the other letters. Not much speaks to the circumstances of any particular church. Although some parts make specific reference to people and places then of concern to Paul, the letter is essentially universal in its thrust.

The questions of introduction that were dealt with above need not be raised again, inasmuch as 2 Timothy shares the same problems in background. Even so, 2 Timothy has unique features that call for discussion.

The date and place of the writing of 2 Timothy. The circumstances of 2 Timothy are different. The important points are these.

Paul was in prison: 1:8, 16; 2:9. Reference to his affliction (1:12) reflects this.

The place of writing was Rome: 1:17 makes this clear. The greetings from people with Latin names (4:21) add a little confirmation, although this point could not stand on its own.

Furthermore, as we have already seen in this chapter, the references to recent events would not fit the Roman imprisonment of Acts 28. Paul had recently left things at Troas (4:13), had left Trophimus ill at Miletus (4:20), and probably left Erastus at Corinth (4:20).

Add to this Paul's very single-minded attitude. He is confident he has finished his course and is about to depart this world (4:6–8). This may be contrasted with the ambivalence of Philippians 1:20–26, for example, or with the hope for release in Philemon 22.

Therefore, 2 Timothy was written from Roman imprisonment very near the end of Paul's life. The tradition is that his arrest was by Nero's order, as an outgrowth of the persecution of Christians that followed the famous fire of AD 64 and that Paul's execution came probably in 66, the approximate date of 2 Timothy.

The events that led to the writing of 2 Timothy. Beyond what has just been noted, little more can be said.

Paul has been arrested by Nero's order, under what circumstances we cannot say. The references to movements involving Miletus, Troas, and Corinth (noted above)—or in some other order—sound like Paul was free at the time. Whether he was seized somewhere else and taken to Rome or went to Rome on his own and was arrested there is also impossible to say. W. J. Conybeare and J. S. Howson speculate that Paul was placed under arrest in Nicopolis, where Titus was to meet him (Tit. 3:12), and transported immediately to Rome.[19]

At some point Onesiphorus of Ephesus had visited in Rome and sought out Paul (1:16–17). That was in contrast to others of Asia who had turned away from him (1:15).

Apparently Paul had had a (preliminary?) hearing, as 4:16 seems to suggest. Unhappily, others had not stood with him on that occasion. Paul expected death (4:6).

Most of Paul's coworkers had gone elsewhere, some on missions for Paul, some having forsaken him (4:10–12). Only Luke was with him (4:11).

Tychichus was being sent, presumably bearing this letter, to relieve Timothy in Ephesus (4:12).

Under these circumstances, then, Paul wrote Timothy this last letter.

The purposes of Paul in writing 2 Timothy. The letter makes several purposes clear.

Paul wrote *to encourage Timothy,* no doubt depressed by Paul's circumstances (1:4), and *to urge him to remain steadfast* in the ministry he was chosen for (1:6, 14; 2:1; 3:14; 4:1–5).

Paul wrote *to prepare Timothy for his departure from the scene,* giving instructions about the requirements of faithful service (2:1–26) and about the "difficult times" that could be expected (3:1–13).

Paul wrote *to warn Timothy,* once more, about the need to resist the false doctrine that had been threatening since before 1 Timothy was written. The wording of passages like 1:13; 2:16–18, 23, which are very much like similar passages in 1 Timothy and Titus, makes it reasonably clear that the same errors were involved.

Paul wrote *to urge Timothy, now relieved by Tychichus* (4:12), *to come quickly* (4:9, 21) and to bring the cloak and scrolls from Troas (4:13).

The destination of 2 Timothy. On Timothy's personal history, see the introduction to 1 Timothy above. Timothy was still at Ephesus. Several references make this clear: (1) the reference to Onesiphorus and his family (1:16–18; 4:19); (2) the sending of Tychichus to Ephesus (4:12), evidently to relieve Timothy; and (3) the probability that Hymenaeus (2:17) is the same as in 1 Timothy 1:20. (It is possible that Philetus [2 Tim. 2:17] is another name for Alexander

[1 Tim. 1:20], but that is tenuous. Or it is possible that the Alexander in 4:14 is the same as in 1 Timothy.)

A question might be raised about Aquila and Priscilla, greeted in 4:19. The last time we knew, they were in Rome (Rom. 16:3), which had been their home earlier (Acts 18:2). However, it is clear they were not in Rome when Paul wrote 2 Timothy because they were wherever Timothy was. Ephesus is a likely place for them, for that is where they had ministered previously (Acts 18:18–26).

The Outline of 2 Timothy

Formal opening, 1:1–2

I. Appeal to Timothy in light of Paul's circumstances, 1:3–18
   A. Grateful remembrance and longing for Timothy, 1:3–5
   B. Appeal to Timothy, 1:6–14
   C. The actions of others, 1:15–18

II. Timothy's responsibilities in ministering the truth, 2:1–26
   A. Exhortation and example for Timothy as a minister, 2:1–13
      1. Timothy's overall responsibility (vv. 1–2)
      2. Lessons from secular occupations (vv. 3–7)
      3. Examples for Timothy to follow (vv. 8–13)
   B. Timothy's responsibility for the purity of the teaching, 2:14–26
      1. Commitment to the truth (vv. 14–15)
      2. Avoiding error (vv. 16–19)
      3. Being a clean, usable utensil (vv. 20–22)
      4. Administering the truth (vv. 23–26)

III. Appeal to Timothy in light of difficult times, 3:1–17
   A. Expectation of opposition to the truth, 3:1–9
      1. The character of "difficult times" (vv. 1–5)
      2. The opposers' capture of others (vv. 6–7)
      3. A biblical example (vv. 8, 9)
   B. The possibility of faithfulness in dangerous times, 3:10–17
      1. Paul's own example (vv. 10–13)

2. The Scriptures as encouragement and resource (vv. 14–17)

IV. Paul's farewell messages, 4:1–18

    A. Paul's concluding charge and testament, 4:1–8

        1. A final appeal to Timothy (vv. 1–5)

        2. The completion of Paul's work (vv. 6–8)

    B. Matters at hand, 4:9–18

        1. Request for Timothy to come (v. 9)

        2. Paul's other coworkers (vv. 10–11a)

        3. Involvements in Timothy's coming (vv. 11b–13)

        4. Warning about Alexander (vv. 14–15)

        5. Paul's hearing (vv. 16–18)

Conclusion, 4:19–22

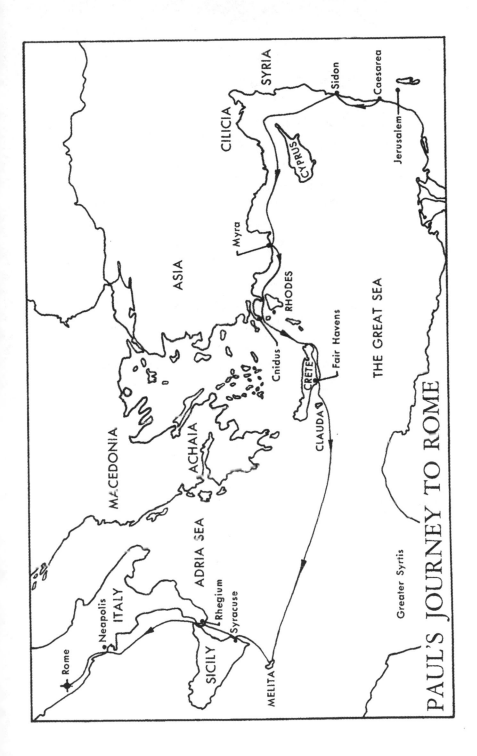

PAUL'S JOURNEY TO ROME

POSTSCRIPT

In about AD 96, Clement of Rome wrote:

Paul, on account of jealousy and strife, showed the way to the prize of endurance; seven times he wore fetters, he was exiled, he was stoned, he was herald both in the East and in the West, he gained the noble renown of his faith, he taught righteousness throughout the whole world and, having reached the limit of the West, he bore testimony before the rulers, and so departed from the world and was taken up into the holy place—the greatest example of endurance.[20]

According to tradition, Paul was beheaded by sword, probably, at Aquae Salviae (now Tre Fontane) near the third milestone on the Ostian Way. Before the end of the second century, a monument was erected where he was said to have been buried, about a mile nearer the city on the same route. About AD 324 Constantine built there a small basilica, replaced by a larger one near the end of that century. That one, in turn, burned in 1823. The present one at the same site was completed in 1854. Underneath the altar is a floor formed by two slabs (discovered in 1835), probably not in their original position.

On these slabs is engraved, in lettering belonging to the fourth century, perhaps to Constantine's time, an epitaph that Paul himself would probably have approved:

PAVLO APOSTOLO MART

Translated, that means, "To Paul, apostle and martyr."[21] Had he been asked, he might have added these additional words from his final letter: "To Him be the glory forever and ever. Amen."

RECOMMENDED RESOURCES

Abbott, T. K. *A Critical and Exegetical Commentary on the Epistles to the Ephesians and Colossians* (ICC). London: Bloomsbury T&T Clark, 2000.

*Barrett, C. K. *The Epistle to the Romans,* revised edition (BNTC). Louisville: Hendrickson Publishers Inc., 1991.

_____. *The First Epistle to the Corinthians,* second edition (NTC). New York: Continuum, 1994.

_____. *The Second Epistle to the Corinthians* (BNTC). Peabody, MA: Hendrickson, 1993.

Barth, Marcus. *Ephesians,* 2 Volumes (AB). Garden City: Doubleday, 1974.

Benko, Stephen, and John J. O'Rourke, eds. *The Catacombs and the Colosseum.* Valley Forge: Judson, 1971.

Betz, Hans Dieter. *Galatians* (Hermeneia). Reprint, Philadelphia: Fortress, 1989.

Bruce, F. F. *Paul: Apostle of the Heart Set Free.* Reprint, Grand Rapids: Eerdmans, 2000

_____. *Commentary on the Book of Acts* (NICNT). Reprint, Grand Rapids: Eerdmans, 1988.

_____. *1 & 2 Thessalonians* (WBC). Reprint, Waco: Word, 2015.

_____. *The Epistle to the Galatians* (NIGTC). Reprint, Grand Rapids: Eerdmans, 2013.

*_____. *1 and 2 Corinthians* (NCB). Reprint, New York City: Harper Collins, 1981.

*_____. *The Epistle of Paul to the Romans* (TNTC). Reprint, Eastford: Martino Fine Books, 2011.

*_____. *The Epistle to the Ephesians.* Reprint, Westwood: Revell, 1976.

Burton, Ernest De Witt. *A Critical and Exegetical Commentary on the Epistle to the Galatians* (ICC). Edinburgh: T & T Clark, 1950.

*Carson, Herbert M. *Colossians and Philemon* (TNTC). Grand Rapids: Eerdmans, 1960.

*Cole, R. A. *The Epistle of Paul to the Galatians* (TNTC). Grand Rapids: Eerdmans, 1978.

Conybeare, W. J., and J. S. Howson. *The Life and Epistles of St. Paul.* Reprint, Grand Rapids: Eerdmans, 1999.

Conzelmann, Hans. *1 Corinthians* (Hermeneia). Philadelphia: Fortress, 1990.

Cranfield, C. E. B. *The Epistle to the Romans,* 2 Volumes (ICC). Edinburgh: T & T Clark, 1987.

Dibelius, Martin, and Hans Conzelmann. *The Pastoral Epistles* (Hermeneia). Philadelphia: Fortress, 1972.

Frame, J. E. *1 and 2 Thessalonians* (ICC). Edinburgh: T & T Clark, 1912.

Furnish, Victor Paul. *II Corinthians* (AB). Garden City: Doubleday, 1984.

*Grosheide, F. W. *Commentary on the First Epistle to the Corinthians* (NICNT). Reprint, Grand Rapids: Eerdmans, 2014.

*Guthrie, Donald. *New Testament Introduction.* Reprint, Downers Grove: InterVarsity, 1990.

_____. *The Pastoral Epistles* (TNTC). Reprint, Grand Rapids: Eerdmans, 1991.

_____, and J. A. Motyer, eds. *The New Bible Commentary,* Revised Edition. Grand Rapids: Eerdmans, 1984.

Harrison, Everett F. *Introduction to the New Testament.* Revised, Grand Rapids: Eerdmans, 1971.

Harrison, P. N. *The Problem of the Pastorals* (Classic Reprint). London: Forgotten Books, 2016.

Hawthorne, Gerald F., and Ralph P. Martin. *Philippians,* Revised Edition (WBC). Grand Rapids: Zondervan, 2015.

*Hendriksen, William. *New Testament Commentary: Exposition of I and II Thessalonians.* Reprint, Grand Rapids: Baker, 1977.

_____. *New Testament Commentary: Ephesians*. Reprint, Grand Rapids: Baker, 1978.

*_____. *Exposition of Philippians*. Grand Rapids: Baker, 1980.

*Hiebert, D. Edmond. *The Thessalonian Epistles: A Call to Readiness*. Chicago: Moody, 1982.

*_____. *Titus and Philemon*. Chicago: Moody, 1957.

*Hughes, Philip E. *Paul's Second Epistle to the Corinthians* (NICNT). Reprint, Grand Rapids: Eerdmans, 1967.

*Kent, Homer A., Jr. *The Pastoral Epistles*, Revised Edition. Chicago: Moody, 1982.

Lightfoot, J. B. *The Epistle of St. Paul to the Galatians*. Reprint, Grand Rapids: Zondervan, 1957.

_____. *St. Paul's Epistles to the Colossians and to Philemon*. Reprint, Charleston: Nabu, 2010.

_____. *St. Paul's Epistle to the Philippians*. Toronto: University of Toronto Libraries, 2011.

Lock, Walter. *The Pastoral Epistles* (ICC). Edinburgh: T & T Clark, 1924.

Lohse, Eduard. *Colossians and Philemon* (Hermeneia). Philadelphia: Fortress, 1988.

Longenecker, Richard N. *Paul, Apostle of Liberty*. Grand Rapids: Eerdmans, 2015.

Machen, J. Gresham. *The Origin of Paul's Religion*. Reprint, Eugene: Wipf & Stock, 2002.

*Marshall, I. H. *1 and 2 Thessalonians* (NCB). Grand Rapids: Eerdmans, 1983.

Martin, Ralph P. *New Testament Foundations: A Guide for Christian Students*, 2 Volumes. Reprint, Grand Rapids: Eerdmans, 1994.

_____. *2 Corinthians* (WBC). Grand Rapids: Zondervan, 2014.

*_____. *Philippians* (NCB). Downers Grove: InterVarsity, 2008.

_____. *Colossians and Philemon* (NCB). Reprint, Grand Rapids: Eerdmans, 1982.

_____. *The Epistle of Paul to the Philippians* (TNTC). Reprint, Grand Rapids: Eerdmans, 2007.

*McDonald, H. Dermot. *Commentary on Colossians & Philemon*. Waco: Word, 1980.

Milligan, George. *St. Paul's Epistles to the Thessalonians*. Reprint, San Bernadino: Ulan, 2012.

Mitton, C. Leslie. *Ephesians* (NCB). London: Oliphant, 1976.

*Morris, Leon. *The Epistles of Paul to the Thessalonians,* Second Edition (TNTC). Downers Grove: InterVarsity, 1985.

*_____. *The First and Second Epistles to the Thessalonians* (NICNT). Grand Rapids: Eerdmans, 2009.

*_____. *The First Epistle of Paul to the Corinthians* (TNTC). Grand Rapids: Eerdmans, 1958.

Moule, C. F. D. *The Epistles of Paul the Apostle to the Colossians and Philemon* (Cambridge Greek Testament). Cambridge: Cambridge University Press, 1968.

*Muller, Jac J. *The Epistles of Paul to the Philippians and to Philemon* (NICNT). Reprint, Grand Rapids: Eerdmans, 1983.

*Murray, John. *The Epistle to the Romans*, New Edition (NICNT). Grand Rapids: Eerdmans, 1980.

Ogg, George. *The Chronology of the Life of Paul*. Eugene: Wipf & Stock, 2016.

Orr, William F., and James Arthur Walther *1 Corinthians* (AB). Garden City: Doubleday, 1976.

Packer, James I. et al., eds. *The Bible Almanac*. Nashville: Nelson, 1980.

Plummer, Alfred. *A Critical and Exegetical Commentary on the Second Epistle of St. Paul to the Corinthians* (ICC). Toronto: University of Toronto Libraries, 2011.

Pollock, John. *The Apostle*. Colorado Springs: Cook, 2012.

Ramsay, W. M. *St. Paul the Traveller and the Roman Citizen*. Reprint, London: Forgotten Books, 2012.

_____. *The Cities of St. Paul*. Reprint, Grand Rapids: Baker, 1997.

*Ridderbos, Herman N. *The Epistle of Paul to the Churches of Galatia* (NICNT). Reprint, Grand Rapids: Eerdmans, 1972.

Robertson, Archibald, and Alfred Plummer. *The First Epistle of St. Paul to the Corinthians* (ICC). Reprint, Edinburgh: T & T

Clark, 1961.

Schürer, Emil. *The History of the Jewish People in the Age of Jesus Christ*, 2 Volumes. Revised and edited by Vermes, Millar, and Black. Reprint, Edinburgh: T & T Clark, 2014.

Sherwin-White, A. N. *Roman Society and Roman Law in the New Testament.* Grand Rapids: Baker, 1992.

*Simpson, E. K., and F. F. Bruce. *Commentary on the Epistles to the Ephesians and Colossians* (NICNT). Grand Rapids: Eerdmans, 1981.

*Tasker, R. V. G. *The Second Epistle of Paul to the Corinthians* (TNTC). Grand Rapids: Eerdmans, 1958.

*Vaughan, Curtis. *Galatians* (Bible Study Commentary). Cape Coral: Founders, 2005.

*_____. *1 Corinthians* (Bible Study Commentary). Grand Rapids: Zondervan, 1984.

*_____. *Romans* (Bible Study Commentary). Grand Rapids: Zondervan, 1976.

*_____. *Colossians and Philemon* (Bible Study Commentary). Reprint, Grand Rapids: Zondervan, 1980.

Vincent, Marvin B. *Philippians and Philemon* (ICC). London: Bloomsbury T & T Clark, 2000.

*Vos, Howard F. *Philippians* (Bible Study Commentary). Grand Rapids: Zondervan, 1980.

*Ward, Ronald A. *Commentary on 1 & 2 Timothy & Titus.* Waco: Word, 1974.

Westcott, B. F. *Saint Paul's Epistle to the Ephesians: The Greek Text with Notes and Addenda* (Classic Reprint). London: Forgotten Books, 2015.

*These will be most helpful to students not prepared for technical studies or unable to read Greek.

NOTES

Foreword

1. See especially I. Howard Marshall, *New Testament Theology: Many Witnesses, One Gospel* (Downers Grove: InterVarsity, 2004); Thomas R. Schreiner, *Paul: Apostle of God's Glory in Christ: A Pauline Theology* (Downers Grove: InterVarsity, 2001); Eckhard J. Schnabel; *Early Christian Mission*, 2 vols. (Downers Grove: InterVarsity, 2004); and Eckard J. Schnabel, *Paul the Missionary: Realities, Strategies, and Methods* (Downers Grove: InterVarsity, 2008).
2. See, for example, Richard N. Longenecker, *The Ministry and Message of Paul* (Grand Rapids: Zondervan, 1971); Charles L. Quarles, *Illustrated Life of Paul* (Nashville: B&H Academic, 2014); and chap. 9: "Paul: The Man and His Message" in Andreas J. Köstenberger, L. Scott Kellum, and Charles L. Quarles, *The Cradle, the Cross, and the Crown*, 2nd ed. (Nashville: B&H Academic, 2016), 437–80.
3. See, in particular, David Wenham, *Paul: Follower of Jesus or Founder of Christianity?* (Grand Rapids: Eerdmans, 1995); cf. Köstenberger, Kellum, and Quarles, *Cradle, the Cross, and the Crown*, 439–48.
4. For a recent selective survey of Pauline scholarship, see N. T. Wright, *Paul and His Recent Interpreters*. I have written a thorough review of this work: http://www.booksataglance.com/book-reviews/paul-recent-interpreters -contemporary-debates-n-t-wright. See also Köstenberger, Kellum, and Quarles, *Cradle, the Cross, and the Crown*, 448–57; and in much greater depth, D. A. Carson, Mark A. Seifrid, and Peter T. O'Brien, eds., *Justification and Variegated Nomism*, WUNT 2/140, 2 vols. (Tübingen: Mohr Siebeck/Grand Rapids: Baker, 2001).
5. For various contributions to this topic on which scholars continue to differ, see Armand Puig i Tàrrech, John M. G. Barclay, and Jörg Frey, eds., *The Last Years of Paul: Essays from the Tarragona Conference, June 2013*, WUNT 352 (Tübingen: Mohr Siebeck, 2015).
6. For full-fledged Pauline theologies, see especially those by James D. G. Dunn, *The Theology of Paul the Apostle* (Grand Rapids: Eerdmans, 1997), though note that Dunn considers only seven letters of Paul to be authentic; Schreiner, *Paul*; and Frank Thielman, *Theology of the New Testament: A Canonical and Synthetic Approach* (Grand Rapids: Zondervan, 2005).
7. As a result, we have chosen to follow a similar chronological approach in our textbooks *The Cradle, the Cross, and the Crown* and the abridged version *The Lion and the Lamb: New Testament Essentials* from *The Cradle, the Cross, and the Crown* (Nashville: B&H Academic, 2012).
8. Andreas J. Köstenberger, *Commentary on 1-2 Timothy and Titus*, BTCP (Nashville: B&H Academic, 2017).

Chapter 1: Paul's Dispersion Background

1. Robert A. Kraft, "Judaism on the World Scene," in *The Catacombs and the Colosseum*, ed. Stephen Benko and John J. O'Rourke (Valley Forge: Judson, 1971), 83.

2. That very road, a major east-west passage, was on the route of the famous expedition of the Persian army, memorialized since ancient times in Xenophon's *Anabasis.*

3. John Pollock, *The Apostle* (Wheaton: Victor, 1972), 5.

4. Sometimes Cilicia and its next door province of Syria were regarded as one: "*Syria et* [and] *Cilicia*"; then, Tarsus and Antioch were regarded as co-capitals. This was probably the case from 25 BC–AD 72 and thus throughout Paul's life. See F. F. Bruce, *Paul: Apostle of the Heart Set Free* (Grand Rapids: Eerdmans, 1977), 33; A. N. Sherwin-White, *Roman Society and Roman Law in the New Testament* (Oxford: Clarendon, 1963), 55–56.

5. This was done at the behest of Anthony, who often spent time in Tarsus. Indeed, he first met Cleopatra there, some forty years before Paul's birth (41 BC).

6. For a more detailed discussion of the difference between free and subject cities, see Emil Schürer, *The History of the Jewish People in the Age of Jesus Christ,* ed. Vermes, Millar, and Black, rev. ed., 3 vols. (Edinburgh: T & T Clark, 1973–79), 2:93–94.

7. Bruce, *Paul: Apostle of the Heart,* 35.

8. Pollock, *The Apostle,* 6.

9. This "assembly" of citizens is the Greek word *ekklesia,* the word the Christians chose for their assemblies, translated "church."

10. Sherwin-White, *Roman Society,* 179.

11. See Bruce, *Paul: Apostle of the Heart,* 34–35.

12. W. M. Ramsay, *St. Paul the Traveller and the Roman Citizen* (Grand Rapids: Baker, 1972), 32; W. M. Ramsay, *The Cities of St. Paul* (Grand Rapids: Baker, 1949), 169–86.

13. In doing this, the cities were imitating the system used by the Roman State, which also grouped Roman citizens into thirty-five "tribes," closely following social and class lines; see Sherwin-White, *Roman Society,* 144–47.

14. That date, too, is debatable, with current scholarship tending to suggest 5/4 BC See Harold M. Hoehner, *Chronological Aspects of the Life of Christ* (Grand Rapids: Zondervan, 1976), 25.

15. Bruce, *Paul: Apostle of the Heart,* 37.

16. Sherwin-White, *Roman Society,* 151.

17. Ibid., 175–76.

18. George E. Wright and Floyd V. Filson, *The Westminster Historical Atlas to the Bible,* rev. ed. (Philadelphia: Westminster, 1956), 77.

19. For a thorough treatment, see James L. Jones, "The Roman Army," in *The Catacombs and the Colosseum,* 187–217.

20. Ibid., 213.

21. See Schürer, *History,* 1:255 (incl. n. 8), 357.

22. John J. O'Rourke, "Roman Law and the Early Church," in *The Catacombs and the Colosseum,* 176.

23. Wright, *Westminster Atlas,* 80.

24. Ibid., 79.

25. Bruce, *Paul: Apostle of the Heart,* 37, mentions a suggestion that a firm of tentmakers would have been very useful to a fighting proconsul.

26. Sherwin-White, *Roman Society,* 151. Two chapters are devoted to the matter of Roman citizenship; see esp. 144–71.

27. Bruce, *Paul: Apostle of the Heart,* 39, which see for further details about certification.

28. O'Rourke, "Roman Law," 176, which see for a helpful section on Roman citizenship.
29. J. I. Packer et al., *The Bible Almanac* (Nashville: Nelson, 1980), 178, which also see for a section on Roman citizenship.
30. Sherwin-White, *Roman Society*, 147.
31. Schürer, *History*, 1:143.
32. Ibid., 2:79.
33. W. J. Conybeare and J. S. Howson, *The Life and Epistles of St. Paul* (Grand Rapids: Eerdmans, 1957), 31ff.
34. Called the Septuagint (often abbrev. LXX) because of the tradition that it was made by a group of seventy. This observation does not imply that only compromising Jews used the Septuagint. No doubt it was in widespread use in the Diaspora. Paul's Old Testament quotations in his letters show that he was well acquainted with the Septuagint. In all likelihood, the Septuagint was predominantly the Bible of the early church.
35. 1 Cor. 9:24–27; Phil. 3:13–14; 2 Tim. 2:5; 4:7–8 are but a few of many examples.
36. Schürer, *History*, 1:309.
37. Sherwin-White, *Roman Society*, 138.

Chapter 2: Paul the Jew

1. In Acts 11:20 Greek-speaking *Gentiles* may be meant: see chap. 4.
2. F. F. Bruce, *Paul: Apostle of the Heart Set Free* (Grand Rapids: Eerdmans, 1977), 38, observes that a Roman citizen would have been given a three-fold Latin name at birth: a forename, family name, and additional (personal) name. In Paul's case we know only the last, perhaps chosen because it rhymed with Saul. Only "the Romans in the ancient world used more than one personal name" (A. N. Sherwin-White, *Roman Society and Roman Law in the New Testament* [Oxford: Clarendon, 1963], 146).
3. W. J. Conybeare and J. S. Howson, *The Life and Epistles of St. Paul* (Grand Rapids: Eerdmans, 1957), 39.
4. "Jew" comes from "Judah," but though the tribe of Judah dominated among the returning remnant, the name came to encompass all Israelites and representatives of all the tribes were and are included. There never have been ten lost tribes.
5. Emil Schürer, *The History of the Jewish People in the Age of Jesus Christ*, ed. Vermes, Millar, and Black, 3 vols. (1891; revised, Edinburgh: T. & T. Clark, 1973–1979), 2:314.
6. Ibid., 2:327.
7. Ibid., 2:336.
8. Hebrew for "pious ones," called "Hasidaeans" in the book of Maccabees.
9. Schürer, *History*, 2:329, 389–90.
10. Joachim Jeremias, *Jerusalem in the Time of Jesus*, trans. F. H. and C. H. Cave (Philadelphia: Westminster, 1967), 243.
11. Schürer, *History*, 2:330–31.
12. See, further, the final paragraph in this section. R. N. Longenecker, *Paul, Apostle of Liberty* (New York: Harper & Row, 1964) demonstrates the interplay of legalism and piety among the Pharisees of New Testament times. See esp. 77–79.
13. Today's fundamentalists are often compared to Pharisees, and the comparison may sometimes be appropriate in limited ways. But in regarding a body of tradition beyond the Scriptures as inspired, they were not like

fundamentalists. In several ways the Sadducees were more like fundamentalists and regarded the Pharisees as modernists. See Bruce, *Paul: Apostle of the Heart*, p. 47; Schürer, *History*, 2:409–11.

14. Cited and commented on by Bruce, *Paul: Apostle of the Heart*, 44.
15. Schürer, *History*, 2:395; all of pp. 389–96 points in this direction.
16. Ibid., 2:405–6.
17. On this point, see Bruce, *Paul: Apostle of the Heart*, 47, for one possible explanation.
18. Schürer, *History*, 1:212.
19. Ibid., 2:213.
20. Ibid., 2:405.
21. Ibid., 2:388.
22. The influence of this group ultimately led to the rebellion that was crushed when Jerusalem was destroyed by the Roman Titus in AD 70. Judas the Galilean mentioned in Acts 5:37 was an early leader of this sect.
23. Schürer, *History*, 2:416.
24. Ibid., 2:419.
25. J. I. Packer et al., eds, *The Bible Almanac* (Nashville: Nelson, 1980), 452.
26. John T. Townsend, "Ancient Education in the Time of the Early Roman Empire," in *The Catacombs and the Colosseum*, ed. Stephen Benko and John J. O'Rourke (Valley Forge, Pa.: Judson, 1971), 154.
27. Ibid., 155–56.
28. Cited by Schürer, *History*, 2:418.
29. Although we cannot be sure this rule was already set in Paul's day, later formulations of rules probably reflected practices of long standing. (See ibid., 1:69.)
30. There were also rabbinic schools in Babylonia, but "they could not vie [in importance] with those of Jerusalem" (Jeremias, *Jerusalem*, 242).
31. Hillel, Shammai, and Gamaliel are titled "Rabban," a degree of greater honor than "Rabbi." They were the first three to win that distinction. According to Conybeare and Howson, *St. Paul*, 47, only seven have ever worn that title.
32. See Bruce, *Paul: Apostle of the Heart*, 49.
33. For source and comment, see ibid.
34. Conybeare and Howson, *St. Paul*, 47.
35. See Bruce, *Paul: Apostle of the Heart*, 50, for reference to a different view of Gamaliel's lineage. See also Schürer, *History*, 2:367.
36. Cited in Conybeare and Howson, *St. Paul*, 47. Bruce, *Paul: Apostle of the Heart*, 50, mentions that a law liberalizing the rules for remarriage after divorce is attributed to Gamaliel.
37. This is one of the reasons Jesus' teaching was in such stark contrast, as in passages like Matt. 7:28–29.
38. Gal. 4:22–31 is an outstanding example.
39. Schürer, *History*, 2:328–29.
40. Cited in Conybeare and Howson, *St. Paul*, 39.
41. Schürer, *History*, 1:207 n. 12.
42. Ibid., 1:319.
43. Ibid., 1:316.
44. These are approximate dates, largely dependent on Josephus. It is possible the last two are one and the same. See ibid., 1:382–83.
45. Ibid., 1:361.
46. Ibid., 1:445.

47. The dates, given by ibid. (1:455–70), are approximate.
48. Jeremias, *Jerusalem,* 222–26.
49. Schürer, *History,* 2:331.
50. It may be coincidence that the disputes that led to Stephen's execution involved, among others, Cilicians (Acts 6:9), or is it possible that this is the way Paul got involved? Was he attending or ministering there?
51. The reference in 2 Cor. 5:16 is not decisive. It may mean nothing more than the fleshly standard of judgment exercised by Paul about Christ before his conversion.
52. Conybeare and Howson, *St. Paul,* 3.

Chapter 3: The Conversion and Commission of Paul

1. Cited by F. F. Bruce, *Paul: Apostle of the Heart Set Free* (Grand Rapids: Eerdmans, 1977), 468.
2. W. M. Ramsay, *The Church in the Roman Empire* (Grand Rapids: Baker, 1954), 32.
3. Cf. 2 Cor. 11:24.
4. F. F. Bruce, *Commentary on the Book of Acts,* NICNT (Grand Rapids: Eerdmans, 1954), 490.
5. Bruce, *Paul: Apostle of the Heart,* 70–71.
6. See Bruce, *Acts,* 193 (incl. n. 9), for discussion.
7. Emil Schürer, *The History of the Jewish People in the Age of Jesus Christ,* ed. Vermes, Millar, and Black, rev. ed., 3 vols. (Edinburgh: T & T Clark, 1973–1979), 2:198.
8. Josephus, *Jewish War* 2.20.2; cf. 7.8.7, where the figure is 18,000.
9. James L. Jones, "The Roman Army," in *The Catacombs and the Colosseum,* ed. Stephen Benko and John J. O'Rourke (Valley Forge: Judson, 1971), 211.
10. W. J. Conybeare and J. S. Howson, *The Life and Epistles of St. Paul* (Grand Rapids: Eerdmans, 1957), 68–69, says, "We neither know how he travelled, nor who his associates were, nor where he rested on his way, nor what road he followed from the Judaean to the Syrian capital."
11. In 9:5–6 the last part of verse 5 and the first part of verse 6 are omitted from most versions and appear in no Greek manuscript. But everything included in these parts *does* appear either in chap. 22 or in chap. 26. See Bruce, *Acts,* 192 n. 4.
12. In the Greek world the saying was commonly used to represent the idea of opposing deity. See Richard Longenecker, *Paul, Apostle of Liberty* (New York: Harper & Row, 1964), 99, for references.
13. Indeed, Paul's recollection of Stephen's appearance, words, and actions was probably the source of Luke's detailed information.
14. Bruce, *Acts,* 491. This understanding seems superior to the view that Paul's conflict was a sensitive Jewish distaste for having to carry out persecution. See Longenecker, *Apostle of Liberty,* 98–101.
15. J. G. Machen, *The Origin of Paul's Religion* (1925; reprint, Grand Rapids: Eerdmans, 1973), resists this view of the goads as suggesting any pre-conversion conviction within Paul. See 58–68 for a thorough discussion of a different approach.
16. Bruce, *Paul: Apostle of the Heart,* 75.
17. Bruce, *Acts,* 197. See also his footnotes on the point.

18. The street is one of Damascus's main thoroughfares, the *Darb al-Mustaqim*. A house traditionally identified as that of Judas is located near its western end.

19. Bruce, *Acts*, 195.

20. For an old and interesting defense of the supenaturalness of Paul's conversion (as a witness to the genuineness of the Christian faith) see Lord George Lyttelton's essay "The Conversion of St. Paul" in *Infidelity* (New York: American Tract Society, n.d. [1840?]). The essay was originally published as a tract, *Observations on the Conversion of St. Paul*, in 1747.

21. "Apostle" is from the Greek *apostolos*, one "sent forth" to represent/serve the sender.

Chapter 4: From New Convert to Missionary Traveler

1. J. Gresham Machen, *The Origin of Paul's Religion* (1925; reprint, Grand Rapids: Eerdmans, 1973), 7–8.

2. For a thorough treatment of the issues involved in dating Paul's life, see George Ogg, *The Chronology of the Life of Paul* (London: Epworth, 1968). This writer does not necessarily agree with all of Ogg's conclusions. Some decisions must always be subjective.

3. This is the only time "Son of God" appears in Acts. It was clearly understood by the Jews of NT times as a messianic title. See F. F. Bruce, *Commentary on the Book of Acts* (Grand Rapids: Eerdmans, 1980), 202–3, for suggestion that Paul's preaching may represent an advance on the way Jesus' messiahship had been preached thus far.

4. "The views which different inquirers take of it will probably depend on their own tendency to the practical or the ascetic life" (W. J. Conybeare and J. S. Howson, *The Life and Epistles of St. Paul* [Grand Rapids: Eerdmans, 1957], 80).

5. Machen, *Origin*, 73–74, suggests that the Jerusalem disciples' later reluctance to accept Paul's conversion might be better understood if most of the three years had been in seclusion rather than public preaching.

6. If Paul's time in Arabia (above) was a preaching mission, he might have offended Aretas in chief cities of Nabataean Arabia. Cf. Bruce, *Acts*, 194, 204.

7. There was serious conflict between Aretas and Herod Antipas, tetrarch of Galilee and Peraea (see p. 44) at this time. Antipas had divorced Aretas's daughter (to marry Herodias), boundary disputes added fuel to the fire, and open warfare came in AD 36. See Emil Schürer, *The History of the Jewish People in the Age of Jesus Christ*, ed. Vermes, Millar, and Black, rev. ed., 3 vols. (Edinburgh: T & T Clark, 1973–1979), 1:340–51. If this were in some way involved, we cannot tell. Did the Jews suggest that Paul was an agent of Antipas?

8. Conybeare and Howson, *St. Paul*, 85.

9. See Bruce, *Acts*, 205, who refers to "an imaginative reconstruction of Barnabas's earlier relations with Saul" by J. A. Robertson, *The Hidden Romance of the New Testament* (London: James Clark, 1923), 46ff.

10. See chap. 2.

11. Some Greek manuscripts of Acts 9:31 have singular "church" (NASB), some the plural "churches" (NKJV).

12. See chap. 1.

13. Bruce, *Acts*, 207.

14. Machen, *Origin*, 77.

15. Remember the elevation: "up" and "down" in Acts have nothing to do with north and south.
16. See the brief contrast between Alexandria and Antioch in chap. 1.
17. Some Greek manuscripts have *Hellenas* (Greeks); some *Hellenistas* (Hellenists); compare NASB and NKJV. But even "Hellenists" could mean Greek-speaking Gentiles. The words have the same root, after all.
18. Acts 4:36; Rom. 12:8; Acts 11:23 all involve the same Greek word *(parakaleo/paraklesis)*.
19. This is the order in which Luke calls their names from now until 13:13, after which it is usually Paul and Barnabas.
20. See Bruce, *Acts,* 242 n. 26, for interesting citations of the earliest secular references to Christians.
21. This fact is the point in such passages as Acts 4:32–37; Gal. 2:10; and in the offering Paul would later sponsor (see chap. 6, below).
22. Bruce, *Acts,* 243 n. 31; he observes, correctly, that "great famine" may well be general rather than specific ("a great famine").
23. Bruce, *Acts,* 244.
24. For a comparison of the Acts account and Josephus's account of Herod's death, see Schürer, *History,* 1:453.
25. It is quite possible Mark was the unidentified young man mentioned in his own gospel of Mark; cf. 14:51f.
26. Bruce, *Acts,* 258.
27. This writer is more inclined to identify Gal. 2:1–10 with Acts 15, but the decision is not crucial to any understanding of the basic truth of the passages involved.
28. See Bruce, *Acts,* 260, for an interesting but unlikely speculation that he might have been the Simon who carried Jesus' cross.
29. He was tetrarch over Galilee and Perea 4 BC–AD 39. (See the insert in chap. 2.)
30. Bruce, *Acts,* 260.
31. Conybeare and Howson, *St. Paul,* 115.
32. Literally, "Son of Jesus"; Jesus/Jeshua/Joshua was a common Jewish name.
33. Bruce, *Acts,* 264.
34. Here called that for the first time in Acts but regularly from here on.
35. As a senatorial province Cyprus was controlled by the Roman Senate and administered by a proconsul. See chap. 1.
36. Bruce, *Paul: Apostle of the Heart Set Free* (Grand Rapids: Eerdmans, 1977), 161.
37. See W. M. Ramsay, *The Bearing of Recent Discovery on the Trustworthiness of the New Testament,* 2nd ed. (London: Hodder and Stoughton, 1915), 150ff., and Bruce's *Acts,* 265, for discussion of the same.
38. A. N. Sherwin-White, *Roman Society and Roman Law in the New Testament* (Oxford: Clarendon, 1963), 121.
39. The Torah, our Pentateuch.
40. This included both the former (our historical books) and latter prophets (our major and minor prophets).
41. Compare Jesus' experiences in Nazareth, when He both read the second lesson and delivered the address (Luke 4:16ff.).
42. Note Paul's attention to "Saul . . . of the tribe of Benjamin," his own name and tribe.
43. Note that Peter used the very same argument in Acts 2:25ff.

44. Bruce, *Paul: Apostle of the Heart,* 129, comments on a suggestion that Paul, before his conversion, had desired to play a role in Jewish missions to make proselytes. That can remain nothing more than speculation.

45. Bruce, *Acts,* 281, suggests appropriately that the implication that Paul's gospel was for Gentiles, too, as dramatically evidenced in the great crowd of them present, would have finally made up their minds against him.

46. Sherwin-White, Roman Society, 78.

47. Ibid.

48. In the Roman system Zeus and Hermes corresponded to Jupiter and Mercury.

49. Note 2 Cor. 11:25, which refers to this incident; note also in Gal. 6:17, written to churches that surely included the Lystrans, that Paul refers to marks on his body, some of which were no doubt scars from this stoning.

50. Bruce, *Acts,* 296.

51. Conybeare and Howson, *St. Paul,* 154–55, provide an interesting discussion of this, theorizing that the Jews aroused the Lystrans with the accusation that Paul and Barnabas were acting not by divine agency but by diabolical magic.

52. Now defined with reasonable certainty as the mound of Kerti Huyiik.

53. It is reasonably clear that the plural "elders" goes with each church (singular), but discussion of questions about offices in the early church is beyond the scope of this text.

54. W. M. Ramsay, *St. Paul the Traveller and Roman Citizen* (Grand Rapids: Baker, 1960), 120.

55. For a reasonable discussion, see Ogg, *Chronology,* 65–67. He concludes that eighteen months is a sufficient time. Conybeare and Howson, *St. Paul,* 158 n. 3, observe: "It is evident that the case does not admit of anything more than conjecture."

56. Everett F. Harrison, *Introduction to the New Testament* (Grand Rapids: Eerdmans, 1971), 254.

57. Of course, our modern system of dating had not begun then.

58. George Milligan, ed., *Selections from the Greek Papyri* (Cambridge: Cambridge University Press, 1927).

59. Ibid., 102–3.

60. Ibid., 60–63.

61. Some scholars theorize that one or two parts of the New Testament, like Matthew, may have had Aramaic originals, but that view need not occupy us here. No such Aramaic "originals" exist.

62. The publication of Adolf Deissmann's *Light from the Ancient East,* in 1910, is often said to mark the full dawning of this realization.

63. J. B. Lightfoot, *Saint Paul's Epistles to the Colossians and to Philemon* (Grand Rapids: Zondervan, 1959), 303.

Chapter 5: The Gentile Mission Expands

1. F. F. Bruce, *Commentary on the Book of Acts,* NICNT (Grand Rapids: Eerdmans, 1980), 298.

2. See the earlier discussion about proselytes in chap. 4.

3. See F. F. Bruce, *Paul: Apostle of the Heart Set Free* (Grand Rapids: Eerdmans, 1977), 174–75.

4. Bruce, *Acts,* 304.

5. Ibid., 309: "If the elders were organized as a kind of Nazarene Sanhedrin, James was their president."

6. J. Gresham Machen, *The Origin of Paul's Religion* (1925; reprint, Grand Rapids: Eerdmans, 1973), 92–95.

7. A longer form of his name is Silvanus, as in 1 Thess. 1:1. It is probably the Roman cognomen, comparable to Saul's "Paul." See Bruce, *Paul: Apostle of the Heart*, 213.

8. See Gal. 2:3, for example.

9. Bruce, *Paul: Apostle of the Heart*, 217.

10. Macedonia was unusual in that it was subdivided into four districts. It may be that Luke's words should be understood to mean that Philippi was in the "first district," but the text is debatable. See A. N. Sherwin-White, *Roman Society and Roman Law in the New Testament* (Oxford: Clarendon, 1963), 93–95.

11. Emil Schürer, *The History of the Jewish People in the Age of Jesus Christ*, ed. Vermes, Millar, and Black, rev. ed., 3 vols. (Edinburgh: T & T Clark, 1973–1979), 1:390; 2:444–45.

12. Bruce, *Paul: Apostle of the Heart*, 220.

13. Bruce, *Acts*, 331.

14. Ralph L. Martin, *Philippians*, NCB (Grand Rapids: Eerdmans, 1980), 7.

15. The Greek word (*strategoi*) translated "magistrates" is rather general, being "the commonest Hellenistic title to render the [technical Latin] term *duoviri*": Sherwin-White, *Roman Society*, 93.

16. Ibid., 81.

17. See the detailed discussions in ibid., 78–83.

18. Gerhard Krodel, "Persecution and Toleration of Christianity Until Hadrian," in *The Catacombs and the Colosseum*, ed. Stephen Benko and John J. O'Rourke (Valley Forge: Judson, 1971), 256, is confident that the concept did not exist in Paul's time.

19. See 2 Cor. 11:25; this is one of the three times referred to there. The other two are not related in Acts.

20. See Machen, *Origin*, 45, for this theory.

21. In the aftermath of the assassination of Julius Caesar, Brutus and Cassius had committed suicide in Philippi in 42 BC.

22. Martin, *Philippians*, 4.

23. "The narrative agrees with the evidence of the earlier period that a Roman citizen of any social class was protected against a casual beating (without trial)"—Sherwin-White, *Roman Society*, 76. See 72–76, 78–83 for a detailed discussion of the Philippian incident.

24. This road crossed Macedonia, joining the Aegean (at Neapolis) to the Adriatic Sea.

25. Jason was a Greek name but one often assumed by Jews named Joshua; see Bruce, *Acts*, 343.

26. Bruce, *Paul: Apostle of the Heart*, 225.

27. Fairly recently discovered inscriptions show that Luke used the correct word for the magistrates in Thessalonica, "politarchs."

28. Bruce, *Paul: Apostle of the Heart*, 225.

29. Sherwin-White, *Roman Society*, 95.

30. John J. O'Rourke, "Roman Law and the Early Church," in *The Catacombs and the Colosseum*, 175.

31. If he *did* stay longer in Thessalonica, he soon joined Paul and Silas in the next place, as seen in v. 14.

32. Sherwin-White, *Roman Society*, 97.

33. Bruce, *Paul: Apostle of the Heart*, 226.

34. Sherwin-White, *Roman Society*, 96.
35. Bruce, *Paul: Apostle of the Heart*, 235, includes the speculation that Paul was originally headed for Rome but diverted south at this point, having learned of Claudius's expulsion of Jews from Rome.
36. W. W. Tarn and G. T. Griffith, *Hellenistic Civilisation*, cited by Martin, *Philippians*, 8.
37. Bruce, *Acts*, 348.
38. Named for their founder, Epicurus (341–270 BC).
39. Founded by Zeno of Cyprus, named for the Stoa (portico) in Athens where he often taught.
40. Bruce, *Acts*, 351.
41. Cf., in the previous chap., comments on Paul's approach at Lystra.
42. A full and helpful discussion of the speech is to be found in Bruce, *Paul: Apostle of the Heart*, 236–47.
43. With Paul's reference to the religiosity of the Athenians, compare Josephus: "The Athenians ... are affirmed by all men ... to be the most religious of the Greeks" (*Against Apion* ii.ll). Paul was not altogether being complimentary; the KJV's "too superstitious" may not be far wrong.
44. Aratus, in turn, may have borrowed from Cleanthes. See Bruce, *Acts*, 359–60, for fuller citation and discussion.
45. Bruce, *Acts*, 362, disagrees with this view.
46. He "shares with the apostle the honour of having a street named after him in present-day Athens" (Bruce, *Paul: Apostle of the Heart*, 247).
47. Victor P. Furnish, *II Corinthians*, AB (Garden City: Doubleday, 1984), 7.
48. Ibid., 14.
49. Schürer, *History*, 1:241.
50. See Bruce, *Acts*, 368, incl. nn. 9, 10, for historical references and possible reasons.
51. Schürer, *History*, 1:393–98.
52. Stephen Benko, "The History of the Early Roman Empire," in *The Catacombs and the Colosseum*, 54.
53. See 1 Thess. 3:6ff. Timothy's report from Thessalonica, in particular, encouraged Paul and led to the writing of 1 Thessalonians, as will be discussed later in this chapter.
54. See 2 Cor. 11:8–9; Phil. 4:15.
55. Many manuscripts give his name as "Titius Justus"; some speculate that his full name was Gaius Titius Justus and identify him with the Gaius mentioned in 1 Cor. 1:14 and Rom. 16:23. See Bruce, *Acts*, 371.
56. For biographical information on Gallio, see Bruce, *Acts*, 373–74.
57. This is the view of Bruce, *Acts*, 374.
58. Suggested by Sherwin-White, *Roman Society*, 102, as an "alternative explanation." See the entire section there (99–107) for detailed discussion of several possibilities.
59. If he is the same as the Sosthenes of 1 Cor. 1:1, he must have been converted later; we cannot be sure. On this whole incident, see Bruce, *Acts*, 375.
60. Sherwin-White, *Roman Society*, 103–4. There is some difference among the Greek manuscripts as to whether "Greeks" is part of the original.
61. See Bruce, *Acts*, 372–74, for a thorough discussion of the dating. See also George Ogg, *The Chronology of the Life of Paul* (London: Epworth, 1968), 104–11.
62. This is Bruce's guess in *Paul: Apostle of the Heart*, 255.

63. See the discussion above relative to the circumcision of Timothy.

64. Not to be confused with our modern usage of "Asia."

65. Schürer, *History*, 1:306.

66. Because Silas is not heard from again, he may have remained in Jerusalem.

67. Some think Timothy also brought a letter from the Thessalonian believers, with questions answered in parts of 1 Thessalonians, but the theory
has a weak foundation. See D. Edmund Hiebert, *The Thessalonian Epistles*
(Chicago: Moody, 1971), 21.

68. For the evidence for this, see Bruce, *Acts*, 374.

69. Though "Jason" is a Greek name, ibid., 343, observes that many Jews
named Joshua took Jason as a Greek name.

70. George Milligan, *St. Paul's Epistles to the Thessalonians* (Grand Rapids:
Eerdmans, 1953), xlvi.

71. Leon Morris, *The Epistles of Paul to the Thessalonians* (Grand Rapids:
Eerdmans, 1959), 18–19, lists eight such purposes.

72. For a more thorough discussion, see I. H. Marshall, *1 and 2 Thessalonians*
(Grand Rapids: Eerdmans, 1983), 23–28; Morris, *The Epistles of Paul to the
Thessalonians*, 25–30; Hiebert, *The Thessalonian Epistles*, 267–70.

73. Donald Guthrie, *New Testament Introduction* (Downers Grove:
InterVarsity, 1970), 569–78.

74. Hiebert, *The Thessalonian Epistles*, 263–67, provides a list of the
parallel passages.

75. Marshall, *1 and 2 Thessalonians*, 45.

76. Guthrie, *New Testament Introduction*, 577.

Chapter 6: The Third Missionary Journey

1. W. M. Ramsay, *The Cities of St. Paul* (Grand Rapids: Baker, 1960), 265.

2. The Greek word is *katechemenos*, whence we get our word *catechism*.

3. F. F. Bruce, *Commentary on the Book of the Acts* (Grand Rapids: Eerdmans,
1980), 382.

4. F. F. Bruce, *Paul: Apostle of the Heart Set Free* (Grand Rapids: Eerdmans,
1977), 289–90, doubts that these twelve were connected with Apollos.

5. Bruce, *Acts*, 396.

6. The question in v. 2 may be read, "Did you receive the Holy Spirit when
you believed?" The Greek simply reads: "Did you, believing, receive the
Holy Spirit?"

7. Bruce, *Acts*, 385–86.

8. With humor, Bruce, *Acts*, 388, wonders whether his parents or his pupils
gave him the name.

9. Ibid., 389.

10. In Ephesus as at Corinth Paul probably worked at tentmaking with Aquila
and Priscilla.

11. Bruce, *Acts*, 390, for a helpful discussion of Jewish involvement in such
practices and for a citation that uses the name of Jesus in a similar way.

12. Many such magical papyri or parchments have survived to this day. Such
items were often called "Ephesian scripts," again testifying to Ephesus's
involvement and reputation.

13. Bruce, *Acts*, 391. He reminds us of Shakespeare's lines describing Ephesus
in *Comedy of Errors*: "They say this town is full of cozenage," etc.

14. The name Erastus also occurs in Rom. 16:2–3 referring to a Christian who
was "treasurer" of Corinth. Whether these are one and the same, "we cannot say certainly; but it is not very likely" (ibid., 395).

15. And, in fact, the Ephesian Artemis was not even technically the same as the original Greek virgin-goddess Artemis. Bruce (ibid., 397) clarifies that she was "the ancient mother goddess of Asia Minor," commonly known as Cybele or by other names as well. See there for further details.

16. The theater is estimated to have seated 25,000 and "is still in quite a good state of preservation" (ibid., 399).

17. A. N. Sherwin-White, *Roman Society and Roman Law in the New Testament* (Oxford: Clarendon, 1963), 83–87.

18. See Bruce and the sources he cites (*Acts,* 400) for a discussion of these "Asiarchs." See also Sherwin-White, *Roman Society,* 89–90.

19. Bruce, *Acts,* 400–401. See also Sherwin-White, *Roman Society,* 83, 86.

20. *Civitas libera;* see chap. 1.

21. See Bruce, *Paul: Apostle of the Heart,* 288.

22. Bruce, *Acts,* 404–5; see also *Paul: Apostle of the Heart,* 314–18.

23. Bruce, *Acts,* 405, suggests Paul planned to use a "pilgrim ship" that took from major ports Jews who wished to be in Jerusalem for the Passover-Pentecost season, but got wind of a plot to kill him on board.

24. According to 2 Cor. 8:6ff., Titus would probably have been along too. The strange fact that Titus is never mentioned in Acts has been theoretically explained by Ramsay as possibly because he was Luke's brother.

25. Bruce, *Acts,* 407.

26. Ibid., 408.

27. Bruce, ibid., suggests that evening was a convenient time for many who were not their own masters and would not have been free in the daytime.

28. Ibid., 409.

29. Richard Longenecker, "The Acts of the Apostles," in *The Expositor's Bible Commentary,* ed. Frank E. Gaebelein, 12 vols. (Grand Rapids: Zondervan, 1979–1992), 9:512.

30. In v. 28, "overseers" is *episkopoi,* the same as is sometimes translated "bishops."

31. Bruce, *Acts,* 421 n. 4.

32. "Half a century later, after Philip's migration to Phrygia, some of his daughters lived on into old age and were highly reputed as informants on persons and events from the early days of Palestinian Christianity" (Bruce, *Paul: Apostle of the Heart,* 343).

33. Bruce, *Acts,* 426, thinks the Greek should, instead, be translated: "bringing us to one Mnason."

34. Donald Guthrie, *New Testament Introduction,* 3rd ed. (Downers Grove: InterVarsity, 1970), 422.

35. Leon Morris, *The First Epistle of Paul to the Corinthians,* TNTC (Grand Rapids: Eerdmans, 1958), 29.

36. Curtis Vaughan and Thomas D. Lea, *1 Corinthians,* Bible Study Commentary (Grand Rapids: Zondervan, 1983), 11.

37. F. W. Grosheide, *The First Epistle to the Corinthians,* NICNT (1953; reprint, Grand Rapids: Eerdmans, 1980), 14.

38. C. K. Barrett, *The First Epistle to the Corinthians,* HNTC (New York: Harper & Row, 1968), 3.

39. Guthrie, *Introduction,* 426.

40. Ibid., 429.

41. Everett F. Harrison, *Introduction to the New Testament,* rev. ed. (Grand Rapids: Eerdmans, 1971), 287 (reflecting Dibelius's suggestion).

42. Philip E. Hughes, *Paul's Second Epistle to the Corinthians*, NICNT (Grand Rapids: Eerdmans, 1962), xviii; see also 356–58.
43. Guthrie, *Introduction*, 439.
44. Ibid., 425–26, 430–37.
45. Ibid., 431: he nevertheless holds to the unity of the latter. For a defense of the view that chaps. 10–13 are from the severe letter, see Alfred Plummer, *A Critical and Exegetical Commentary on the Second Epistle of St. Paul to the Corinthians*, ICC (Edinburgh: T & T Clark, 1960), xxvii-xxxvi.
46. C. K. Barrett, *The Second Epistle to the Corinthians*, HNTC (New York: Harper & Row, 1973), 9.
47. This is the view of Hans Dieter Betz, explained in his recent Hermeneia volume, *2 Corinthians 8 and 9* (Philadelphia: Fortress, 1985).
48. See Donald A. Carson, *From Triumphalism to Maturity: An Exposition of 2 Corinthians 10-13* (Grand Rapids: Baker, 1984), esp. 14–16, for the view that there was a lengthy break between 1–9 and 10–13, during which Paul received further news.
49. J. B. Lightfoot, *The Epistle of St. Paul to the Galatians* (Grand Rapids: Eerdmans, n.d.), 36.
50. Ibid., 19–20.
51. For a good, brief discussion, see F. F. Bruce, *The Epistle to the Galatians*, NIGTC (Grand Rapids: Eerdmans, 1982), 8–9.
52. Ibid., 11–13.
53. Ibid., 43–56 (Bruce's commentary on Acts may also be consulted).
54. Ibid., 44.
55. Herman N. Ridderbos, *The Epistle of Paul to the Churches of Galatia*, NICNT (Grand Rapids: Eerdmans, 1982), 31–35.
56. Lightfoot, *Galatians*, 45–48.
57. Bruce, *Galatians*, 54.
58. Ridderbos, *Paul to the Churches of Galatia*, 33.
59. Bruce, *Galatians*, 58.
60. W. H. Griffith Thomas, *St. Paul's Epistles to the Romans* (Grand Rapids: Eerdmans, 1946), 23.
61. Frederic Godet, *Commentary on St. Paul's Epistle to the Romans* (Grand Rapids: Zondervan, n.d.), x.
62. F. F. Bruce, *The Epistle of Paul to the Romans*, TNTC (Grand Rapids: Eerdmans, 1963), 21.
63. For a clear and helpful discussion of the date, see C. E. B. Cranfield, *The Epistle to the Romans*, ICC, 2 vols. (Edinburgh: T & T Clark, 1975–79), 41:12–16.
64. C. K. Barrett, *A Commentary on the Epistle to the Romans*, HNTC (New York: Harper & Row, 1957), 6.
65. Cranfield, *Romans*, 1:21.
66. Guthrie, *Introduction*, 397.
67. Ernst Käsemann, *Commentary on Romans* (Grand Rapids: Eerdmans, 1980), 19.
68. Bruce, *Romans*, 31–32 (citing Lightfoot).
69. Barrett, *Romans*, 1.
70. Guthrie, *Introduction*, 400–414; see also Bruce, *Romans*, 25–31.
71. The observations along these lines as well as concerning travel to and from Rome in the original ICC volume by W. Sanday and A. C. Headlam (*The Epistle to the Romans* [Edinburgh: T & T Clark, 1902], xxvi, xxvii) are helpful.

72. Guthrie, *Introduction*, 401.
73. James Denney, "St. Paul's Epistle to the Romans," in *Expositor's Greek Testament*, 5 vols. (Grand Rapids: Eerdmans, 1951), 2:581 (citing Gifford).

Chapter 7: Paul the Prisoner

1. Emil Schürer, *The History of the Jewish People in the Age of Jesus Christ*, ed. Vermes, Millar, and Black, rev. ed., 3 vols. (Edinburgh: T & T Clark, 1973–1979), 1:361.
2. Ibid., 1:367–68.
3. Ibid., 2:218.
4. Ibid., 2:223.
5. Ibid., 1:363.
6. Ibid., 1:366.
7. Ibid., 1:380.
8. Ibid., 1:379.
9. Most of this is taken from Joachim Jeremias, *Jerusalem in the Time of Jesus*, trans. F. H. and C. H. Cave (Philadelphia: Fortress, 1967), 21–25, 79–80.
10. Schürer, *History*, 1:458.
11. Ibid., 1:460.
12. The Roman historian Tacitus, quoted by ibid., 1:462.
13. See ibid., 1:372–76, 381, 401–4, 2:197.
14. Ibid., 1:464.
15. We do not know how many elders represented the believers in Jerusalem. F. F. Bruce, *Commentary on the Book of Acts* (Grand Rapids: Eerdmans, 1980), 429, speculates that in view of the thousands of believers, there might well have been seventy, over which James presided, as sort of a Nazarene counterpart to the regular Sanhedrin.
16. Ibid., 430.
17. Josephus, *Antiquities* 19.6.1, tells of an occasion when Herod Agrippa I bore the expenses of a large number of Nazirites in a similar manner, probably as a public demonstration of his piety.
18. Notices were placarded at the barrier, which led inside to warn Gentiles of this very fact. See Bruce, *Acts*, 434, for reference to the discovery of original notices.
19. See A. N. Sherwin-White, *Roman Society and Roman Law in the New Testament* (Oxford: Clarendon, 1963), 35–43.
20. For a helpful discussion about Lysias, see ibid., 154–66, who suggests that he had equestrian status in the auxiliary army.
21. Schürer, *History*, 1:305.
22. Ibid., 1:330.
23. See the discussion on Roman citizenship in chap. 1. Lysias had purchased his, and the adopted name Claudius would indicate that "he had done so in the reign of Claudius, under whom Roman citizenship became increasingly available for cash down" (Bruce, *Acts*, 446).
24. Ibid., 447.
25. It is inconceivable that Paul could not tell that Ananias was high priest, even though he might not have known him personally or by face. "I wist not" must be used in the sense "I did not take account," "I forgot myself." Bruce, *Paul: Apostle of the Heart Set Free* (Grand Rapids: Eerdmans, 1977), 352 n. 52, suggests that Paul's words were ironic: "I didn't know that a man who acted thus illegally could be the high priest!" This Ananias was in the high priest's office for eleven or twelve years, beginning in AD 47.

26. Bruce, *Acts*, 457 n. 29, cites the Mishnah as making "provision for relief from such vows as could not be fulfilled 'by reasons of constraint.'"

27. Ibid., 457.

28. Sherwin-White, *Roman Society*, 5.

29. Bruce, *Acts*, 461–62.

30. "In the NT [*praetorium*] is used of the official residence of a Roman provincial governor" (ibid, 462). The building was actually a palace originally built by Herod the Great for his own residence. Herod built Caesarea during a twelve-year period (22–10 BC) with its central structure a temple dedicated to Caesar. See Schürer, *History*, 1:306, 361.

31. Cited by Bruce, *Acts*, 462. See Bruce for more detail.

32. Sherwin-White, *Roman Society*, 49.

33. Or else they are but generally summarized by Luke. No doubt he was present and made notes. Although "we" does not occur from 21:27 to 26:32, that is not indicative; there really are not any places where "we" would have applied in this section.

34. Christians are still known as Nazarenes in Hebrew and Aramaic (Bruce, *Acts*, 465).

35. See Sherwin-White, *Roman Society*, 49–50.

36. Ibid., 53.

37. Bruce, *Acts*, 472.

38. See Sherwin-White, *Roman Society*, 53.

39. See Schürer, *History*, 1:465.

40. Bruce, *Acts*, 474.

41. Bruce, *Paul: Apostle of the Heart*, 363.

42. John J. O'Rourke, "Roman Law and the Early Church," in *The Catacombs and the Colosseum*, ed. Stephen Benko and John J. O'Rourke (Valley Forge, Pa.: Judson, 1971), 177.

43. Apparently the procurator could judge the case of the Roman citizen who did not make such an appeal. See Schurer, *History*, 1:369, and Sherwin-White, *Roman Society*, 60–66.

44. Sherwin-White, *Roman Society*, 67.

45. Felix's wife, Drusilla, was also their sister.

46. Schürer, *History*, 1:370 n. 80.

47. So does ibid., 1:475 n. 21.

48. Bruce, *Acts*, 503.

49. Ibid., 506.

50. W. M. Ramsay, *St. Paul and Traveller and Roman Citizens* (1897; reprint, Grand Rapids: Baker, 1960), 322ff. suggests that a ship's council was held and Paul was invited to give his opinion as an experienced traveler.

51. Notice the "we" in vv. 15, 16, 19; the passengers—even physician Luke—were pressed into duty in the serious circumstances.

52. Bruce, *Acts*, 510.

53. Bruce, ibid., 517, suggests that perhaps the number appears right here because they had to count to divide the food.

54. Compare the distress of the Philippian jailer in Acts 16:27.

55. For the traditional location, see James Smith, *The Voyage and Shipwreck of St. Paul*, rev. by W. E. Smith, 4th ed. (London: Longmans, 1880); for an alternative, see W. Burridge, *Seeking the Site of St. Paul's Shipwreck* (Valletta, 1952).

56. The Greeks coined the word "barbarian" *barbaros* by onomatopoeia; to them, other languages sounded like so much "bar-bar-bar."

57. As recently as 1960, a set of stamps of Malta celebrated the 1900th anniversary of Paul's shipwreck there.
58. Bruce, *Acts*, 525–26.
59. J. D. Douglas, ed., *The Illustrated Bible Dictionary*, 3 vols. (Wheaton: Tyndale, 1980), 3:1351.
60. G. A. Buttricks, ed., *The Interpreter's Dictionary of the Bible*, 4 vols. (New York: Abingdon, 1962), 4:126.
61. Thomas W. Africa, *Rome of the Caesars* (New York: Wiley, 1965), 8.
62. Ibid., 9.
63. Edwin Yamauchi, *Harper's World of the New Testament* (New York: Harper & Row, 1981), 112.
64. See James L. Jones, "The Roman Army," in *The Catacombs and the Colosseum*, 198–99.
65. See Sherwin-White, *Roman Society*, 108–10, for technical discussion of several possibilities.
66. O'Rourke, "Roman Law," 174.
67. Sherwin-White, *Roman Society*, 112–19.
68. Ibid., 117.
69. Ralph P. Martin, *Colossians and Philemon*, NCB, rev. ed. (Grand Rapids: Eerdmans, 1981), 27.
70. Donald Guthrie, *New Testament Introduction*, 3rd ed. (Downers Grove: InterVarsity, 1970), 472–78, has a helpful discussion on the possibility of an Ephesian imprisonment, which he is inclined to reject.
71. For a presentation and defense of this view, see Martin, *Colossians and Philemon*, 22–32.
72. Cited by Guthrie, *Introduction*, 556. (Italics Dodd's.)
73. "The present-day site is uninhabited and not yet [1973] excavated" (Martin, *Colossians and Philemon*, 3).
74. See ibid., 4–5, for a helpful description.
75. Guthrie, *Introduction*, 546–50.
76. See Martin, *Colossians and Philemon*, 10–12, for a detailed discussion.
77. J. B. Lightfoot, *Saint Paul's Epistles to the Colossians and to Philemon*, rev. ed. (Grand Rapids: Zondervan, n.d.), 73–113.
78. Martin, *Colossians and Philemon*, 8–19.
79. Eduard Lohse's summary in *Colossians and Philemon* (Philadelphia: Fortress, 1971), 127–31, given after his exegesis of chapter 2, is a reasonably temperate description of the heresy and of Paul's response; even so, the conclusions must remain tentative.
80. Martin, *Colossians and Philemon*, 9, summarizing J. Ferguson.
81. E. K. Simpson and F. F. Bruce, *Commentary on the Epistles to the Ephesians and Colossians*, NICNT (Grand Rapids: Eerdmans, 1957), 17.
82. C. Leslie Mitton, *Ephesians*, NCB (London: Oliphant, 1976), 11.
83. For a good summary of objections and of Goodspeed's view, see ibid., 2–11.
84. Guthrie, *Introduction*, 479–508; the even more detailed investigation by Marcus Barth, *Ephesians*, 2 vols., AB (Garden City: Doubleday, 1974), 1:3–50, is also helpful. Barth concludes that "the tradition which accepts Paul as the author of Ephesians is more recommendable than the suggestion of an unknown author" (41).
85. Guthrie, *Introduction*, 671–84.
86. Mitton, *Ephesians*, 17–18.
87. See Guthrie's helpful use of this point, *Introduction*, 493–94.

88. The three are P 46, Aleph, and B. Two or three other late cursives also omit the words.

89. Guthrie, *Introduction*, 508.

90. Mitton, *Ephesians*, 16.

91. Ibid., 32.

92. J. B. Lightfoot, *Saint Paul's Epistles to the Colossians and to Philemon* (Grand Rapids: Zondervan, 1959), 321.

93. Ibid., 322.

94. See, for example, Arthur Rupprecht, "Christianity and the Slavery Question," *Bulletin of the Evangelical Theological Society* 6:2 (May 1963): 64–68; Edwin Yamauchi, "Slaves of God," in the same journal 9:1 (Winter 1966): 31–49, esp. 36–44.

95. Lightfoot, *Colossians and Philemon*, 318–19.

96. See C. F. D. Moule, *The Epistle of Paul the Apostle to the Colossians and to Philemon* (Cambridge: Cambridge U., 1958), 34–35.

97. Lightfoot, *Colossians and Philemon*, 303.

98. Guthrie, *Introduction*, 635–38.

99. Lightfoot, *Colossians and Philemon*, 312.

100. H. A. A. Kennedy, "Philippians," in *The Expositor's Greek Testament*, ed. William Robertson Nicoll, 5 vols. (Grand Rapids: Eerdmans, 1951), 3:473.

101. J. B. Lightfoot, *Saint Paul's Epistle to the Philippians* (reprint; Grand Rapids: Zondervan, 1953), 30–46.

102. For the best presentation (from whom much of the following is taken) see Ralph P. Martin, *Philippians*, NCB (Grand Rapids: Eerdmans, 1980), 36–57.

103. Gnilka, quoted by ibid., 52.

104. See F. F. Bruce, *Paul: Apostle of the Heart*, 294–99, for a thorough discussion of the possibilities.

105. Ibid., 390.

106. Martin, *Philippians*, 56.

107. Guthrie, *Introduction*, 535.

108. See Martin, *Philippians*, 40–42; compare Lightfoot, *Philippians*, 36–38.

109. A. N. Sherwin-White, *Roman Society*, 177.

110. See the lengthy discussion in ibid., 93–95.

111. Ibid., 94.

112. Martin, *Philippians*, 5, 9.

113. Ibid., 21.

Chapter 8: The Last Years of Paul

1. For details, see Homer A. Kent, Jr., *The Pastoral Epistles*, rev. ed. (Chicago: Moody, 1982), 45–47.

2. Gerhard Krodel, "Persecution and Toleration of Christianity Until Hadrian," in *The Catacombs and the Colosseum*, ed. Stephen Benko and John J. O'Rourke (Valley Forge: Judson, 1971), 360.

3. See the full citation at the end of this chapter.

4. Cited by F. F. Bruce, *Paul: Apostle of the Heart Set Free* (Grand Rapids: Eerdmans, 1977), 449.

5. There is one traditional source that claims Paul went as far as Great Britain on his westward journey, but that strand of tradition is too weak to inspire much confidence.

6. Cited by Bruce, *Paul: Apostle of the Heart*, 442.

7. W. J. Conybeare and J. S. Howson, *The Life and Epistles of St. Paul* (Grand Rapids: Eerdmans, 1957), 767.

8. See, for example, F. J. Babcock, *The Pauline Epistles and the Epistle to the Hebrews in their Historical Setting* (n.p., 1937).

9. Donald Guthrie, *New Testament Introduction*, 3rd ed. (Downers Grove: InterVarsity, 1977), 584–622; see also his commentary, *The Pastoral Epistles* (Grand Rapids: Eerdmans, 1957), and his booklet *The Pastoral Epistles and the Mind of Paul* (Madison: TSF, n.d.).

10. Guthrie, *Introduction*, 600.

11. Walter Lock, *The Pastoral Epistles* (Edinburgh: T & T Clark, 1924), xix.

12. For detailed citations see (using English) Kent, *Pastoral Epistles*, 23–37; (using Greek) Newport J. D. White, "The Pastoral Epistles" in *The Expositor's Greek Testament*, ed. William Robertson Nicoll, 5 vols. (Grand Rapids: Eerdmans, 1951), 4:75–82.

13. Guthrie, *Introduction*, 620. He devotes a helpful appendix to this question (671–84).

14. Ibid., 675–76.

15. See Kent, *Pastoral Epistles*, 15, 21, 50, for an attempt to make a detailed reconstruction. Kent postulates two visits east, with the trip to Spain in between. This moves the composition of 1 Timothy and Titus up to AD 62 or 63. White, "Pastoral Epistles," 74–75, also suggests two eastern journeys but puts 1 Timothy and Titus in the last journey and so would follow the dating given above.

16. Martin Dibelius & Hans Conzelmann, *The Pastoral Epistles* (Philadelphia: Fortress, 1972), 2.

17. Guthrie, *The Pastoral Epistles*, 183.

18. For a thorough discussion of the history and tradition involved in the question of whether Paul had a ministry beyond Acts, see Bruce, *Paul: Apostle of the Heart*, 441–55.

19. Conybeare and Howson, *St. Paul*, 764–65.

20. 1 Clement 5:5–7.

21. See Bruce, *Paul: Apostle of the Heart*, 450–51.